The Spirituality of Anorexia

Widely popularized images of unobtainable and damaging feminine ideals can be a cause of profound disjunction between women and their bodies. A consequence of this dissonance is an embodied performance of these ideals with the potential development of disordered eating practices, such as anorexia nervosa. This book develops a spirituality of anorexia by suggesting that these eating disorders are physical symptoms of the general repression of feminine nature in our culture. Furthermore, it puts forward Goddess feminism as a framework for a healing therapeutic model to address anorexia and more broadly, the "slender ideal" touted by society.

The book focuses on the female body in contemporary society, specifically the development of anorexia nervosa, and what this expression communicates about female embodiment. Drawing upon the work of a variety of theorists, social commentators, liberation theologians and thealogians, it discusses the benefits of adopting female-focused myths, symbols and rituals, drawing upon the work of Marion Woodman and Naomi Goldenberg. Ultimately, it theorizes a thealogical approach to anorexia aimed at displacing the damaging discourses that undermine women in the twenty-first century.

Offering an alternative model of spirituality and embodiment for contemporary women, this book will be of keen interest to scholars of theology, religious studies, gender studies and psychology.

Emma White holds a PhD from the University of Winchester, UK. Her research focuses on the spirituality of gender and embodiment, particularly regarding eating disorders. Her article titled 'Starved by Society: An Examination of Judith Butler's Gender Performance and Society's Slender Ideal' has been published in *Feminist Theology*.

Gender, Theology and Spirituality
Edited by Lisa Isherwood
University of Winchester, UK

Public Theology and the Challenge of Feminism
Edited by Anita Monro and Stephen Burns

Searching for the Holy Spirit
Feminist Theology and Traditional Doctrine
Anne Claar Thomasson-Rosingh

God and Difference
The Trinity, Sexuality, and the Transformation of Finitude
Linn Marie Tonstad

Christian Goddess Spirituality
Enchanting Christianity
Mary Ann Beavis

Schooling Indifference
Reimagining RE in Multi-Cultural and Gendered Spaces
John I'Anson and Alison Jasper

Shame, the Church and the Regulation of Female Sexuality
Miryam Clough

Living Out Sexuality and Faith
Body Admissions of Malaysian Gay and Bisexual Men
Joseph N. Goh

The Spirituality of Anorexia
A Goddess Feminist Thealogy
Emma White

For more information about this series, please visit: www.routledge.com/religion/series/GTS

The Spirituality of Anorexia

A Goddess Feminist Thealogy

Emma White

Routledge
Taylor & Francis Group
LONDON AND NEW YORK

First published 2019 by Routledge

2 Park Square, Milton Park, Abingdon, Oxfordshire OX14 4RN
52 Vanderbilt Avenue, New York, NY 10017

Routledge is an imprint of the Taylor & Francis Group, an informa business

First issued in paperback 2020

British Library Cataloguing-in-Publication Data
A catalogue record for this book is available from the British Library

Library of Congress Cataloging-in-Publication Data
A catalog record for this book has been requested

ISBN: 978-1-138-47806-0 (hbk)
ISBN: 978-0-367-58957-8 (pbk)

Typeset in Sabon
by Apex CoVantage, LLC

Contents

Preface

The female body in contemporary society is at the heart of this book which was born from my desire to understand the drive towards a slender idea that so many of us have internalized as a very personal goal. The extreme outcome of this drive to narrow our bodies' boundaries is the development of eating disorders, such as anorexia nervosa. Drawing upon a variety of multidisciplinary research, I argue that anorexia develops as a consequence of living in a patriarchal society that creates a disjunction between women and their bodies. The consequence of this destructive rhetoric has kept women disempowered, disembodied and disconnected from a strong and powerful female heritage.

As a young woman living in the UK, it is painfully clear that the size and shape of our bodies represents a lot more than physical health. They come to represent our moral virtues, values, cleanliness, drive, passions, intelligence, and it is hard not to internalize these culturally communicated lessons. When I was growing up, the valorization of the slender form was largely limited to the television, film, magazines and the fashion advertisements promoting clothes, underwear, make-up, perfume. etc. – at least, this is where my friends and I gained the majority of our exposure – but today we are also influenced by our favourite bloggers and vloggers and the people who invite us in with promises of friendship and instead feed these deep-seated insecurities with cleverly marketed adornments as they sell a lifestyle model which promises acceptance, happiness and success. When there is money to be made from "selling" the slender ideal, there will be new and initiative ways created to market it.

My discussions here are not just limited to the development of anorexia, but the dieting behaviours that we find ourselves engaged in at various stages throughout our lives. I discuss this in the context of a Slender Performance; an act that we engage in, not for health reasons, but to obtain cultural legitimacy. I find it troubling that despite the growing awareness of eating disorders, there is not more literature available on the female body in contemporary society. Is the slender ideal so desirable that we do not want to question the belief systems lying at its heart? Are we all so sensitive about growing levels of obesity, that we ignore those who fall at the opposite end of the scales? My personal aim at the inception of this book was to understand why women diet so aggressively, why they believe their self-worth is limited to the size and shape of their bodies. Is it born from a biological imperative or is there something more toxic in our environments which creates this deep-seated discontent?

Since writing this book, more body behaviours have been identified and named. We now read about orthorexia, defined as an obsession with the consumption of "healthy" and "pure" foods and bigorexia (also known as muscle dysmorphia; a subtype of body dysmorphic disorder) which, broadly speaking is a disorder in which people experience their bodies as small and weak instead of large, muscular and strong. I will not speculate here on the aetiology of such expressions but, what I can say is that it appears that we are increasingly being driven towards extreme behaviours and it is not resulting in embodied, healthy and happy people. We need to explore the underlying features of these human drives if we are to construct creative strategies towards healing these damaging expressions and dismantle the features of contemporary living which lend themselves to these disembodied realities.

The Spirituality of Anorexia tracks my journey to understand the drives underpinning anorexia and the desire towards slenderness that consumes the time and energy of so many women. Starting with an examination of the medical classification systems, the history of anorexia, current treatment programmes and the influence of biology and society on our conceptualizations of self, I explore contemporary understandings of anorexia. Arguing that this behaviour develops as a consequence of patriarchal society, heavily influenced by our Judeo-Christian heritage and Greek dualistic thought, I explore the aspects of contemporary society which create an environment in which self-worth is derived from the attainment of certain beauty prerequisites. Slenderness and all it represents, is high amongst that list. Moving to the political aspects of self-starvation, I explore the work of Judith Butler on gender performativity and the concept of a slender performance is developed as I consider the ways in which excess flesh has become taboo and how those occupying it are subject to stigmatization as lazy, weak and gluttonous. The price of these judgements is high. The female body as historically mediated is also discussed as I explore the connection between agoraphobia, hysteria and anorexia as gender specific maladies and the political ramifications of such an assertion. I also discuss the question of whether there is any psychological benefit or spirituality to result as a consequence of the anorexic expression in the context of "cutting" and religious self-harm practices. Finally, equipped with the knowledge gleaned from this research, I move towards exploring the potential benefit of Goddess feminism and thealogy in addressing the features that manifest in the development of anorexia.

I sincerely hope that this book goes some way towards helping deconstruct the debilitating features of anorexia and that it will offer a helpful perspective to those new to this field of study, those already working within treatment programmes, the family and friends watching someone they love suffer, and also to the women who are currently trapped by this behaviour, within the cyclic routines of stringent exercise and restrictive food consumption. Whilst I discuss the benefit of the symbolism of the Goddess on female perceptions of self, I do not intend this to be a limiting factor. There are many positive and powerful role models and frameworks at our disposal and many more creative strategies to be fleshed out. Of central importance is understanding how destructive and "disordered" behaviour takes it shape, so we can work towards the construction of healing frameworks that foster positive perceptions of self, healthy human connection and a strong basis for the development of self-esteem. The goal must be empowered and embodied women. This book works towards that end.

Introduction

The aim of this book is to develop a Spirituality of Anorexia as I draw upon evidence that eating disorders, such as anorexia nervosa, are physical symptoms of the general repression of feminine nature in our culture. The research and theories of a number of social commentators and female psychotherapists, feminist liberation theologians, thealogical commentators and thealogians will be discussed as I aim to rediscover the lost Goddess not only in society but within every woman. My work is explicitly concerned with the psychology of women and what anorexia and the slender ideal communicate about their place within contemporary society. As you shall see in the following pages, anorexia is still a predominantly female disorder and as such, the experiences and voices of women are my primary concern.

A central focus of this book will be the theorizing of a thealogical response to society's construction of the feminine[1] as I explore how destructive female stereotypes and idealizations directly affect female embodiment and lends itself to the development of anorexia in women. This work marks the start of a broader research project concerned with developing alternative therapeutic responses to anorexia which utilizes the symbolism of the Goddess within a thealogical framework providing women with access to empowering and embodying symbols of the feminine. As you will see in the following pages, anorexia here is understood as symbolic of a female yearning for meaning, significance and value (expressed through utilizing cultural preoccupations with the slender female body) in a patriarchal society which continues to value male over female virtues. I argue that the mainstream societal adoption of a thealogical framework will help to displace and subvert damaging female idealizations and stereotypes that contribute to the individual's utilization of the anorexic expression, whilst offering empowering symbols of female embodiment and a connection to a broader empowering framework. Despite my focus on theory, current therapeutic responses will be touched upon throughout when necessary to provide a thorough overview of the theories I am discussing.

Themes of control, low self-esteem, disempowerment, rejection, suffering and the desire for a youthful aesthetic are recurring themes throughout literature on eating disorders. A plethora of writing, spanning decades, speculate on the aetiology of anorexia and focuses, with increasing rapture, on the observation that appearance norms have become increasingly invasive and oppressive for women.[2] In less than two decades the acceptable female body size has dropped by one third[3] and most women not only do not fit it, but attempting to do so is threatening their lives and significantly damaging their place in this world. Increasing amounts of time, money and attention is spent on reducing the body and maintaining their weight loss, an activity that has become a requirement of modern womanhood. This had led many social commentators[4] to conclude that these beauty norms are a form of female oppression aimed at keeping women suppressed, sedated, numb and politically castrated. This slender ideal has become mainstream and the "norm" for girls and women in contemporary society. This slender/reductionist rhetoric has been internalized by billions of women all over the globe and the message is painfully clear – the only way to be happy, successful, desired and loved is by adhering to these strict beauty demands at all costs. The normalization of this slender standard is evidenced by the lack of social enquiry and personal probing of the damaging rhetoric; we are not questioning why we feel this way, why we are policing these body boundaries so aggressively. We are so busy trying to drop pound-after-pound of "fat" that we forget to question why – to probe below the surface of this body hatred and disgust to discover the real issues underpinning this obsession with control and power over female flesh. This is what the following body of work is concerned with. As such, themes I shall explore throughout the following chapters include anorexia as a form of "male interpretation" in which women seek to sever their relationship with the traditionally ample and curvaceous female body and escape their sexuality, the influence society and visual images have on our perceptions of self and the mind/body dualisms inherent within the images and advertisements generated by the fashion, beauty, food and diet industries, the similarities anorexia shares with earlier female maladies such as hysteria and agoraphobia and how the Judeo-Christian tradition with its dualistic and patriarchal heritage has contributed to this discontent between society and the bodies of women. I argue that the aetiology of this disorder can be found within reflections on society, the politics of the female body and the influence religion has had on these body ideals within the environments we inhabit.

Drawing on the work of Michael Foucault, I work from the premise that the female body is constantly under the control and "in the grip" of cultural practices, and that what we know of the "natural" body is actually a performance of what we believe natural should look and feel like.[5] It is evident that society significantly influences our thoughts and feelings about our bodies; that our bodies are constituted by culture and 'the map on which we mark our meanings'.[6] This message is further solidified when reflecting upon the anorexic female frame.

The female body has historically borne the brunt of extreme cultural manipulation and one reason for this might be because women have been associated with bodies in ways that men have not.[7] Bodies in general have been considered women's "sphere" in mythology, family life, philosophical, scientific and religious ideology.[8] It is within the writings of Foucault that we are led to consider the way that bodies and sexualities are shaped by social pressures and have been the subject of a vast array of different practices and discursive regimes. Some feminist writers, such as Susan Bordo[9] and Sandra Bartky[10] have expanded upon this platform by arguing that femininity can be viewed as a disciplinary regime in which femininity is 'achieved (if it is ever achieved) through a long process of labor to force the body into compliance with a feminine ideal, through depilation, cosmetics, exercise, dieting and attention to dress'.[11] The very act of dieting and restricting the consumption of food creates an all-consuming fear of hunger as it comes to symbolize how out of control the body is with its dangerous eruptions and needs. This hunger and struggle for control fosters within women an increasing sense that their bodies need for sustenance is wrong, dangerous and can overpower their carefully constructed and controlled self-restraint. The culmination of this is a tense balancing act and increasing intoxication and obsession with food in which food becomes the evil villain, threatening to take away the purity and innocence of the young woman.

Any response to anorexia must be as multifaceted as the disorder itself. My understanding of anorexia is distanced but not unconnected to those early instances of self-starvation, the female mystics who were encouraged to starve their bodies to stop menstruating and become honouree men[12] and the medieval fasting saints,[13] but its increasing prevalence marks a modern-day reaction to the environments in which we live and the ideals and values of those environments. Furthermore, my work is broader than a discussion limited to the boundaries of anorexia. It is about all those women who obsess about food and the consequences of eating too much. Their desire to emulate the slender ideal and conform to prevailing standards of beauty – that identify slenderness as an essential attribute – which are so deeply ingrained in their psyche that they are literally starving themselves to death.[14] I do not mean to simply blame men for all female wrongs, to unearth an age-old conspiracy to keep women from taking an equal position next to their male counterparts, or to place the blame on any one group for the social forces that keep women located firmly as "the second sex". As written by Bordo – quoting Foucault – that although a

> perfectly clear logic, with perfectly decipherable aims and objectives, may characterize historical power relations, it is nonetheless "often the case that no one was there to have invented" these aims and strategies, either through choice of individuals or through the rational game plan of some presiding "headquarters".[15]

People will consciously pursue goals that will better their own situation but this does not mean that they are conscious of the overall direction these actions might advance in. They might even be unaware of the consequences these "harmless" decisions have on others. However, it is certainly true that what we know of the world we live in today has, on the whole, been constructed by men and as such, created to suit their needs and desires. Taking this further, Naomi Wolf calls for us to look at how society 'makes use of a manufactured conflict with women's shapes'[16] instead of focusing all our efforts on individual women's psychology. She reminds us that 'individual men don't spin out fashionable images . . . multi-national corporations do that'.[17] This is part of a larger political movement[18] to critically explore the advanced capitalist roots underpinning the dis-ease between women and their bodies. She cites the overwhelmingly powerful message of our culture as the reason why girls and young women diet so aggressively, something that 'no amount of parental love and support [is] strong enough to override'.[19] She believes that until our culture tells girls and young women that their bodies are valued simply because they are inside them, that women are valuable with or without the excuse of "beauty", they will continue to starve. Polly Young-Eisendrath argues that for centuries all facets of a woman's life – motherhood, sex, spirituality, appearance, money, career – have been defined by male desires and standards which are so ingrained within our psyches that we struggle to break the rules. She argues that the breaking down of these boundaries is of paramount importance if we are to become self-determining women. She writes that '[a]t the very essence of what it means to be human . . . is the freedom to change. And this can be realized only when we know our own intentions, when we know what we want'.[20] Following from this position, I believe that the starting point for liberation from anorexia and the broader slender ideal is through understanding the nature of the void these obsessive behaviours are filling and what we truly want and desire from our lives. This book works towards this end as I search for symbols, stories, myths and rituals powerful enough to help these girls and young women re-appropriate their bodies and psychologies. It marks a pursuit towards female embodied consciousness utilizing some of the core features of Goddess thealogy within a political framework. Here we engage in a search for the divine feminine nature buried deep within the anorexic body and more broadly speaking, within every woman in society tightrope walking from one diet to another. It is in search of a reconnection to this hidden feminine nature, our desires, understanding our true hungers and emotions and as a political striving towards full equality and freedom within the environments in which we live. If we understand anorexia to be a deep-seated unease with the consequences of being a woman in our culture and as embodying a struggle for control and agency, I argue that liberation can take place through the search for meaning, authenticity and embodiment as a new way to understand and experience the world in which we live.

To unpack this further we need to delve into the literature of feminist spirituality which, in the last thirty years, has 'emerged as an expression of the creative transformations envisioned by feminist approaches to the study and practice of religion'[21] and has been used to 'denote the positive aspects of the ancient religious traditions, unencumbered by the "dead hand" of the church, and yet something which provides a liberation and solace in an otherwise meaningless world'.[22] I am concerned with using the term "spirituality" as a model within which to deconstruct and subvert the patriarchal and androcentric agenda that still presides over the lives of women. I use the term spirituality in the place of religion as I believe that the latter carries a deeply androcentric heritage that is too deeply ingrained to shake off. As argued within the writings of Mary Daly, Naomi Goldenberg, Nelle Morton, Carol Christ and others,[23] language and metaphor are of central importance in the re-visioning of structures that keep us oppressed. Alison Jasper writes that spirituality is a 'concept or metaphor for feminist-friendly thinking . . . that has the capacity to flourish . . . expanding – when it is strongly defended – public capacity for understanding the implications of difference/s and articulating in consequence some important and transformative visions'.[24] These difference/s have been manipulated into hostile "otherness" in the past as we see when it comes to gender inequality and the subjugation of women. In using this term, my intention is to disrupt the gender binaries that reinforce androcentric society as I work towards a gender-neutral space (initially focusing on female empowerment) for human flourishing. Here we work towards disabling the potential for this sex difference debilitating hostility that results in psychological maladies, such as anorexia. I argue the term spirituality has the potential to penetrate social norms and values in a way that might be restricted by the term religion given its patriarchal heritage.

Alongside this adoption of the term spirituality, my framework for unpacking and disseminating these cultural trends will draw from the academic discourses of feminist liberation theology, body theology and thealogy. My aim is to identify and isolate the damaging societal "norms" and feminine stereotypes that keep women at a dis-ease with their bodies which in turn limits their full and uncompromised participation in society and from disrupting the gender status quo in challenging androcentric rule. My focus, therefore, is on the desirability of the slender female aesthetic indicative of contemporary society and the attributes it is understood to represent. My work therefore carries a political agenda as I seek to create an alternative reality from the patriarchal undercurrents of contemporary society that find their roots within traditional Judeo-Christian theologies and Greek dualistic thought.[25] The disembodied rhetoric that results as a consequence of these patriarchal discourses of power become manifest within contemporary bodily practices as we see when we take a closer look at anorexia, extreme emaciation, eating disorders and diet culture more broadly. Through a lens of feminist liberation theology, and drawing upon the resources and developments made by body theology and thealogy, I work towards the development of a model of healing through which the possibility of dismantling and subverting the damaging rhetoric underpinning these actions and desires becomes possible. These discourses play a central role in my examination of anorexia and society as they each contribute a unique perspective on the contemporary human condition whilst challenging outdated assumptions about who is valued and why. This becomes clear as we explore the core principles of Feminist Liberation Theology and its central focus on the praxis of theology from the perspective of women. At the heart of this discourse lies a striving towards liberation from all forms of oppression whilst advocating the full humanity of every individual.[26] Here we call for the equal representation of women within theological discourse whilst placing female bodily knowing as a central component in the interpretation and re-visioning of the Christian faith, something far removed from the traditional theology espoused by the church fathers. It is a movement towards constructing 'theological doctrine whereby the experience of women, whether described in terms of oppression or the positive aspects of a women's world, plays a particular and significant role in shaping Christian theology'.[27] Thus, one of the core arguments is that patriarchal and androcentric hierarchies of power have historically been central to a wide range of theologies and traditions and it is these disorders that need to be re-imagined if humanity is to become liberated from the current structure of gender hierarchy and the inequality of sexism. As experience and incarnation are central aspects of the Judeo-Christian tradition, it is impossible for women to become equal partners in its construction if their experiences, participation and dialogue are excluded from the debate. As such, throughout this body of work, I take the female body as normative. Whilst so doing, I understand the constraints of this position as the very principles of feminist liberation theology limit the construction of a universal definition of what it means to be a woman. The consequence of this position means the very foundation of my work will continuously fluctuate as I work towards a model of subversion. It is important, however, to state that my own perspective is that of a white, Anglo-American female living within the United Kingdom, subject to all the vagaries of such a position. I write from my perspective of the damaging diet/slender/reductionist rhetoric this position affords me. The foundation I find within the patriarchal and androcentric Western world view finds its grounding within traditional Judeo-Christian theologies. As Rosemary Radford Ruether reminds us, the foundation of Western society has been heavily influenced by both historical and theological reflections, that 'religion has been not only a contributing factor, it is undoubtedly the single most important shaper and enforcer of the image and role of women in culture and society'.[28] Religion, as a social institution, has been the cultural sanctioner of the ideological reflection of our cultures sexual domination and subjugation.[29] Therefore, it follows that if we are to dismantle contemporary beauty ideals we must first understand how religion contributed to the Western world view that created them. She urges us to understand liberation in terms of political action and that is where I start, as you will see in the pages that follow. Sitting alongside Feminist Liberation Theology within this text is the discourse of Body Theology and more centrally, the advancements made by Thealogy over the last twenty years.

Broadening the reach of Feminist Liberation Theology, Body Theology places bodily knowing as central to the construction and imaging of the divine and our relationship with it. A theology of the body is based on a cycle of reflection, identification and action, as we identify damaging disembodied and dismembered rhetoric about the female body and its place within theological discourse. This reimagining of the female condition is further strengthened by the development of Goddess feminism and the religio-political discourse of Thealogy which emerged out of the late twentieth-century's re-emergence of a reverence for female deities. Within this discourse the 'Goddess can be seen as the symbol, the normative image of immanence'[30] as she 'represents the divine embodied in nature, in human beings, in flesh'.[31] I argue that thealogy provides the basis for a liberating and empowering framework towards which women can begin to understand and re-appropriate their bodies within society, to reclaim the feminine nature that has not just been lost but torn from their bodies. The basic premise of my argument is that it is only through understanding and engaging with the underlying features and drives of anorexia (by which I also include the broader slender ideal) that we can fully liberate ourselves from the patriarchal constraints that underpin these actions. I believe that the Judeo-Christian tradition is inherently and irredeemably patriarchal and so within a framework of theology where we are unable to satisfactorily liberate ourselves from the inequality of sexism, there will always be a hierarchy and men will always reside at the top. I strongly argue for a female, strong, powerful, empowering and embodied divinity located within the reality of our lives. This divine being carries the power to challenge our androcentric society and our patriarchal lineage asking why men are worth so much more than women and why the female body continues to be the battleground for this gender war. In this, we start to conceive of a new future modelled on equality. In reclaiming female power and liberating the crone, hag, cat lady, witch, harlot, whore from demonization and the mocking humor cruelly thrown at those women who do not fit into the "normal" role ascribed by our patriarchal society. This divinity advocates full embodiment with an aim to fully bind together the body and mind as we breach the gap made by our dualistic heritage. To work away from the concept of the body as an object to be refitted and reshaped at will. Whilst feminist liberation theology can help transgress these boundaries, to truly liberate ourselves from these patriarchal ideologies we need an alternative divine image to reflect upon. With this in mind, following an examination of the female body in contemporary society, and having taken a close look at the anorexic form, I will explore the benefits of a model of healing located within Goddess feminism as providing access to powerful female role models, sitting comfortably within their own flesh. Unashamed, unabashed and powerful, calling out and demanding freedom from these discourses that would see them starve themselves until they disappear. In doing this, I have divided the following body of work into five chapters.

In Chapter 1 I define what is meant by the term anorexia nervosa. This chapter identifies key characteristics as we explore the strengths and weaknesses of the medical classification systems used to make a diagnosis, alongside a consideration of the triggers and risk factors associated with disordered eating as we unpack the complex aetiology of anorexic behaviour. I argue that the aetiology of anorexia is multifaceted but ultimately develops out of our society's insistence that 'thin is good'.[32] As we shall critically explore in Chapter 2, this message is relayed in myriad ways throughout our environments, from the moment we are born to the moment we die. This slender, diet and reductionist rhetoric envelopes every sphere of our public and private life as our ultimate fear becomes succinctly embodied by the calories and fat caught between the crinkled edges of a muffin wrapper. In Chapter 3, on the female body as a politically mediated form, I discuss the "docile body" as conceptualized by Foucault and how the female body in society is constructed according to a very specific definition of femininity. As we shall see, adherence to the pejorative definition of femininity is essential if we are to become legitimate subjects within society. This idea of a legitimate performative subject is unpacked and analyzed from within the writings of Judith Butler and the idea of a slender performance is explored as we consider the ways in which fat as taboo has become an entrenched concept within our environments with dire consequences for women. Chapter 4 unpacks the female body as a historically mediated form as we look more closely at how anorexia is situated next to diagnoses of agoraphobia and hysteria indicative of the nineteenth and twentieth centuries. The female body as an area of control and domination is also broached as we explore, amongst others, the work of Richard Gordon, Naomi Wolf, Paula Saukko and Kim Chernin. The second half of this chapter focuses on the question of whether there is any psychological benefit or spirituality to result from the anorexic experience in the context of "cutting" and other self-harm practices. In Chapter 5 we take a look at discourses on the Goddess as we explore Goddess feminism and thealogy as a challenging to our patriarchal heritage and the inherently androcentric world view. It is here that I theorize on the idea that it is through thealogy and Goddess feminism that women, through the creation of individually meaningful myths, can reconnect with their bodies and experience a greater sense of embodiment as women. Drawing upon the idea of the Goddess, I explore ways to subvert and ultimately break down and destroy the power these oppressive female body standards hold over us.

The Spirituality of Anorexia examines the different facets of women's entry into culture and society. It addresses issues surrounding control, low self-esteem, disempowerment, rejection, suffering and the desire for a youthful aesthetic. In assessing the relationship between the individual and society through an examination of body theology and thealogy – which draws upon the childhood struggle for identity and issues surrounding sexuality – we may re-evaluate our approaches and create a healing thealogy based upon empowerment and embodiment. Literature from the academics referred to in this body of work show us that liberation from an obsession with food and weight takes place slowly. It is a central aim of this book to transform an obsession with food into an authentic ritual of transformation.[33]

Notes

1 Society's construction of the feminine in this work refers to a distorted female ideal. By this I mean the socially constructed feminine ideals and stereotypes ("beauty" prerequisites such as: slenderness, cosmetics, face and body shapes etc.) "sold" to us with the underlying message that the attainment of these aesthetic principles will result in a happy, loving and fulfilling life; that possessing these qualities will improve the individual's experiences of embodiment.

2 See Chernin, K. (1994) *The Obsession: Reflections on the Tyranny of Slenderness*. New York: HarperPerennial; Orbach, S. (1998) *Fat Is a Feminist Issue*. London: Arrow Books; Heywood, L. (1996) *Dedication to Hunger: The Anorexia Aesthetic in Modern Culture*. Berkeley: University of California Press; and Bordo, S. (1999) *Twilight Zones*. Berkeley: University of California Press.

3 This was cited by Patricia Fallon, Susan Wooley and Melanie Katzman in 1994. See Fallon, P., Wooley, S. C., Katzman, M. A. (1994) *Feminist Perspectives on Eating Disorders*. New York: The Guilford Press, ix.

4 Bordo, S. (2003) *Unbearable Weight: Feminism, Western Culture, and the Body*. London: University of California Press; Wolf, N. (1990) *The Beauty Myth: How Images of Beauty Are Used Against Women*. London: Vintage Books; and Wolf, N. (1994) Hunger. In: Fallon, P., Katzman, M. A., Wooley, S. C. (eds.) *Feminist Perspectives on Eating Disorders*. New York: The Guildford Press, 94–115.

5 As written by Susan Bordo 'it is not a matter of cultural *repression* of the instinctual or natural body. Rather, there is no "natural" body. Cultural practices, far from exerting their power *against* spontaneous needs, "basic" pleasures or instincts, or "fundamental" structures of body experience, are already and always inscribed'(Bordo 2003: 142; Author's emphasis).

6 Warner, M. (1985) *Monuments and Maidens: The Allegory of the Female Form*. London: Weidenfeld & Nicolson, 331. Quoted in Wykes, M., Gunter, B. (2004) *The Media and Body Image: If Looks Could Kill*. London: Sage Publications, 62.

7 As discussed in greater detail in Chapter 1, it is estimated that 89 per cent of anorexic sufferers are female. As such, it is the issue of contemporary female embodiment that I am principally concerned with here.

8 Bordo (2003: 143).

9 Bordo (2003; and 1999).

10 Bartky, S. L. (1988) Foucault, Femininity and the Modernization of Patriarchal Power. In: Diamond, I., Quinby, L. (eds.) *Feminism and Foucault: Reflections on Resistance*. Boston: Northeasten University Press.

11 Mills, S. (2003) *Michael Foucault*. London: Routledge, 93.

12 Bynum, C. W. (1987) *Holy Feast and Holy Fast: The Religious Significance of Food to Medieval Women*. London, England/Berkeley and Los Angeles, California: University of California Press.

13 Despite the similarities between the accounts of medieval fasting saints (described as 'Holy' anorexia by Rudolph Bell) and contemporary experiences of anorexia (namely, an unwillingness to consume sustenance, the physical symptoms of malnutrition, struggle for power and acceptance), as culturally situated forms of

female protest (as we explore throughout this body of work), they are unique and distinct expressions which culminate as a consequence of the female idealizations, stereotypes and identity restrictions of their time. These women, separated by decades, are driven by different social forces and influences but common to accounts from both periods, is a renouncing of food because they abhor the consequences. The drive for the fasting saint or Holy anorexic is holiness whilst, as this body of work will attest, the drive for women utilizing the anorexic expression in contemporary society, is thinness. This thinness comes to symbolize a number of social ills, whilst expressing a drive towards a more meaningful existence, is nevertheless framed by the cultural influences of contemporary society and the pervasive slender ideal. For more information, see Bell, R. M. (1987) *Holy Anorexia*. London: The University of Chicago Press; and Bynum 1987.

14 Anorexia is commonly cited as having the highest death rate of any psychiatric illness. Frequent causes include suicide and organ failure as a direct result of starvation. For more information, see Rachelle, L., Lilenfeld, R. (2016) Suicidal behaviour in Eating Disorders. In: Latzer, Y., Stein, D. (eds.) *Bio-Psycho-Social Contributions to Understanding Eating Disorders*. New York: Springer International Publishing, 65–77 (66).

15 Foucault quoted in Bordo (2003: 144–145).

16 Wolf (1994: 98).

17 Wolf (1994: 98).

18 Explored further in Chapter 4.

19 Wolf (1994: 104).

20 Young-Eisendrath, P. (2001) *Women and Desire: Beyond Wanting to Be Wanted*. London: Judy Piatkus Ltd, xv.

21 Mantin, R. (2001) Carol Christ: Feminist Spirituality and Narrative Thealogy. In: Erricker, C., Erriker, J. (eds.) *Contemporary Spiritualities: Social and Religious Contexts*. London: Continuum, 93–113 (93).

22 Carrette, J., King, R. (2005) *Selling Spirituality: The Silent Takeover of Religion*. London: Routledge, 1.

23 Daly, M. (1992) *Beyond God the Father: Towards a Philosophy of Women's Liberation*. Boston: Beacon Press; Goldenberg, N. (1979) *Changing of the Gods: Feminism and the End of Traditional Religions*. Boston: Beacon Press; Morton, N. (1985) *The Journey Is Home*. Boston: Beacon Press; and Christ, C. (1997) *Rebirth of the Goddess: Finding Meaning in Feminist Spirituality*. Reading: Addison-Wesley.

24 Jasper, A. (2015) Womanspirit Still Rising? Some Feminist Reflections on 'Religious Education' in the UK. In: *Feminist Theology* 23, no. 3: 240–253 (246).

25 Two dualistic philosophies are referred to throughout this body of work as a consequence of the damage their imagining of the separation between the mind and body has caused to contemporary female experiences of embodiment, namely Greek and Cartesian dualisms. The former finds its location within the philosophy of ancient Greece and operates under the premise that the mind and body are two ontologically separate categories. This is commonly attributed to the work of Plato (428–348 BCE) who separated ideas from the rest of human existence by stressing the ideal over empirical reality, encouraged the use of the mind as a mechanism to overrule the body. His philosophy took many forms and heavily influenced early Christian theologies. Within this philosophy, women were associated with the body, whilst men found a closer association with the mind. This is evident when reflecting on the work of Aristotle who wrote that the ruling-class Greek males exemplified the mind (spirit) whilst women, slaves and barbarians represent the "body" in their need to be controlled by the ruling elite. Thus, a hierarchy was established based on a male elitist system of values. In a similar fashion, Cartesian dualism, a philosophy which originated from the work of French thinker Rene Descartes (1596–1650), distinguished the mind and body as

different forms and elevated the mind and "rational" thought as superior to the physical aspects of human existence. Within this philosophy, the mind belonged within the realm of the spirit. He encouraged the belief that human value resided in our thinking ability whilst our physical nature was conceptualized in animal and base terminology. This served to further perpetuate the pre-Christian Greek division of the world into polarities of black and white, good and bad, mind and body. The way of dealing with this dualism was to transcend the body by striving to be a disembodied being. For more information on Greek and Cartesian dualisms see McKim, D. K. (2014) *The Westminster Dictionary of Theological Terms*. Louisville: Westminster John Know Press, 238. For information on how this dualistic heritage has been addressed from a feminist liberation theological perspective, see Isherwood, L., McEwan, D. (2001) *Introducing Feminist Theology*. Sheffield: Sheffield Academic Press, 78; and Martin, F. (2011) *The Feminist Question: Feminist Theology in Light of Christian Tradition*. Eugene: Wipf & Stock Publishers.

26 Peacore, L. (2008) Feminist Theologies. In: Dyrness, W. A., Karkkainen, V.-M. (eds.) *Global Dictionary of Theology: A Resource for the Worldwide Church*. Nottingham: Inter-Varsity Press, 317–322.

27 Peacore (2008: 317).

28 Ruether, R. R. (1974) *Religion and Sexism*. New York: Simon and Schuster, 9.

29 Here I refer to the damage that dominant patriarchal readings have wrought on the integrity of the belief systems they come to represent. Within the context of the patriarchal readings of biblical narratives, women have been undermined, beaten, raped, demonized and named as the source of male sin. A plethora of research has been generated by feminist liberation theologians in the hope that in identifying the damaging misogynist undercurrents, work can be done to re-appropriate these biblical narratives and improve the situation of women today. For more information, see Ruether 1974; Long, A. P. (1992) *In a Chariot Drawn by Lions: The Search for the Female in Deity*. London: The Women's Press Ltd; Condren, M. (2002) *The Serpent and the Goddess: Women, Religion and Power in Celtic Ireland*. Dublin: New Island Books; and Isherwood, L. (2007b) *Patriarchs, Prophets and Other Villains*. London: Equinox Publishing.

30 Starhawk (1982a) *Dreaming the Dark: Magic, Sex & Politics*. Boston: Beacon Press, 9.

31 Starhawk (1982a: 9).

32 Lynn, C. (2012) *Hope With Eating Disorders*. London: Hay House UK LTD, 231.

33 This ritual of transformation works towards the evolution of a new type of female identity, a theme we shall explore throughout this text. Chernin, K. (1985) *The Hungry Self: Women, Eating and Identity*. New York: HarperCollins Publishers, xxii.

1 Anorexia nervosa

The starting point for our discussions surrounding the complex aetiology of anorexia must be on its definition, the basis upon which a diagnosis is made, its location alongside other eating disorders, risk factors and triggers. As such, in the following pages, I will examine the current medical classification systems used to make a diagnosis of anorexia and the complications of applying this to such a multifaceted and complex cluster of symptoms. In this we start to unpack the undercurrents of anorexia and to identify the meaning behind the statistics that show a growth in incidences over the twentieth and twenty-first centuries. The second and third sections of this chapter will provide an overview of the history of anorexia as we explore the aetiology of this eating disorder and identify common risk factors as drawn on by researchers in the field. The aim of this chapter is to provide an overview of contemporary research and developing understandings of anorexia before examining contemporary therapeutic and medical responses to the expression.

The term "Anorexia Nervosa" was first named and identified in medical literature by Sir William Gull in 1873. However, very similar afflictions dating back to the fourteenth century of fasting girls and Catholic saints have been found in historical accounts. Features common to these accounts include, but are not limited to, deliberate self-starvation, excessive activity, amenorrhea (absence of menstrual cycle for at least three months in post-menarcheal women), a fear of being fat or gaining weight and 'a fear and terror of food and an obsession – although secretive – interest in food'.[1] Those who suffer from anorexia express their preoccupation with food by becoming thin 'to the point of emaciation and sometimes even to the point of death through starvation'.[2] The term anorexia, originates from the Greek *an* meaning "little", and *orexis* which translates as "appetite". Thus, the literal translation can be summed up as a lack of desire to eat. This could not be further from the truth as anorexic individuals do not escape the pangs and cramps of hunger, rather 'this extreme form of self-starvation is distinguished by a *struggle* to transcend hunger signals'[3] and to *control* the hungers and desires of the body. Thus, medical conditions and mental disorders that lead to significant weight loss should be excluded from a diagnosis of anorexia as the individuals desire to reduce their weight is absent. Therefore, the primary distinction made should be whether or not the weight loss is intentional.

Anorexia is considered a mental illness and is therefore classified according to a clinically approved list of symptoms and behaviours. The most common of which are taken from *The Diagnostics and Statistics Manual for Mental Health Disorders* (DSM-5) and the *International Statistical Classification of Diseases and Related Health Problems* (ICD-10). There is a slight discrepancy between these two definitions but for the most part the following description covers the "essence" of the disorder from a medical and treatment perspective. In the ICD-10 anorexia is defined as:

> A disorder characterised by deliberate weight loss, induced and sustained by the patient. It occurs most commonly in adolescent girls and young women, but adolescent boys and young men may also be affected, as may children approaching puberty and older women up to the menopause. The disorder is associated with a specific psychopathology whereby a dread of fatness and flabbiness of body contour persists as an intrusive overvalued idea, and the patients impose a low threshold on themselves. There is usually under nutrition of varying severity with secondary endocrine and metabolic changes and disturbances of bodily function. The symptoms include restricted dietary choice, excessive exercise, induced vomiting and purgation/purging, and use of appetite suppressants and diuretics.[4]

A different focus is captured in *The Diagnostics and Statistics Manual for Mental Health Disorders* (DSM-5), which places more importance on self-evaluation (as opposed to the ICD-10's 'dread of fatness and flabbiness of body contour'). The DSM-5, a slightly amended version of the previous DSM-4, was revised from the following diagnosis classification system: 'refusal to maintain body weight over minimum expected for age and height'[5] (usually a body weight less than 85 per cent of what is expected); an intense 'fear of gaining weight or becoming fat';[6] a disturbance in 'the experience of body weight and shape, undue influence of body weight or shape on self-evaluation, or denial of the seriousness of low body weight';[7] and, amenorrhea (the absence of three consecutive menstrual cycles). The updated version removes the word "refusal" as it infers intention on the part of the individual which can be difficult to diagnose along with the amenorrhea as this previously excluded men, women taking contraceptives, premenarchal or post-menopausal women. A patient exhibiting partial criteria would fall into the Eating Disorder Not Otherwise Specified (EDNOS) diagnosis. Both of these definitions require the individual to have lost a significant amount of weight (although the actual weight lost in order to constitute a diagnosis is ambiguous and open to interpretation in both classification systems). This ambiguity can lend itself to the pejorative understanding that anorexia is limited to those individuals who display extreme emaciation; a common misconception. For example, a study carried out by researchers at Australia's Murdoch Children's Research Institute found that between 2005 and 2010, there was a 'fivefold increase in the incidence of hospitalised adolescents who, apart from not being underweight, met all of the criteria for the diagnosis of anorexia nervosa'.[8] Professor Susan Sawyer, director of The Royal Children's Hospital Centre for Adolescent Health maintains that '[e]ating disorders can emerge at any weight'[9] and can be indicated by any sudden weight loss, even if 'the young person is not underweight at the time they present'.[10] She argues that many health professionals overlook or delay a diagnosis of anorexia based on the individual's weight loss and because of this, the patients may be extremely unwell before they are finally admitted to hospital. Carrie Arnold identified the moment she became anorexic as follows 'I wasn't clinically underweight . . . but I was unable to start eating on my own, I was terrified of gaining weight, and I was unable to see what the issue was'.[11]

The clinical classifications used to make a diagnosis of anorexia, whilst standardizing the symptoms and allowing for a common approach towards diagnosis and treatment, have been criticized for their limited scope and exclusionary nature. For example, the previous inclusion of amenorrhea meant that a diagnosis of anorexia in post-menopausal women[12] and pre-menarcheal women was prevented although, as we have discussed, steps have been taken to make the criteria more inclusive. Anorexia varies between individuals and it is quite possible for a person to exhibit eating disordered emotions and behaviours whilst meeting only partial ICD-10 and DSM-5 criteria. Also, standardized criteria lend themselves to a similarly standardized approach in therapy which, as we will explore throughout this book, can be problematic. The use of bespoke therapies that utilize a number of approaches whilst working towards recovery is often necessary in order to truly unpack the varied and complex factors that led to utilizing this expression. Whilst I will not go into detail here about the pros and cons of the diagnostic criteria (which is by-and-large far beyond the scope of this work), it is important to clarify that questions have been raised about the absolute nature of the classification criteria and where the line should be drawn between dieting behaviour and anorexia. Incorporating all aspects of eating disordered behaviour into one working definition is a problematic task. The clinical criteria are clearly an attempt to recognize the physical effects of anorexia and to move away from, what could be criticized as, vague psychological features such as the inability to recognize internal states and emotions (as we shall examine later with the work of Hilde Bruch) and a deficient sense of self. The inclusion of amenorrhea was an example of this. However, the criteria are clearly moving towards becoming more inclusive. It is worth remaining mindful of the classification systems subjective nature and what the consequence of a diagnosis might mean for the women suffering from such extreme eating behaviours. For example, by including anorexia nervosa, bulimia nervosa, and EDNOS into the DSM-5 and ICD-10, we pathologize disorders and label them as "abnormal", which is in itself damaging for the individual exhibiting symptoms. This movement towards pathologizing mental health disorders, which finds its grounding within biological and "concrete" developmental explanations, may also result in people seeking pharmaceutical interventions[13] instead of considering the benefits of behavioural and therapy driven strategies – the latter of which is usually side-effect free.

Anorexia shares many of its traits with other mental illnesses, such as mood and anxiety disorders and obsessive-compulsive disorders, which can lead to additional complications when it comes to correctly diagnosing and treating the underlying issues. Furthermore, the effects of starvation can exacerbate some characteristics. For example, anhedonia (the inability to feel pleasure in usually pleasurable situations), insomnia (an inability to sleep) and depressed mood can be explained as a consequence of starvation and malnutrition. The same could be said for the anorexic's obsessive and secretive interest in food and the ritualization of eating. Therefore, a depressed mood and anxiety diagnosis should not be made if the symptoms could also be explained as features of anorexia. The same is true for the compulsive desire to calculate calorie intake, which should not be confused with obsessive-compulsive syndromes and the need to keep belongings in a certain order (although commonalities clearly exist). Other common features of anorexia can be identified as social phobia and reluctance towards eating food in front of family and friends for fear of being challenged or judged. This judgement is not just limited to the quantity of food being consumed (whether too much or too little) but also the act of eating itself. Other common features of anorexia are the presence of body image disturbance 'in the forms of fear of weight gain or denial of the seriousness of low weight'[14] and a fixation on the body as an arena for control and discipline.

Anorexia often begins with the decision to diet which provides the individual with powerful feelings of control and mastery for both internal (power, control and euphoria for someone who previously felt weak, depressed and empty) and external reasons (conforming to the slender ideal in an environment where the thin body represents a great achievement). A secondary satisfaction might also be gleaned from the power of manipulation that the individual exerts over her family and friends. As Richard Gordon writes: 'in a situation in which she may have felt herself discounted, the refusal of food evokes a powerful response from others, an assertion of her presence that can no longer be ignored'.[15] In addition to these social and psychological factors, there will be physiological consequences that result from the effects of starvation. These factors can be independent of the causes that produced the initial symptoms. As dieting becomes fasting and fasting becomes wilful starvation, the body has little energy left to heat the outer extremities and focuses instead on keeping the internal organs warm; this results in the anorexic individual feeling continuously cold. Malnutrition can also lead to heart irregularities (bradycardia) and electrolyte disturbances such as low potassium and chloride levels. As the body is put through gruelling exercise regimes, the consequences of starvation can become even more exacerbated. The "fasting high" that is often experienced at the start of this disorder is quickly replaced by feelings of hopelessness, emptiness and depression. It is these feelings that come to have dominance throughout the life of the disorder. When the weight loss becomes extreme, tactics of deception and secrecy are employed by the individual to defend herself from reprisal. She attempts to fool both the people in her immediate environment and herself as she seeks to justify this behaviour by denying the seriousness of her condition. This denial can often extend to families and friends who seek to rationalize this behaviour as a "passing phase". Thus, when the diagnosis is finally made, the individual is already caught in a complex web of physiological disturbances and psychological attitudes. Similar effects were captured by the Minnesota studies which examined the mind-set of the conscientious objectors of World War Two. Attitudes identified here included an obsessive preoccupation with food, social withdrawal, difficulty concentrating and depression.

Anorexia has been identified as a disorder of adolescence (with peak ages between fourteen and eighteen) as the disorder is typically 'triggered by stresses that challenge the individual's sense of personal identity and competence'[16] which is pivotal during this period especially in an environment which values the slender disciplined body.[17] Issues here are resolved by weight loss and bodily discipline. For some young women, the adolescent period offers challenges that are more easily masked by the development of anorexia than by addressing them directly. These challenges can be identified as independent decision-making, the intimacy of sexual relationships and the need to identify and pursue self-chosen activities and goals. Playing a significant part in this is their desire to please others and "be good" which can be exacerbated over time when coinciding with other pressures (exams, puberty and the development of "womanly curves") or experiences (loss of a friend, failure to live up to personal expectations, romantic rejections). These experiences can increase feelings of powerlessness and trigger (for those who already have low self-esteem and a tendency towards perfectionism) an eating disorder such as anorexia. Whilst these experiences are not limited to adolescence, they are most common during this period. If the underlying issues are not addressed, when faced with similar experiences in later life, they can once again resurface.

In terms of gender as a risk factor, women are approximately nine times more likely to be diagnosed with anorexia than men.[18] As we will explore in the following chapter, this is commonly attributed to the differences between male and female body image ideals within Western societies. This indicates the importance of environmental factors on the development of eating disorders. This is not just the case within contemporary accounts of anorexia but this bias towards female prevalence has been a common feature throughout the history of the disorder.

History

Although the term was first coined in 1873,[19] as a clinical entity, accounts of anorexic behaviour have been identified as far back as two centuries earlier. One of the first documented cases was recorded in 1689 when Richard Morton, an English physician, detailed two cases of a "wasting" disease of nervous origin. The primary symptoms were a radical weight loss and a loss of appetite that he attributed to 'sadness and anxious cares'.[20] One of his female patients experienced indifference to extreme cold conditions, amenorrhea and spent a significant amount of time 'poring upon Books'.[21] On receiving her diagnosis, she rejected treatment and died following a fainting fit. The second case documented was of a 16-year-old boy who abandoned food and bodily needs whilst focusing, with increasing rapture, on his studies and pursuits of the mind. However, he regained health following the recommendation that he abandon his studies and 'pursue his health in the country'.[22] Over the next two centuries very few accounts of this disorder make their way into medical reports.

It was in 1945 that interest really started forming around this "new symptom" with Dr Ludwig Binswanger documenting the case of Ellen West, described as an intelligent young woman, who exhibited symptoms that had rarely been exhibited outside the religious community until this point. Exhibiting many symptoms common to contemporary accounts of anorexia, at the age of twenty, she started to develop a 'dread of becoming fat, avoided food, and went on long hikes'.[23] This change in body perception is identified as a consequence of her brother becoming fatally ill, her father's rejection of her engagement to a 'romantic foreigner'[24] and appears to have been triggered by a holiday with friends where she was 'teased for being fat'.[25] This obsession took its grasp and lasted thirteen years until she died at the age of thirty-three. Throughout these years she struggled to understand this obsession but reported feeling spiritually satisfied because she was thin.[26] She later admits to her husband 'that she is living her life only with a view to being able to remain thin, that she is subordinating every one of her actions to this end, and that this idea has gained a terrible power over her'.[27] She understood the dangers of her situation as her reason rebelled against her attempts to starve herself but she was choked by her obsession and was ultimately unable to free herself. West grew up at a time when women were seeking greater freedoms and access to previously male-dominated domains. It was also a time of changing fashions as the voluptuous female body gave way to the slender aesthetic ideal. Her internal struggles and conflicts (her desire for freedom pitted against her wish to meet and exceed her family's expectations), in the context of her personality and family, met in the desire to control and reduce her body and the space it demands. The conflicting aspects of her personality (passionate, creative and sensual in opposition to her desire for control, order and success and their gender associations) developed as a reaction to the dilemmas of the culture she lived in. She rebelled against the constraints of the female role seeking to reject its limitations. This took its root during childhood, a time when she longed to be a boy and pursue her ambitions and thirsts. In her diary she wrote 'you realize that the existing social order is rotten . . . rotten down to the root, dirty and mean; but you do nothing to overthrow it'.[28] She struggled but was unable to find a meaningful means of deposing the system. Bound by the 'iron chains'[29] of her life, she instead focused on her desire to be 'delicate and ethereal'.[30] During the thirteen years of this obsession, West took up to sixty to seventy laxative tablets every evening, became a vegetarian (skipping meals but consuming up to twenty oranges and several pounds of tomatoes per day), hid food at meal times and attached weights to her body whenever she was weighed. Her menstrual cycle ceased following a miscarriage, she suffered from severe depression and anxiety, developed an obsession with death which culminated in four suicide attempts, the final one resulted in death. She wrote: 'I am in a prison and cannot get out. It does no good for the analyst to tell me that I myself place the armed men there, that they are theatrical figments and not real. TO ME THEY ARE VERY REAL'.[31] The prison and the armed men were real. They came to represent the entire unknown cultural, social and psychological forces within which West was fighting against. As they remained unknown and unnamed, they suffocated and ultimately destroyed her. The final hours of her life make for an uncomfortable read:

> On her third day at home [she is transformed], Ellen ate more freely – so much so that for the first time in 13 years she felt satisfied and really full. In the afternoon she ate coffee creams and Easter eggs. In the evening she went for a walk with her husband and read poetry. She appeared cheerful. Later that evening, however, she took a lethal dose of poison, and on the following morning she was dead.[32]

For West, developing an understanding of the underlying issues and ultimately finding equilibrium was the only way she could save herself from the condition but despite searching for an answer, her desperation consumed her. The decision to take her life in the face of irreconcilable feelings can be understood as an act of release from the crushing pressures of her life. Her anxiety surrounding the consumption of food and the size of her body meant that she felt trapped and unable to find a meaningful existence.

Over the next twenty to thirty years, psychoanalytic interpretations emerged from American psychiatry that theorized on the sexual origins of anorexia and the hypothesis that anorexic women were defending themselves 'against fantasies of oral impregnation, or against promiscuous impulses'.[33] This appeared to follow the footsteps of Freud who attributed self-starvation in girls and young women to depression caused by sexual underdevelopment in 1896. However, significant breakthroughs in contemporary understandings of this disorder emerged following the publication of Hilde Bruch's work *Eating Disorders* in 1973 in which she distinguished between two types of anorexia; primary and secondary. She argued that the development of anorexia took its form from body insecurities but that it also indicated problems in the young women's psychological development. She stated that there were intimate connections between disorders of the body (and anxieties over its shape and weight) and disorders where the consumption of food became a psychological conflict. She categorized the primary type as a determined refusal to eat as opposed to a loss of appetite. The attributes displayed by individuals categorized by this type were identified as a distorted body image and delusional misconceptions surrounding the body's size and shape, being unable to identify internal feelings and needs (such as hungers and emotions), and a powerful and overwhelming sense that their actions, thoughts and feelings are ineffective and simply products of external expectations as opposed to expressions of the self. She argued that this behaviour (particularly the deficient sense of self) was grounded in childhood experiences which helped explain why the disorder typically becomes manifest in adolescence (a time when self-mastery, independence and identity is essential to achieve independence from parents). Secondary anorexia was understood as a more diverse condition and its central feature was weight loss due to psychogenic (emotional or mental) distresses. These involved psychological conflicts arising from underlying personality difficulties. Distinguishing between these anorexic "drives" helps us to identify the most helpful (and thus, potentially beneficial) path towards healing. For example, someone driven by the cultural slender female ideal will need a different approach to treatment than someone suffering from anorexia as a consequence of depression or an anxiety disorder. Despite how beneficial the theory of Bruch's was in understanding the aetiology of anorexia, it has not been fully accepted and incorporated into the contemporary criteria within the diagnostic manuals (aspects of this classification are however, closely linked with the diagnostic criteria for EDNOS).

At the time of publication in 1973, Bruch was still able to describe anorexia as 'rare indeed'.[34] However, in the years that followed the incidences experienced a meteoric rise. It was in the 1980s, Gordon writes, that anorexia was 'widely publicized, glamorised, and to some extent romanticized'[35] which led to it becoming an acceptable vehicle 'for the expression of mental illness in Western, industrialised culture'.[36] As written by George Devereux, anorexia became the prescribed template for mental illness '[d]on't go crazy, but if you do, do it this way'.[37] It was labelled the "disease of the 80s", which reflected how easy it is for diseases to become "fashionable". Gordon wrote that the central feature of anorexia is the intense pursuit of thinness and a morbid fear of getting fat which he saw as a cultural, not just a clinical problem. So, it was in 1984 that Susan Bordo (one of the leading experts in the aetiology of anorexia) wrote that 'one in every 200–250 women between the ages of thirteen and twenty-two suffer from anorexia, and that anywhere from 12 to 33 percent of women control their weight through vomiting, diuretics, and laxatives'.[38] Moving forward thirty-one years from Bordo's figures, in a report commissioned by B-eat (the leading UK charity for people with eating disorders) and produced by PwC in 2015 titled *The Costs of Eating Disorders – Social, Health and Economic Impacts* estimates that more than 725,000 people in the UK are affected by an eating disorder of which 11 per cent are male.[39] B-eat also references estimates provided by the NHS information centre (which draws upon the 2007 Adult Psychiatric Morbidity Survey[40]) which suggest that up to '6.4% of adults displayed signs of an eating disorder'[41] and (in contrast with the B-eat report) that 25 per cent of reported cases result in males. Also cited are figures published by The Health and Care Information Centre in February 2014 which demonstrated 'an 8% rise in the number of inpatient hospital admissions in the 12 months previous to October 2013'.[42] The same report says this is indicative of trend as research shows that the percentage is increasing year-on-year: 'a 34% increase in admissions since 2005–06 – approximately 7% each year'.[43] B-eat claim that of those with eating disorders, 10 per cent are suffers of anorexia, 40 per cent are bulimic, and the remaining 50 per cent fall into the EDNOS category which includes, for example, binge eating disorders and those individuals that only partially meet the criteria for anorexia or bulimia (most will be aged between 14 and 25 years old although cases of young children and post-menopausal women have also been recorded).[44] This however, does not represent the many women who have eating habits which give cause for concern or are dieting and/or exercising excessively. When reflecting on the statistics, it is also worth noting that they are limited to those who are affected by eating disorders who have received inpatient NHS treatment and they therefore exclude all those who have not come forward, have not been diagnosed, are receiving private treatment, are being treated as an outpatient in the community or who do not currently meet the diagnostic criteria used for diagnosing an eating disorder. There is definitely a need for more reliable statistics and for broader understandings of what constitutes an eating disorder if we are to understand and treat the issues lying at the heart of a diagnosis of anorexia.

The aetiology of anorexia

As a multifaceted disorder, determining the aetiology of anorexia can be a highly contentious and emotive issue. From cultural influences, fashion and feminine ideals to biological predispositions, discussions surrounding the "starvation gene", the construction of identity and the influence of family members, there are a plethora of causes cited as providing the bedrock for the development of anorexia. Whist these will be discussed in greater detail in the chapters that follow, we shall explore some of these theories now.

Cultural and environmental factors are often cited as providing the groundwork for a negative relationship with the body. These factors include society's emphasis on thinness, the link between self-control, self-discipline and dieting, the participation in sports with emphasis on a lithe, svelte physique and the attainment of a slender body as a consequence of desiring attention and respect from peers and family members. These factors make up the underlying features which lead to the development of low self-esteem and the desire towards perfectionism that find their expression within the development of anorexia. These values are communicated throughout media and advertisement campaigns and find reassurances though family and friends who have themselves internalized such ideals. We live in a society that endorses a fear of fat and a repulsion of gaining weight. Within this framework fear of rejection becomes the "drive" or "motivation" for weight loss. As Susie Orbach writes, it is clear that 'our bodily codes and behaviours constitute who we are'.[45] Our bodies communicate crucial aspects of our identities and affiliations, as has been the case throughout history. The way we display ourselves marks us as belonging to a particular group of people as bodies communicate the period, religious values and geography through displaying forms of body modification such as lengthening the neck, tattooing skin, decorating faces, binding feet, covering heads, etc. The body 'is neither natural nor pure but a body that is inscribed and formed by the accretion of myriad small and specific cultural practices'.[46] Within Western society, anorexia has come to symbolize a great achievement as control and discipline have been implemented to reduce the body's boundaries. This all takes place within our androcentric and patriarchal society which has been heavily influenced by our dualistic heritage which values domination, control and order over the bodies of those who inhabit its spaces. Overlaying these cultural features, Victor Turner in *The Body in Society*, writes that anorexia expresses patriarchal anxieties regarding women's bodies and conveys the contemporary view of thinness as beauty. Although anorexia has been a predominantly Western disorder,[47] in recent years the incidence of anorexia in non-Western cultures has experienced an increase.[48] One reason cited for this growth is that globalization has 'caused popular culture to infiltrate non-western cultures'[49] and with it, thinness as a beauty necessity has become popularized. The debate surrounding the role of social factors in the development of anorexia is ongoing. It is widely accepted that anorexia is both culturally and historically situated and that sociocultural factors play a significant part in its development and continuation amongst girls and young women. The industries culpable for these insidious messages and values are the beauty and fashion industries, advertising and marketing campaigns (focusing solely on desirability of the slender form and the associated attributes) and television shows which relay, through visual representation, that success, wealth, happiness and love are granted to those who conform to these narrowly defined ideals (Gossip Girl, Sex and the City, Friends . . . the list is endless!). This has led to the understanding of anorexia as a culture-bound syndrome. This will be the focus of the following chapter as we explore and critically analyze the cultural factors that culminate in the development of low self-esteem and body anxieties in women.

Whilst some features of anorexia appear to be culturally bound, there is a plethora of research that argues the aetiology lies within our biology. The biological risk factors include genetic vulnerability, obsessive-compulsive traits, depression, perfectionism along with exactness and precision, the early onset of puberty and sexual maturation, low self-esteem and the constant desire for approval and reassurance, the need for control, restrictive dieting, avoiding risk and harm and the pursuit of an eating disorder identity.[50] Broadly speaking, for many cultural analysts and those operating within the medical community, it is argued that our genes 'load the gun but the environment pulls the trigger'.[51] For example, Joan Brumberg in *Fasting Girls: The History of Anorexia Nervosa*[52] writes that anorexia develops as a consequence of cultural, biological and psychological variables but that the two latter factors are "culturally neutral" and therefore, not shared by all dieters. This would account for why only some women will develop anorexia. She argues that individuals diagnosed with anorexia require objective psychiatric treatment which might not be granted if the assumption made is that the condition is purely the consequence of sociocultural factors. Gordon takes a similar approach as he refers to 'developmental vulnerabilities'[53] to describe the difference he sees between anorexic women and "normal" dieters. The key argument here is that there must be some biomedical or psychological problem that would account for why some, and not all, women develop an eating disorder such as anorexia. However, what appears to go unacknowledged is that each of us will experience the world differently. Whilst there are culturally bound ideals and stereotypes that are universally acknowledged, each of us will have unique experiences of these in the context of our individual lives; not everyone will live or experience these social discourses in the same way. Whilst the clinical model may be to identify and treat the "internal" causes (internal to both families and individuals), cultural theorists such as Susan Bordo focus on anorexia as a "crystallization" of numerous cultural streams which revolve around the body as a site of control.[54] Anorexia becomes an internalization of sociocultural ideals that express an extreme or exaggerated form of "normal" behaviour. Within this model, under the right conditions, anyone can develop an eating disorder such as anorexia. Thus, with what we already know about the glamorization of anorexia in the 1980s, this position might go some way to explain the dramatic rise in diagnoses.

Other arguments that gravitate towards biological risk factors identify the importance of hormone imbalances. One such argument is that anorexia is caused by a serotonin imbalance in the brain (a popular stance within the medical community that the 'common cause of depression and eating disorders is located in brain chemistry'[55]), that tiny differences in the HT2A serotonin receptor could have people 'pre-wired for anorexia from birth'.[56] When triggered by a weight loss diet, these differences can 'set off a series of events that trip . . . [these] neurochemical wires . . . out of control'.[57] Other research looks at the relationship between anorexia, depression, obsessive-compulsive disorder and anxiety disorders. Arnold in *Decoding Anorexia* believes that a large number of suffers also show signs of having an anxiety disorder that could predate the eating disorder. As such, she argues that if 'anxiety is a pathway into the disorder . . . finding alternative ways to manage anxiety is a pathway out'.[58] She argues that anorexia is a biologically based mental illness and not the sole consequence of our environments, parents or peers. Continuing along this thought process, there is increasing interest in gene and environmental interaction and how a combination of the two may be involved in the aetiology of eating disorders. For example, advancements in technology have resulted in an increase in the number of studies that focus on epigenetics, the 'study of changes in gene expression that occur without any alteration in the sequence of the DNA'.[59] These epigenetic modifications to the gene expression can take place at different stages throughout the life of the individual and can also be influenced by the environments we live in. In the case of anorexia, it has been suggested that prenatal risk factors such as maternal malnutrition, stress and the early development of the foetus, acute environmental changes (exposure to malnutrition or high calorific foods) and the epigenetic processing in learning and memory[60] can have an influence on the development of eating disorders. However, despite recent advancements, research regarding epigenetics and eating disorders is still in the early stages of development[61] and so the conclusions we can draw are limited. I do not wish to enter into a debate about how likely modifications in the gene expression are in the development of eating disorders such as anorexia. The literature demonstrates that our environments, development and learning play a significant role in these gene modifications. If a biological risk factor is present, it is clear that without an environmental pressure, this would remain dormant. For now, focus should still be applied to sociological factors and pressure should be applied to those social discourses that encourage and promote anorexic behaviours.

Research has also been carried out to ascertain the familial transmission of anorexia as some studies have shown that it may reoccur in families affected by eating disorders.[62] It is the role of our genes that takes centre stage here as 'molecular genetic studies have pointed to a number of possible genetic variations that may be linked'[63] to a risk of developing anorexia. The theory goes that an episode of dieting or weight loss can trigger this change in the gene and this is when anorexia takes its hold. However, these studies have not been replicated and a starvation gene has not, and is unlikely to be, identified. As Arnold writes:

> [r]esearchers haven't found a single gene that causes anorexia, and it's unlikely they will . . . genes generally increase and decrease your risk of developing the disorder . . . [which is] subsequently influenced by the environment in which a person lives.[64]

Consideration should not only be given to the processes that occur prior to the anorexic symptoms but also to the effects on the body throughout the illness. In terms of psychobiology (the use of biology to study normal and abnormal cognitive and emotional processes) and the effects that starvation can have on the body, studies have shown that brain matter can actually decrease in patients with anorexia.[65] Research has identified reductions in the right dorsal anterior cingulate cortex (ACC), an area of the brain related to both weight loss and weight recovery.[66] It is believed that studying this area of the brain can lead to an accurate prediction regarding the individual's recovery and changes to this area prior to diagnosis might indicate risk towards a later development of the disorder.

As we have seen, there are a number of studies that focus on the effect our biology and our genes have on the development of eating disorder behaviour and the development of anorexia and this is still a growing area of academic interest. From changes to our gene expressions and hormone imbalances to the influence of depression and anxiety disorders on the physical body, the argument for biologically based explanations in the development of anorexia is strong. However, this research is relatively new and still under development. As such, there are a few things that we must remain wary of. For example, assigning biological responses typically necessitates the use of drugs in treating the "underlying" causes that are viewed in terms of abnormal bodily functioning. This can be a "one-size-fits-all" fix for doctors who are under increasing pressure to turn patients around and limit the need for further tests and expensive surgery bills. These drugs can also have damaging side effects and act only as a plaster to mask the underlying issues that become dormant and may manifest in other ways later in life. In applying this understanding to the treatment of anorexia, we also move away from the benefits of a multidisciplinary approach that values the use of therapy and ritual in helping the individual to find a path away from an eating disorder.

As evidenced whilst examining the medical classification systems used for a diagnosis of anorexia, in the majority of cases, this eating disorder becomes manifest during puberty at a time when the construction of identity is pivotal in the development of self-identity and attaining independence from parents. It is a process that depends on both social and individual factors that bring together 'divergent and conflicting aspects of his or her social experience'[67] which is influenced by 'historical and sociological conditions, the particularities of family experience, biological predispositions, and the accidents of development'.[68] This is a process that occurs throughout the life of the individual but the most critical period is during adolescence, as the individual must navigate the process of merging the experiences of childhood, which structured the foundation of the self, with the challenges and demands associated with early adulthood. Threats to this process can come in the form of dramatic changes in cultural expectations and social roles that can lead to identity confusion; an extreme example of this can be found within the development of anorexia. Gordon, in his book *Eating Disorders*,[69] argues that 'eating disorders are the extreme expression of radically altered social expectations on women that have emerged on a mass scale since about the mid-twentieth century, but particularly since the 1960s'.[70] He writes that new pressures and expectations that focused on attributes oriented towards achievement, independence and competitiveness were suddenly expected of young women within a relatively short time frame. These values found themselves in sharp contrast to the traditional Western embodiment of the female role. This shift in social expectations heralded confusion with developing identities as these young women struggled to embody both worlds. For some it caused self-doubt, confusion and fragmentation. Within this framework, anorexia (which holds at its core issues surrounding self-esteem, achievement, perfectionism and the struggle for autonomy) can be understood as a magnified reflection of these conflicting demands. He writes that anorexia can be understood as a core expression of the stresses, tensions, anxieties and unresolved problems of a particular culture or historical period, that it reflects a crisis of identity following the contradictions of being female in Western society. Within this environment, the only way the individual can manage this crisis of identity is through controlling various aspects of her life. Here, controlling the body becomes an attractive source of reassurance as an area completely at her disposal in an environment where control of the body communicates themes of transcendence, invulnerability and adherence to society's strict body ideals. Seeking to both survive and subvert, the young woman strictly monitors her food intake and attempts to weave a web of control. This act embodies both a protest of the conflicting female roles whilst also conforming to the pejorative definition of femininity. Gordon writes that 'anorexics and bulimics draw upon the common cultural vocabulary of their time, through latching onto the contemporary mania about dieting, thinness, and food control that have become endemic to the advanced industrial societies'.[71] They utilize cultural preoccupations as defences that enable them to escape from, and achieve some sense of control over, unmanageable personal distress as they achieve specialness through deviance. Thus, resonating throughout discussions on eating disorders is a political undercurrent since they are so closely connected with the issue of control of the female body. As a political act, anorexia is a striking visible statement that takes place on the public stage. It's not just her size and weight that become the most visible feature, but the refusal to eat, her adamant *NO!* in the face of family and friends. This becomes an act of rejection, of building boundaries and a foundation upon which she can start to build her identity which becomes increasingly disembodied, dualistic and cellular as she departmentalizes the different elements that make up the life that she knew to make way for the life that she desires. In this, she attempts to address her unbalanced world and to make sense of, and ultimately change, her social position. Within the individual we see a thoroughly schizophrenic pattern take its form as 'one side of the personality is in fierce rebellion against the society that is starving them . . . [and] the other side is killing them in order to attain the image that society requires'.[72]

Discussions surrounding the part played by families in the development of anorexia usually focus on the relationship between the daughter and her mother. As written by psychotherapist Marilyn Lawrence in *The Anorexic Experience*: 'I can say with certainty that I have never worked with an anorexic woman who has a "straightforward" relationship with her mother'.[73] She states that the relationship is usually complex and baffling for both the mother and the daughter. Broadly speaking, "mothering" is associated with caring, feeding and the giving of life, sustenance, nourishment and love and therefore it is easy to see how the rejection of food can symbolize a rejection of her mother's love especially given the timing of the anorexic symptoms which typically take shape around major life events (examinations, starting a new career, leaving home to progress studies at university). The stresses of such periods 'may involve conflicts surrounding achievement, but the difficulties of these situations are often described by anorexics in terms of separation . . . [of] leaving home . . . [and] leaving mother'.[74] This is a time when opposing feelings clash, when desires for independence, autonomy and separation conflict with a desire for closeness, support and safety. Rejecting the mother's love through the rejection of food can ease this separation anxiety by emotionally distancing the daughter from her mother. One anorexic woman wrote that her mother prepared the food for her family and so the act of wilful starvation became an act of metaphorically rejecting her without actually severing the relationship.[75]

Another common observation of the family dynamics concentrates on the behaviour exhibited by the mother. Bruch writes that 'nearly all of the mothers . . . [are] submissive to their husbands but very *controlling* of their children'.[76] She therefore advocated the position that anorexia had to be understood in terms of the 'development of the total personality in the *context* of the family'.[77] The mother is also a source of guidance, providing information about the world and her place in it. It's through the mother that her daughter learns about her body and so the transference of both positive and negative body esteem can be gleaned from this relationship.[78] For example, if the daughter sees her mother critically analyzing her body in the mirror, pinching her thighs in disgust and wishing away wrinkles, her daughter may be more at risk of developing the same critical view of her body. Parents can play a significant role in their children learning cultural obedience as they, like their children, are subjected to the same demands of society. Everyone operates in cultural time and space, as Bordo writes, 'no one lives in a bubble of self-generated "dysfunction" or permanent immunity – especially today, as mass media culture increasingly has provided the dominant "public education" in our children's lives'[79] and no one develops anorexia overnight. As written by Tania Kindersley and Sarah Vine: 'it is a gradual process, fostered by a culture which insists that if you are a very thin woman you can conquer the world'.[80] A message transferred in myriad ways. Whilst parents may not be the root cause of the development of anorexia, the relationship with their daughter can exacerbate her feelings and thus contribute towards the developing problem.

With regards to the wider network within the home, anorexic women are typically raised in families that place a great importance on achievement, external appearance, weight control and the individual may put considerable value on these attributes. These young women have an overwhelming desire to please their families and loved ones and so engage in damaging behaviours that appear to meet these expectations. However, underneath this façade of good behaviour and success they feel weak, unworthy and obliged to live up to these unrealistic and relentless demands for perfection. Underlying these feelings is a sense of powerlessness that can be triggered by experiences that challenge the brittle façade. It is through the control of food that the anorexic woman feels she is in a position to regain power and control over her experiences. However, Wolf writes, political and economic retaliation against female appetite is so much stronger than family dynamics at this point. For example, she states that 60–80 per cent of college women struggle against the slender ideal and that it is very hard to believe that 60–80 per cent of families are dysfunctional in this specific way. Anorexic behaviour 'can no longer be explained as a private issue'.[81] So, whilst the family may put considerable importance on their daughters displaying attributes of perfectionism, achievement, beauty and weight control, for Wolf these values have been constructed and reinforced by our environments and internalized by our families.

Treatment

There are a number of approaches adopted by clinicians and therapists to treat patients presenting with anorexic symptoms. Treatment can utilize one or more of the following approaches: Cognitive Analytic Therapy (CAT); Cognitive Behaviour Therapy (CBT); Interpersonal Therapy (IPT); Focal Psychodynamic Therapy (FPT); Family Intervention; Compulsory Treatment; and, Medication. The focus of Cognitive Analytic Therapy is on behavioural patterns. The belief is that mental health conditions such as anorexia are caused by unhealthy patterns of thought and behaviour which date back to childhood experiences. The three stages of Cognitive Analytic Therapy are: reformulation – understanding the influence past events have on present behaviour and patterns of thought; recognition – helping the individual understand the link between current patterns of behaviour and childhood experiences; and, revision – helping the individual identify changes that can break these unhealthy patterns of behaviour.

Central to Cognitive Behavioural Therapy is the belief that how we think about a situation can affect how we feel and subsequently act. When considered in the context of anorexia, the therapist will explore how the condition is associated with unhealthy and unrealistic thoughts and beliefs about food, diet and their body. The focus here is exploring the roots underpinning this body, food and weight negativity. Ultimately the aim is to encourage the adoption of healthier and more realistic ways of thinking that are conducive to disrupting the cycle of harming behaviour whilst Interpersonal Therapy focuses on the consequences of relationships with others and their environment. A first step may be to identify the root cause of self-esteem, self-doubt and bodily anxiety through analysis of relationships with peers and family members. Here, healing is associated with transforming, resolving or disconnecting from negative and destructive relationships that feed body insecurities. Central to Focal Psychodynamic Therapy is the idea that past unresolved conflicts or traumas are being played out in the present through a refusal to eat. For the individual this can take the form of body punishment for what is perceived as an earlier weakness or as a coping mechanism to deal with unresolved negative feelings resulting from an earlier trauma. A focus for therapy in this instance could be on helping the individual to come to terms with the underlying tensions so alternative expressions can be utilized in the present to acknowledge and subsequently address these unresolved feelings within a safe and healing framework.

Family interventions draw family members into the healing process. As anorexia can be traumatic for both the individual and wider family network, bringing everyone together in order to establish underlying tensions and negativities can help the process of healing. Compulsory treatment is implemented when the individual exhibiting anorexic symptoms refuses treatment despite being severely ill and putting their life at risk. In this scenario doctors can decide to section their patient under the Mental Health Act in order to treat the individual compulsorily. In this setting the individual exhibiting anorexic symptoms may be prescribed medication to address elements of depression, anxiety, obsessive-compulsive disorder etc. There are two main medications: selective serotonin reuptake inhibitors (a type of anti-depressant medication that is prescribed to help people manage additional psychological problems such as depression and anxiety); and, olanzapine (used to help reduce feelings of anxiety as a "last resort" when the individual is unresponsive to previous treatments). Medication is usually only prescribed when the individual has started to gain weight, as the side effects can be more serious for underweight patients. Patients under 18 years of age are prescribed these medications cautiously due to the possible side effects. Psychological treatments undertaken by the NHS typically last between six and twelve months, the length of which is identified by a care plan established early in the treatment process. A central element of this plan will focus on weight gain usually at a rate of 0.5–1kg per week. This is achieved through small increases in food consumption.[82] These approaches can be incorporated into intensive inpatient programmes, residential and partial hospitalization programmes and various levels of outpatient care where the individual has access to general medical treatment, nutritional counselling and individual/group/family therapy sessions. A difficulty for both health care professionals and patients can be identifying the best course of treatment as many geographical locations outside urban locations can struggle to offer the varied resources often needed to offer bespoke treatment programmes.[83]

The statistics discussed at the beginning of this chapter capture those individuals who met the definition of at least one of these classification systems. It therefore calls into question the accuracy of these statistics when we consider how many people may suffer from anorexia but do not lose three consecutive menstrual cycles or who are not considered sufficiently underweight by their physicians. As Bordo writes, do the college girls who chew pizza and then spit it out have an eating disorder? 'Of course not – look, they're eating pizza'.[84] My point here is that I believe that a high proportion of women within Western society (to varying degrees at some point in their lives) experience low self-esteem related to their body shape and size as a result of our society's high and unrealistic expectations regarding women's bodies but this is displayed most extremely in the aestheticism of the anorexic. As a consequence we diet, restrict calorie intake and experience a sense of hopelessness and depression. To a certain extent we have all bought into the beauty myth and it is damaging and limiting our development within society.[85] As we see when reflecting on the story of Ellen West, her obsession with starving her body came to symbolize a spiritual struggle for her very soul only she did not have the language to vocalize it as such. This struggle was instead hidden by the obsession of maintaining society's desired slender aesthetic. In attempting to forgo her feminine nature and embody masculine ideals she became alienated and distanced from an essential part of her "inner self". This alienation heralded the obsession with the thinness ideal and all the associated attributes (purity, transcendence, perfection, cleanliness). Therefore, food came to symbolize so much more than simple nourishment. It came to represent a reconnection with her female nature whilst the rejection of it represents her desire to embody masculine ideals and her despair and dissatisfaction of not being able to within a female body. Her hunger was misdirected and embodied a spiritual longing. Food merely provided a distraction, hiding the true desire. As Chernin writes: '[t]he demonic quality of obsessive longing arises from the fact that human beings cannot bear this alienation from an essential part of the self'.[86] When it finally came to it, the consumption of food was an inadequate substitute for the female psyche that had been lost. Hunger came to represent 'a state of being, a unified condition of the self, rather than for a piece of food'[87] as food cannot adequately satisfy the real nature of the longing. West writes: 'I even dread to go into the grocery store. The sight of groceries awakens longings in me which they [the groceries] can never still. It is as though a person tried to quench his thirst with ink'.[88] Ultimately, the obsession symbolizes both the will to destroy the "inner self" and body and a longing to be reunited with it. As we shall explore in the chapters that follow, this experience is also indicative of many contemporary accounts of anorexia and the sense of desperation and longing are no less real. Whilst the medical classification systems may be an attempt to recognize disordered eating from a clinical perspective, it negates the development of a cultural model as an explanation in its focus on the biological features. This can severely hamper treatment and the way the anorexic individual comes to regard her situation. This in turn restricts her developing understanding of not just the "disorder" but also her place in society and the politics surrounding the slender ideal she desperately attempts to emulate.

I understand anorexia to be a contemporary disorder. A core argument throughout this work is that anorexia is a characteristic expression of our culture that highlights some of the central ills in our environments. I understand anorexia as an expression of the contradictions of the female role and expectations in an environment where women still struggle to define themselves in a patriarchal world. It embodies a struggle for control over her body and her immediate environment. I believe these to be some of the central issues lying at the foundation of the development of anorexia. The goal must be to understand the primary causes so the right therapeutic model for healing can be established. It is through unpacking the political and cultural undercurrents that women can work towards liberation and subversion of the androcentric ideologies inherent within our social structures that manifests within women as eating disorders such as anorexia. So, it is to the influence of society that we now turn our attention.

Notes

1 Orbach, S. (1998) *Fat Is a Feminist Issue*. London: Arrow Books, 151.
2 Orbach (1998: 152).
3 Orbach (1998: 152, author's emphasis).
4 World Health Organisation (2012) Anorexia Nervosa. In: World Health Organisation (eds.) *International Statistical Classification of Diseases and Related Health Problems*. Geneva: WHO, 583–589.
5 Gordon, R. A. (2000) *Eating Disorders: Anatomy of a Social Epidemic*. Oxford: Blackwell Publishers, 189.
6 Gordon (2000: 21).
7 Gordon (2000: 21).
8 Anon. (2014) *Eating Disorders Not Exclusive to those Who Are Underweight*. Available at: www.mcri.edu.au/news/2014/august/eating-disorders/ [31/01/2015].
9 Anon (2014).
10 Anon (2014).
11 Arnold, C. (2013) *Decoding Anorexia: How Breakthroughs in Science Offer Hope for Eating Disorders*. East Sussex: Routledge, 2.
12 Hill, R., Haslett, C., Kumar, S. (2001) Anorexia Nervosa in an Elderly Woman. In: *Australian and New Zealand Journal of Psychiatry* 35: 246–248.
13 For more information on the use of anti-depressants on patients diagnosed with both anorexia and depression, see Jaafar, N. R. N., Daud, T. I. M., Rahman, F. N. A., Baharudin, A. (2007) Mirtazapine for Anorexia Nervosa and Depression. In: *Australian and New Zealand Journal of Psychiatry* 41: 768–769. In this study, major depression was diagnosed by depressed mood exhibited as a consequence of anhedonia, poor concentration, insomnia and recurrent death wishes.

This particular case utilized a number of approaches which included therapeutic treatment alongside medical, dental and nutritional support.

14 Keel, P. K., McCormick, L. (2010) Diagnosis, Assessment, and Treatment Planning for Anorexia Nervosa. In: Grilo, C. M., Mitchell, J. E. (eds.) *The Treatment of Eating Disorders: A Clinical Handbook*. London: The Guildford Press, 3–28 (4).

15 Gordon (2000: 23).

16 Gordon (2000: 21).

17 The manifestation of anorexia is not limited to development within this adolescent period. Anorexia can occur at any age and may be triggered by an event or trauma. Onset in middle age may be the consequence of earlier diagnoses rematerializing or new stresses which challenge the individual's sense of identity (such as divorce or a relationship breaking down, death of a loved one etc.). For more information, see Anon. (2017) *Eating Disorders Can Strike in Mid-Life*. Available at: www.bbc.co.uk/news/health-38635082 [24/01/2017].

18 Recent studies show an increase in male diagnoses of anorexia, as more men step forward for treatment of anorexia. Reasons for the increased prevalence include changing understandings of anorexia as broader than a disorder limited to the female sex alongside more reliable statistical data. Whilst there is a general lack of research in the area, there appears to be commonalities between female and male incidences. These include: age of onset (typically times of transition such as puberty, middle age etc.); its employment as a coping mechanism; expression of underlying emotional stress; as a consequence of dieting; peer pressure (losing weight); and, the influence of the media and advertising campaigns. Whilst looking good appears to be low on the list of things boys worry about, it is becoming clear that pressure from social media, from advertising and celebrity images, are influencing the way men reflect on their embodiment too. There is also debate surrounding the growing prevalence of anorexia in gay or bisexual male communities. It is suggested that these men may be judged on attractiveness in the same way as women, leading to increased body anxieties. The "perfect body" is becoming increasingly aspirational for the male sex as focus is given to "sculpting" and "building" the body for a more "chiselled" aesthetic. This has led to the development of "bigorexia" (focus on getting bigger and engaging in body building activities). For more information, see Anon. (2016) *Men Get Eating Disorders Too*. Available at: http://mengetedstoo.co.uk/ [15/01/2017]; B-eat (2016) *New Report Gives Insight Into Body Image Issues Among Boys*. Available at: www.b-eat.co.uk/latest/5397-new-report-gives-insight-into-body-image-issues-among-boys [15/01/2017]; and Langley, J. (2006) *Boys Get Anorexia Too: Coping With Male Eating Disorders in THE Family*. London: Sage Publications.

19 Catherine Garrett in *Beyond Anorexia* writes that the labelling and defining of anorexia at the end of the nineteenth century was part of a strategy by the medical community to control knowledge of the body and mind in a period of increasing political power and freedom for women. Garrett, C. (1998) *Beyond Anorexia: Narrative, Spirituality and Recovery*. Cambridge: Cambridge University Press, 48.

20 Gordon (2000: 14).

21 Richard Morton quoted in Treasure, J., Alexander, J. (2013) *Anorexia Nervosa: A Recovery Guide for Sufferers, Families and Friends*. London: Routledge, 18.

22 Gordon (2000: 15).

23 Russell, G. R. M (1997) The History of Bulimia Nervosa. In: Garner, D. M., Garfinkel, P. E. (eds.) *Handbook of Treatment for Eating Disorders*. New York: The Guilford Press, 11–25 (17).

24 Russell (1997: 17).

25 Russell (1997: 17).

26 Chernin, K. (1994) *The Obsession: Reflections on the Tyranny of Slenderness*. New York: Harper Perennial, 174.

27 Ellen West quoted in Chernin (1994: 174).

28 Ellen West quoted in Chernin (1994: 170).
29 Chernin (1994: 170).
30 Chernin (1994: 172).
31 Ellen West quoted in Chernin (1994: 176; author's emphasis).
32 Russell (1997: 17).
33 Gordon (2000: 17).
34 Bruch, H. (1973) *Eating Disorders*. New York: Basic Books, 4.
35 Gordon (2000: 3).
36 Goldstein, L., Rissman, J. (2008) Anorexia. In: Gilman, S. L. (ed.) *Diets and Dieting: A Cultural Encyclopaedia*. New York: Routledge, 7–11 (7).
37 George Devereux quoted in Gilman, S. L. (1980) *Diets and Dieting: A Cultural Encyclopaedia*. New York: Routledge, ix.
38 Bordo, S. (2003) *Unbearable Weight: Feminism, Western Culture, and the Body*. London: University of California Press, 140.
39 B-eat in conjunction with PwC adopted a new methodology for this trial believing that the results are more robust than previous similar studies. The National Institute of Health and Clinical Excellence estimates around 11per cent of cases are reported by men. For more information, see B-eat (2016) *Eating Disorder Statistics*. Available at: www.b-eat.co.uk/about-beat/media-centre/information-and-statistics-about-eating-disorders?gclid=CMSWhIKync4CFUJmGwod17kFMQ [03/08/2016].
40 Quoted by B-eat: B-eat (2016) *Eating Disorder Statistics*. Available at: www.b-eat.co.uk/about-beat/media-centre/information-and-statistics-about-eating-disorders?gclid=CMSWhIKync4CFUJmGwod17kFMQ [03/08/2016].
41 NHS information centre referenced by B-eat. For more information, see B-eat (2016) *Eating Disorder Statistics*. Available at: www.b-eat.co.uk/about-beat/media-centre/information-and-statistics-about-eating-disorders?gclid=CMSWhIKync4CFUJmGwod17kFMQ [03/08/2016].
42 Quoted by B-eat: B-eat (2016) *Eating Disorder Statistics*. Available at: www.b-eat.co.uk/about-beat/media-centre/information-and-statistics-about-eating-disorders?gclid=CMSWhIKync4CFUJmGwod17kFMQ [03/08/2016].
43 Quoted by B-eat: B-eat (2016) *Eating Disorder Statistics*. Available at: www.b-eat.co.uk/about-beat/media-centre/information-and-statistics-about-eating-disorders?gclid=CMSWhIKync4CFUJmGwod17kFMQ [03/08/2016].
44 B-eat (2016) *Eating Disorder Statistics*. Available at: www.b-eat.co.uk/about-beat/media-centre/information-and-statistics-about-eating-disorders?gclid=CMSWhIKync4CFUJmGwod17kFMQ [03/08/2016].
45 Orbach, S. (2009) *Bodies*. London: Profile Books Ltd, 7.
46 Orbach (2009: 7).
47 Anorexia is often referred to as a culture-bound syndrome indicative of contemporary Western society as a consequence of the popularized slender ideal. This is a theme unpacked in greater detail in Chapter 2 (society's slender ideal) and Chapter 4 (the political undercurrents of anorexia as a culture-bound syndrome).
48 As we explore in Chapter 2.
49 Goldstein, Rissman (2008: 10).
50 Goldstein, Rissman (2008: 8).
51 Anon. (2015) *General Information*. Available at: www.anad.org/get-information/about-eating-disorders/general-information/ [03/01/2015].
52 Brumberg, J. (2000) *Fasting Girls: A History of Anorexia Nervosa*. New York: Vintage Books.
53 Gordon (2000: 96).
54 This concept is discussed throughout this book but for more information on the work of Bordo, see Bordo (2003).

55 Goldstein, Rissman (2008: 9).
56 Arnold (2013: 5).
57 Arnold (2013: 5).
58 Arnold (2013: xi).
59 Pjetri, E., Schmidt, U., Kas, M. J., Campbell, I. C. (2012) *Epigenetics and Eating Disorders*. Available at: www.researchgate.net/profile/Martien_Kas/publication/225056288_Epigenetics_and_eating_disorders/links/0deec51a335cb9dce2000000.pdf [15/08/2015].
60 This is of particular interest when you consider that learned behaviour contributes to the development and maintenance of eating disorders.
61 There is a lack of live brain tissue to study and this will continue to hamper progress within the area of psychiatric disorders.
62 Becker, A. E., Keel, P. K., Anderson-Fye, E. P., Thomas, J. J. (2004) Genes (and/or) Jeans?: Genetic and Socio-Cultural Contributions to Risk for Eating Disorders. In: *Journal of Addictive Diseases* 23: 81–103.
63 Keel, McCormick (2010: 9).
64 Arnold (2013: 11).
65 Keel, P. K. (2005) *Eating Disorders*. Upper Saddle River: Pearson Prentice-Hall.
66 McCormick, L. M., Keel, P. K., Brumm, M. C., Bowers, W., Swayze, V., Anderson, A. (2008) Implications of Starvation-Induced Change in Right Dorsal Anterior Cingulate Volume in Anorexia Nervosa. In: *International Journal of Eating Disorders* 41: 602–610.
67 Gordon (2000: 96).
68 Gordon (2000: 96).
69 The work of Gordon is based heavily on the work of George Devereux, a psychologist and anthropologist, who was interested in the complex relationship between culture and psychopathology. His key interest was the relationship between the normal and the abnormal and the link between cultural anxieties and the manifestation of these in individuals. He developed the concept of an "ethnic disorder" (which can also be described as a culture-bound syndrome) as we will explore in Chapter 4.
70 Gordon (2000: 96)
71 Gordon (2000: 12).
72 Woodman, M. (1982) *Addicted to Perfection: The Still Unravished Bride*. Toronto, Canada: Inner City Books, 30.
73 Lawrence, L. (1995) *The Anorexic Experience*. London: The Women's Press Ltd, 67.
74 Moorey, J. (1991) *Living With Anorexia and Bulimia*. Manchester: Bell and Bain Ltd, 59.
75 Arnold (2013: 3).
76 Bordo (2003: 156, my emphasis).
77 Roth, G. (2010) *Women, Food and God: An Unexpected Path to Almost Everything*. London: Simon and Schuster UK LTD, 18, my emphasis.
78 Problematizing the mother is fraught with tensions. Bruch's work relies heavily on family theory to analyze the manifestation of anorexia which was said to result from isolated and uncommunicative families where the mothers had failed to instil independence and self-sufficiency in their daughters. Thus, anorexia was framed as a result of poor mothering as the young woman rejected social and sexual maturity. Whilst my work rejects this supposition (as anorexic is discussed in the context of damaging patriarchal discourses of power), the mother's reflection on her embodiment does, I believe, influence the child's growing opinion surrounding her own body's development. Both are the consequence of social discourses. For more information on the tensions surrounding mother blaming, see Malson, H. (1998) *The Thin Woman: Feminism, Poststructualism and the*

Social Psychology of Anorexia Nervosa. East Sussex: Routledge; and Dignon, A. (2007) *All of Me: A Fuller Picture of Anorexia*. Oxford: Peter Lang.
79 Bordo (2003: xx).
80 Kindersley, T., Vine, S. (2009) *Backwards in High Heels: The Impossible Art of Being Female*. London: Fourth Estate, 44.
81 Wolf, N. (1994) Hunger. In: Fallon, P., Katzman, M. A., Wooley, S. C. (eds.) *Feminist Perspectives on Eating Disorders*. New York: The Guildford Press, 100.
82 For more information, see NHS (2016) *Anorexia Nervosa – Treatment*. Available at: www.nhs.uk/Conditions/Anorexia-nervosa/Pages/Treatment.aspx [15/10/2016].
83 For more information, see Keel, McCormick 2010: 3–28.
84 Bordo (2003: xxvii).
85 A theme we shall explore further in Chapters 3 and 4.
86 Chernin (1994: 191).
87 Ellen West quoted in Chernin (1994: 191).
88 Chernin (1994: 191).

2 The female body as mediated by society

The idea that anorexia is a metaphor of our time has been heavily drawn upon throughout research on female bodies in the late twentieth and early twenty-first centuries. First mentioned by Kim Chernin in *The Hungry Self*, and drawn upon by Susie Orbach, it has been clearly asserted that '[f]ood is the medium through which women are addressed . . . (and) in turn, food has become the language of women's response'.[1] Writings on this disorder proliferate in theories surrounding the aetiology, triggers and risk factors with an aim to identify, isolate and ultimately destroy the disabling foundations of anorexia. The following chapter aims to examine and contextualize current understandings of anorexia through an investigation of psychological, sociological and anthropological responses to this expression. As in many areas, language is an important factor as it is so tied up in power rhetoric. I use the term disorder throughout this body of work in reference to society. It is my intention to demonstrate that anorexia is a culturally induced syndrome symptomatic of a larger societal disorder. In anorexia we see an individual's response to society's control and manipulation of the female form, as I argue that women are increasingly driven by the culturally motivated desire to embody the slender ideal. In expanding on the reasons behind the argument that anorexia is a culturally induced syndrome, some of the questions I will answer in the following chapter are: is anorexia the consequence of nature, nurture or both? Can popular culture, the media and advertising campaigns be held accountable? Can we blame the pressures of today's society? And, is it a physical condition or a mental illness?

Two positions can be said to dominate discussions surrounding the aetiology of anorexia. One view is that they are deeply private and emotionally motivated mental illnesses. This view disregards media factors, such as airbrushing and fashion, as patronizing and irresponsible. At the other end of the spectrum, there are those that argue it is impossible to ignore the increasingly artificial and unrealistic beauty demands made through the media and advertising campaigns, and that the pressure on young women to conform to these ideals is enough to set eating disorders, such as anorexia, in motion. My work is situated firmly within the latter of these two views. Here the aetiology of anorexia is multifaceted, but ultimately develops as a response to our society's gender stereotyping and idealizations of what it means to fully embody femininity. These "lessons" are communicated and reinforced by family, peers, husbands, lovers, the media and advertising campaigns, they are viciously and insidiously borne upon us at conception, the point of our making, and not surprisingly, collectively embraced by the populations of women seeking to fit in, to attain that evanescent, sparkling dream of normality presented on an elite pedestal. These social pressures will be the focus of this chapter. I will examine the female body in Western society, principally the United Kingdom and the United States of America, with the intention of contextualizing current societal influences and pressures.

This chapter will start with a critical examination of the cultural "trends" which have been identified as contributing to the development of anorexia within Western society. These factors include media and advertising representations of women (which utilize airbrushing and Photoshop applications) that focus on the desirability of an increasingly slender form, creating unrealistic and destructive standards of "beauty" for women. These images "sell" a deeply damaging ideal for girls and young women whilst teaching them powerful lessons about the value and place of women within our society. From this starting point we will examine the capitalist agenda underpinning these constructions whilst exploring the link between patriarchal society's inherent sexism and how sex-based differences have traditionally been translated into sexist discourse which in turn contributes towards this construction of femininity. This will be discussed in relation to neurosexism and the many academics that are today arguing that there are fundamental differences in the male and female brain, which in turn, determines our strengths and weaknesses throughout life. We will explore how this argument can be used to reinforce gender-based stereotypes and contribute towards limiting gender roles. Female stereotypes and the sexualization of childhood is explored next as we take a look at how these factors combine to create the tensions we see within the anorexic expression. Here, we explore the tensions of consumer culture and the part they play in the development of anorexia as we analyze eating disorders as a social formation as opposed to a personal psychopathology. In this chapter I hope to demonstrate that anorexia is a powerful symbol of female discomfort which has a complex aetiology that is heavily influenced by the environments in which we live.

The female body in contemporary society

Historical cultural attitudes concerning the female body in society, which value attributes of vulnerability, frailty and helplessness, are finding new and worrying expressions within contemporary society. I am interested in why our culture appears to be so obsessed with maintaining tight, slim and young bodies that, as Bordo writes, when '500 people were asked what they feared in the world, 190 replied, "getting fat"'.[2] I want to understand why, as Susie Orbach writes, we live in a culture that praises thinness and frailty in women. Anthropologist Mary Douglas argued that the 'body often becomes the symbol of the social and religious structures to which it belongs and the anxieties of the society are played out on the human body'.[3] She states that we must understand the body as a symbol of society; 'to see the powers and dangers credited to social structure reproduced in small on the human body'.[4] It is only then that we may be capable of interpreting rituals that concern the body and thus, understand rituals concerning eating.

As we will explore in the following pages, many social commentators, therapists and psychologists have drawn parallels between the images glamorizing slender models in the media and advertising campaigns and the development of eating disorders such as anorexia, but this is only part of the story. Contributing to this situation are the contemporary realities of gender inequality, female stereotypes, control and power over female flesh, alongside our dualistic heritage and the contradictions of being a woman (wife, mother, cleaner, and businesswoman. Let Go! You can have it all!). In an environment where weight, appearance and popularity are synonymous[5] it is not surprising that teenagers and young women would come to associate success with the slender form. As Orbach writes in *Hunger Strike*, whatever their manifestation, eating disorders are a 'complex personal response to a set of interpersonal, intra-psychic, social and political phenomena that structure the individual women's relationship to self and other'.[6] The relationship women have with food and body image can be understood as a social phenomenon connected to women's social and psychological existence. Women are 'constantly engaged in trying to mediate the harrowing effects of culturally induced body insecurity . . . (and) anorexia . . . is perhaps the most dramatic outcome of the culture's obsession with regulating body size'.[7] In examining the relationship between women and food she argues that anorexia is a response to the inequality of the sexes. Finding its root in patriarchal culture, anorexia 'exemplifies through the language of the body the woman's attempt to enter and at the same time disappear from a culture that derogates and defies her'[8] and it is only by challenging the principles lying at the heart of this discursive system that women may find liberation.

Men and women are aiming for perfection in new and damaging ways and the result of this is the development of body dysmorphia syndromes,[9] eating disorders and a general discomfort or dis-ease with their bodies. This, alongside the development of new technologies, allows those who can afford to, to trade in the 'messiness and fragility of life, the vulnerability of intimacy, the comfort of human connection, for fantasies of limitless achievement'.[10] This all happens within an environment where cultural imagery cultivates, reinforces and constantly raises the bar of bodily "perfection". We are being trained to see defects in our bodies as we compare them to airbrushed celebrities on the front cover of magazines. The idea that bodily perfection is the gateway for a happy life is the undercurrent of such imagery adding additional pressure and urgency for the requirement of such procedures.

A lifestyle of love, acceptance, happiness and wealth are all displayed. The problem now is that the discontent many women experience with their bodies does not just manifest in anorexia or bulimia, but in their daily rituals. The most devastating consequence is that many girls and young women with seemingly healthy eating habits are secretly analyzing every morsel of food they consume and, in many cases, exercising obsessively. The glamorization of eating disorders and exercise (particularly jogging and marathon running in recent years) and their association with the middle class, successful, businesswoman is one of the most debilitating images to be implemented by the media and marketing campaigns. To some extent, it has made anorexia (and emaciation) "fashionable".

Media

Fashion magazines, TV, movies, the internet and advertising campaigns, all types of media, play a central role in the development of eating disordered behaviour. A plethora of emaciated, glamorized and artificially created images are promoted and idealized by these industries. The messages communicated to the audience are often unbalanced and misleading. They provide information about dieting and exercise whilst highlighting none of the dangers associated with extreme weight loss or exercise. Nor do they discuss healthy body shapes and sizes or what the models have done to attain their body shapes. Putting it into context, many of the celebrities displayed in the magazines have gruelling exercise regimes constructed for each day of the week coupled with strict diets in order to maintain their body shapes. As well as these measures, photographers use computer technologies, such as Photoshop and Lightroom, to perfect certain features, be it spot cover-ups, removing signs of old age, or distorting the body to reflect fashionable curves and desirable sizes. Despite repeated calls to display equal representation of diverse body shapes and to reduce the use of underweight models, this industry continues to "sell" one ideal. The avid consumers of such literature happen to be the most influenced and insecure, teenagers and young women who strive to "fit in"; after all, it's only the thin, beautiful, popular girls in the advertising campaigns of Hollister and Jack Wills who are truly happy! A mistake is often made of regarding slenderness as a surface ideal; it's not, these marketing messages are internalized and unreal standards and expectations are established in the minds of these young women and become manifest in unconscious and damaging ways. For example, Bordo writes that images of slenderness are never "just pictures", as many fashion magazines are quick to quip. Not only are the 'artfully arranged bodies in the ads and videos and fashion spreads powerful lessons in how to see (and evaluate) bodies, but also they offer fantasies of safety, self-containment, acceptance, immunity from pain and hurt',[11] aspirations for many women (and increasingly men) today. In *Unbearable Weight* she describes the postmodern body which is increasingly fed on 'fantasies of rearranging, transforming, and correcting, limitless improvement and change, defying the historicity, the morality, and, indeed, the very materiality of the body'.[12] The extreme outcome of such an understanding is the conceptualization of the biological body as a fiction, a canvas for change, often at the will of fickle fashions. We have become distanced from an appreciation of the sacredness of our bodies and the beauty of individuality and uniqueness. As new technologies designed to control and overcome our numinous biological clocks become commonplace, we are distanced from an appreciation of the biological consequences of such extreme procedures. As Bordo notes, our bodies have 'become alienated products, texts of our own creative making, from which we maintain a strange and ironic detachment'.[13] Only it is not *our* making but the making of a society that inscribes upon us what aesthetic we should project! Demonstrating just this, in her research on the effects of the media on body satisfaction and the development of eating disorders, Bordo discusses a study conducted by anthropologist Anne Becker back in 1995 when the first, single station television was introduced to a remote location in the Fiji Islands. The programmes broadcast originated from Great Britain, the United States and Australia and before its introduction 'Fiji had no reported cases of eating disorders . . . [and] showed that most Fijian girls and women, no matter how large, were comfortable with their bodies'.[14] After three years of viewing this channel, in 1998, '11 percent of the girls surveyed reported vomiting to control weight, and 62 percent of the girls surveyed reported dieting during the previous months'.[15] Quite surprising statistics when you consider these women had previously celebrated voluptuous bodies and encouraged the consumption of food.

It is not just media images promoting the slender ideal that consumers need to be wary of, but the exercise routines that are promoted as a means of achieving the "look". Images of Beyoncé, Madonna, Jennifer Lopez and more recently Kim Kardashian (to name a few) are flaunted and recommended as the means of achieving the same aesthetic in terribly patronizing and animated language. Take, for example, an article from *Ebony* in 2008 about the exercise routine of Beyoncé. Apparently 'star bodies are not necessarily born'[16] but sometimes they are actually made! The "good news" is that you can have that body too and all it takes is motivation. Taking into consideration that this magazine is aimed at the African American population in the United States, the average size of which is just over 11 and a half stone[17] which, with an average height of 5 feet and 4 inches, makes it highly improbable that motivation *is* all it will take. The consequence of such articles is to make millions of women feel dejected, hopeless and lacking (ironically crushing any motivation they might have started with).[18]

What many magazines fail to acknowledge is the manipulation these visual images go through prior to publication. No amount of exercise or healthy eating will change the contours of your face or body in the same way that computer-enhancing technology will. Airbrushing and Photoshop have a big part to play in the illusion portrayed by the magazines.

Looking more closely, airbrushing can be defined as a 'process of retouching or altering photographs used in advertising numerous products'.[19] Following the patenting of the technology in 1876, by the makers of the Stanley Steamer, the technology was intended for use in painting watercolours and for artistic purposes. However, now the term is almost solely associated with fashion photography. Its use here is to eliminate imperfections and change the size and shape of the models photographed. This practice, implemented by advertising campaigns, is said to trigger negative body esteem for teenagers and young women. For example, a study conducted by the University of Missouri has shown that 'after just one-to-three minutes of exposure to the type of advertising routinely found in magazines . . . young women just entering adulthood, [increasingly] hate themselves'[20] as they desperately seek to embody the impossibly flawless features. The study was carried out with eighty-one European-American women who were divided into two groups. The first group were provided with "neutral" images (ten images which did not include people) whilst the other group viewed five appearance-related images (of European-American women who could be said to embody the desired beauty aesthetic) and five neutral images. The findings revealed that repeated exposure to this ideal, over time, had a significant negative effect on individual women's self-esteem.[21] This effect was the same regardless of the specific body shape or size of the individual viewing the imagery – 'thin or heavy, confident or prone to self-objectification, the result was the same: the women were equally affected by viewing the images of thin women and showed increased dissatisfaction after viewing appearance-related images'.[22] Through this visual communication, these airbrushed images reinforce the socially constructed standard of beauty by demonstrating a "better" version of the model. Many actresses in recent years have sought to educate their audiences by demonstrating the before and after effects of extensive make-up and hair sessions. Jamie Lee Curtis for *More* magazine[23] asked her photographer to take pictures of her without makeup, professional hairstyling, jewellery or high couture, in unforgiving lighting and at a full body angle. As you would expect, she looked human, just like the rest of us. She said, 'I don't have great thighs. I have very big breasts and a soft, fatty little tummy. And I've got back fat. People assume that I'm walking around in little spaghetti-strap dresses. It's insidious, Glam Jamie, the Perfect Jamie, the great figure, blah, blah, blah. . . . It's such a fraud. And I'm the one perpetuating it'.[24] In a similar manner, Emma Watson in the *Sunday Times Style* magazine said, 'with airbrushing and digital manipulation, fashion can be an unobtainable image that's dangerously unhealthy'.[25] Over the years, Watson has also been transparent about the beauty products, time and attention spent on getting her digital images "just right". In the last few years, regulations have been imposed which demand that advertisers are transparent about what is enhanced or altered in the photographs published; they are now required to provide disclaimers. In addition, marketing campaigns that advertise the benefits of beauty products with computer-enhanced and airbrushed models have come under heavy criticism and in some cases, have been banned by the Advertising Standards Authority, as they are 'not representative of the results the products could achieve'.[26]

While we cannot change the media representations of women overnight, what we can do is change the way we think about them. We can see the manipulation and disempowering rhetoric for what it is and attempt to rationalize and navigate the fear of our bodies, of food and the hatred we feel for our perceived imperfections. As Jennifer Nelson writes in *Airbrushed Nation* '[k]nowing you're being force-fed an unreal paradigm makes it easier to withdraw yourself from that which strips you from your sense of self'.[27] It is also worth remembering that "the media" also encompasses those individuals, organizations and publications that work ethically to promote a change in the way body image is represented in these industries. For example, in 2004, Dove launched their *Campaign for Real Beauty* following the findings of *The Real Truth About Beauty: A Global Report* which proved the hypothesis that the 'definition of beauty had become limiting and unattainable'.[28] The study found that only 2 per cent of the global population of women would describe themselves as beautiful. Since then Dove has implemented various campaigns to challenge beauty stereotypes and broaden the discussion on beauty. In 2010 this effort was renewed when they launched the *Dove Movement for Self-Esteem*. Following this, the 2011 study (*The Real Truth About Beauty: Revisited*) of over 1,200 10- to 17-year-olds (predominantly girls) found that 72 per cent felt a great deal of pressure to conform to these narrowly defined ideals and that 'only 11% of girls around the world feel comfortable using the word beautiful to describe their looks'.[29] For the campaign this demonstrated that there has been a universal increase in the pressure these girls feel to meet prevailing standards of beauty that results in a decrease in their confidence as they enter adulthood. The Dove survey also revealed that 'the number of women who would like to see "real" models used in advertising has risen from 74 per cent to . . . 95 per cent'.[30] Whilst low self-esteem resulting from exposure to these images of beauty may not be the sole cause of the development of anorexia, they do demonstrate a connection between advertising and the development of low self-esteem and confidence. These reinforced ideals also create an anxiety and negativity about the body and food at a time when their bodies are still developing. As I shall demonstrate later, choices made about food at these young ages significantly shape a women's relationship with her body years down the line.

My position is clear, as I have demonstrated, but there are many academics in the field that disagree with this argument and advocate the position that people do not passively internalize these moral values. The premise is that there are many different factors – such as political outlook, race, social class and value systems – at play when we make day-to-day decisions and that any messages gleaned from the media that are inconsistent with these values will ultimately be rejected. Following this argument, only those individuals with a biological predisposition towards low self-esteem and confidence are truly influenced by these messages and therefore, the images of slender, computer-enhanced women portrayed in the media will not leave all women pre-disposed to developing an eating disorder such as anorexia. For example, Lucy Howard-Taylor in *Biting Anorexia* writes that whilst the 'media plays a role in furthering anorexia and, indeed, in seeding it in some young people . . . it is by no means a major factor'.[31] Instead she cites self-criticism, 'defeatism, an inability to deal with things, a need to absolve oneself of expectation, of one's SELF in its entirety'[32] as the building blocks. She argues that biological disposition, temperament and the genes we are born with have the most significant bearing on the development of anorexia and that environmental factors can do nothing more but set the spark which ignites the underlying neurosis. At face value this appears to be a fairly innocuous comment, but the consequences of a biological standpoint can be deeply damaging for women as has been demonstrated throughout history. This position reinforces the nineteenth- and twentieth-century belief that women are of a delicate disposition 'unequipped for anything but the most sheltered domestic life'[33] as written by Sigmund Freud in a letter to John Stuart Mill, 'I implore her to withdraw from the strife into the calm . . . activity of my home'.[34] It also does not explain why diagnoses continue to increase year-on-year or the developing increases in male diagnoses. An argument for the biological underpinning of anorexia also plays into the hands of neurosexism. Something I will explore further in the next section.

As the media are 'both a reflection and a shaper of social reality',[35] their influence and potential for transformative subversion is tantalizingly attractive. However, this industry is so entrenched in this damaging rhetoric that our only hope is to view and understand these images differently. It is through education and awareness, questioning and challenging these visually communicated messages that we have the power to subvert them. And how do we know that these unrealistic standards of beauty are still a problem? We know because a discomfort about our bodies is now considered standard and the "norm". As explored in the previous chapter, a text book case for the development of anorexia takes place during puberty and often develops out of a desire to be more 'fit, healthier and slimmer'[36] because she 'wasn't pretty enough . . . didn't have quite the right figure' or 'didn't feel as attractive to the boys in the class',[37] reinforcing the message that the development of anorexia is heavily influenced by the aesthetic pressures produced within societies that value the slender ideal. Literature on the development of anorexia spans decades and yet it remains an issue, only now it has been popularized and made mainstream by our generation's increasingly exaggerated female idealizations (that go far beyond the dimensions of the natural body). Bordo notes 'you can be as cynical as you want about the ads . . . and still feel powerless to resist their messages',[38] no matter what parents, teachers and clergy tell us, '"inner beauty" is a big laugh in this culture'.[39]

Neurosexism[40]

Differences in the male and female brain are often cited as the bedrock for developmental differences between the sexes and are therefore of interest as we explore the aetiology of anorexia. In the blurb of *Why Gender Matters*, Leonard Sax claims to demonstrate and subsequently teach us 'hardwired differences [between the sexes] to help every girl and every boy reach their fullest potential'[41] with research that follows in the footsteps of Simon Baron-Cohen in *The Essential Difference*. On the opening page of his book Baron-Cohen plainly states the claim that '*[t]he female brain is predominantly hard-wired for empathy. The male brain is predominantly hard-wired for understanding and building systems*'[42] and his book systematically takes us through the research that led to the assertion that men 'make the best scientists, engineers, bankers and lawyers'[43] whilst women make the best 'counsellors, primary-school teachers, nurses, carers, therapists, social workers, mediators [and] group facilitators'.[44] Broadly speaking, he argued that there are two different "brain types": empathizers (who are better at identifying the thoughts and feelings of other people) and systemizers (who are more interested in braking down and analyzing systems). Whilst there are variations within each gender group, on the whole, he associates the systemizing brain with males and the empathetic brain with females. He does not believe that this is the product of cultural conditioning but that the different levels of hormones the foetus is exposed to in the womb can influence the way brains work and thus influence subsequent behaviour.[45] These researchers would have us believe that there are fundamental gender differences that start within the very structure of the human brain. This brings to mind the age-old misogynist comment that women are not *inferior*, simply *different*. In *The Sexual Paradox* Susan Pinker asks us why women, with all the equal opportunities of men, choose different career paths. The answer is complicated as, after a lifetime of cultural conditioning, are the choices we make truly representative of what we want or what society wants? Is the world as equal as she would have us believe? Whilst the jury is out on the part biology plays in the decisions we make, there is much evidence to demonstrate that our environments and the social discourses to which we are exposed, have a significant impact on our conceptualizations of self. In an interesting programme on just this, Horizon on BBC Two, aired a documentary asking *Is Your Brain Male or Female?* hosted by Dr Michael Mosley and Professor Alice Roberts. Their goal was to determine 'whether gender differences are innate or shaped by the outside world'.[46] Mosley argued these differences are 'hard-wired into us from the womb'[47] supporting the "nature" position within this debate and Roberts supported the argument that these behavioural differences are learned as a consequence of 'social and cultural pressures'[48] or "nurture". Roberts worries that placing too much emphasis on biological factors may discourage girls and young women from progressing with careers in the sciences saying 'we live in a country where fewer than three out of ten physics A levels are taken by girls, where just 7% of engineers are women . . . and where men still earn on average nearly 20% more than their female colleagues'.[49] Whilst no firm conclusions were reached, the experiments conducted in the search for an answer were thought provoking and indicated that cultural pressures play a significant part in both our physical traits and our biological development (which I will come to explain in a few moments). Whilst it was demonstrated that, '[m]en scored higher in a special awareness exam[s] . . . [and] women prevailed in emotion recognition',[50] it was unclear if this was the result of cultural conditioning as opposed to inherent differences in the biological make-up (encouraging boys to be good at Maths, providing Lego for building etc. whilst encouraging girls to excel in language, to care and look after people, to play with dolls from a young age). Another examination involved 'a troop of Barbary macaques [who] were given toys to see if males were drawn to trucks and females to dolls'.[51] It turned out that this was correct; the females were drawn to the dolls whilst the trucks drew the attention of the males. However, as the female Barbary macaques raise the young, it may be that the males recognized that connection and drew their attention to the only remaining foreign object, the truck. The experiment that yielded the most definitive results involved babies. The children were each presented to an adult as the opposite sex (the boy was presented as a baby girl and vice versa). Without realizing it, the adults limited the children's activities and picked the toys most associated with the assumed gender role. The children appeared ambiguous towards the different choices but the adults continued to encourage the "girl" to play with the doll and the "boy" to play with the cars and trucks – gender-specific toys. The show also found that mother's 'pushed boys to achieve more than girls'[52] which, Roberts notes, 'would affect their ambitions and carry over into adulthood. . . . It would become a self-fulfilling prophecy'.[53] Research has shown that the human brain is plastic, throughout life it continues to change and adapt as per our surroundings, the experiences and people who influence us. As Roberts tells us '[t]he human brain is malleable, particularly during adolescence, and any differences you see could simply be the product of stereotyping and social pressure'.[54]

Whether or not you endorse them, your brain will make unintended associations based on your environments. In basic terms, for example, if you see women behind a hoover or cleaning, over time, you will subconsciously associate women with cleaning or housework. Likewise, if you see the glamorization of slender female models in magazines and advertising campaigns, you will associate that image with desirability and come to assign success with those attributes. In terms of development, this is 'an effortless and efficient way to learn about the world around you'[55] as associations are constructed 'without the need for awareness, intention and control'.[56] However, unlike explicitly held knowledge (that you choose to take on board) this in unconsciously communicated and therefore, not filtered. Nilanjana Dasgupta and Shaki Asgari at the University of Massachusetts have carried out numerous studies to demonstrate how influential, damaging and limiting these associations can be for the development of women. Their study showed how life itself, the people in our environments and the media can give rise to these associations and demonstrated that 'seeing women leaders reduced implicit self-stereotyping relative to controls . . . when they were portrayed as similar to one's ingroup . . . and oneself'.[57] We would expect then, that women surrounded and taught by powerful women in senior positions, would encourage the implicit association of women with words associated with strength, intelligence, power, decision-making etc. One of their experiments examined the effects of counterstereotypic information by asking a group of women to list words they associate with their sex both before and after reading biographies of powerful and influential women (Ruth Ginsburg, US Supreme Court Justice and the then CEO of e-Bay, Meg Whitman). Following exposure to powerful female figures, the women in the study were more likely to associate leadership words with women. This demonstrates, at least in part, that 'the patterns of their environment . . . altered the gender stereotypes represented in the implicit mind'.[58] Basically, gender inequality becomes not just a part of our minds, but also part of our biology. The circuits of our brains are a product of our 'physical, social and cultural environments'[59] as well as our thoughts and behaviours. What we do and experience 'creates neural activity that can alter the brain, either directly or through changes in gene expression'.[60] This is known as neuroplasticity. The idea that gender difference is the result of biological factors, such as hormone levels in the womb, is often referred to as neurosexism as it categorizes us according to our sex and values, as is always the case in a patriarchy, men over women. As Cordelia Fine writes in *Delusions of Gender* 'if you cuddle a baby, get a promotion, see billboard after billboard of near-naked women or hear a gender stereotype that places one sex at a higher status than the other, don't expect your hormonal state to remain impervious. It won't'.[61] The biological turns out to be cultural after all.

Taking this information about the development of the brain, society's gender hierarchy and anorexia together, we start to see the myriad affects this can have on women. Arguments for a biological basis ultimately portray women as the "second sex". This reinforces gender inequality and ends up validating female stereotypes and the objectification of women (they are prescribed worth by way of the male gaze). This creates an insecurity regarding their bodies and begins a constant struggle for equality whilst simultaneously desiring to take up as little space as possible, to reduce their body boundaries. Here there is a fine line to negotiate as young women seek to meet the female stereotypes (in order to belong) whilst striving for increased meaning and substance. In reflecting upon the development of anorexia – in light of neuroplasticity – we can see how cultural influences can be far more destructive and damaging than we might have first thought. If what we see and hear can actually change the way our brains function and operate, we start to understand how important our environments are for our development throughout life and how damaging arguments for gender difference can be. One of the consequences of gender difference is stereotyping and assigning the normalized or "natural" – perceived as "acceptable" – gender performance on the populations of people that inhabit that space. It has been theorized that eating disorders, in particular anorexia, can develop within this environment as a struggle to meet these normalizing standards and expectations. As Naomi Goldenberg writes 'the very concept of "essential" biological differences has itself been rendered problematic since no perception of male and female uniqueness can ever be separated from its political and social underpinnings'.[62] It is the subject of female stereotypes that we will explore further now.

Female stereotypes

Gender traits, often referred to as "femininity" and "masculinity" 'reflect stereotypes about the beliefs and behaviours typically attributed to men and women, which are acquired as they learn about the world and their roles in it'.[63] This knowledge shapes and structures gendered behaviour and serves to reinforce the pejorative understanding of femininity and masculinity. For example, whilst the gendered divide may be less exaggerated today than the twentieth century, or the beginning of the twenty-first century, it remains the case that gendered slogans, gender-specific colours and toys still permeate mainstream toy stores and many social commentators have commented on the damage this has wrought on both sexes. We still see the marketing of dolls,[64] pushchairs and other toy child-rearing paraphernalia marketed directed towards daddy's little princess. This appears in sharp contrast to the "boys" toys for the budding builder, driver, knight in shining armour. Focus here is given to building materials, Lego blocks, their favourite Marvel Characters – do not get me started on Wonder Woman! – remote control fighting toys etc. Amongst the shelves of blue merchandise, our little soldiers can find everything they need to build and protect their little den whilst the girls (in what some would call a complementary manner) are equipped with the mini hoover, kitchen appliances and button-nosed dolls to complete these make-shift homes. How very helpful for fulfilling their gender roles in adulthood. Furthermore, with the aid of dressing up costumes, girls are even encouraged to become the dolls they worship, to become their favourite Disney princesses.[65] Whilst the film and television industry has historically played a significant role in reinforcing these stereotypes, in recent years, a small shift has started to take place; the industry is starting to grow up and show a more empowering role for the female sex. On the silver screen we now see Sleeping Beauty take on her father, the dominating and controlling patriarch with the help of Maleficent, the powerful and feared matriarch of the Disney original back in 1959 and in a complementary fashion, in *Frozen*, the next generation are exposed to alternative models of love, as the story moves away from the "knight in shining armour"/saviour ideal which has been touted since the inception of the Disney brand, in favour of a story surrounding the love and powerful bounds between two sisters. It is a shame that each of these characters reflected one model of embodiment; that Angelina Jolie (cast as Maleficent) and the characters of Anna and Elsa (*Frozen*) were portrayed as conforming to the thinness ideal, but hey – we have to start somewhere!

The fact is that we live in a patriarchal society and so men tend to be in positions of power and authority.[66] Even in the twenty-first century, this gender division still permeates every sphere of public and private life. The consequence of this position is that desirable, "normal" and valuable attributes tend to be associated with masculinity and men, and so cultural preoccupation is on men and the things they do. In such an environment, 'both sexes are brought up to behave the same: to worship men and deride women'.[67] Tahmima Anam writes:

> [t]he world is unequal . . . at some point, probably between college and your first job, you will realise that the cards are stacked against you. It may start from a very small thing, for instance being interrupted at a meeting at work; or something quite significant, such as discovery that your salary is less than half your male counterpart's . . . you will start to see the world differently, and realise that every moment of your life, every experience has been coloured and influenced by your gender.[68]

Faced with this gender-biased environment, it is understandable that a woman might seek to embody masculine traits whilst masking evidence of her femininity. Many scholars[69] examining the manifestation of anorexia draw upon society's stereotypes, ideals of femininity and a fear of developing sexuality to explain the underlying features of the disorder. For example, in her research, Bruch[70] records voices of anorexic women who struggle to escape the female body as femininity is often associated with softness, and softness is associated with body fat, weakness and a lack of control, all negative attributes in the eyes of a patriarchal order which values control, discipline, competency and action. It really is no surprise that some women would strive towards "looking like a man" in this environment by rejecting the markings of femininity. However, as Lesley Heywood writes, this ultimately ends up reinforcing the status quo:

> Anorexia is a reaction to pervasive cultural symbols related to femininity, and it tries to create its own symbols, a female body that "can do as much as any man can do," that signifies competence, rather than dependence. But in the creation of this "new" symbol and body, the anorexic ironically upholds the very definition she fights against, accepting the pejorative definition of femininity.[71]

It is my belief that a woman living with a deep-seated dis-ease with her body, the extreme manifestation of which takes its form in anorexia, is the consequence of living in a patriarchy. As written by Isherwood,

> it is difficult for women to be fully embodied under patriarchy, as it has been demonstrated in works relating to sexuality, and it may just be that food is seen as just as physical and sensual, as so to be restricted in women in a way it is not with men.[72]

I also think it's important to remember that, as with any system, the people in power make the rules and it follows that these rules will suit them. Since we live in a world largely ruled by men, it is men who benefit and women who come to be evaluated in relation to male-defined norms. As de Beauvoir writes, 'one is not born, one rather becomes a woman'[73] and her making is in order to support the male status quo. Furthermore, as marketing and advertising industries focus on catching the interests of younger consumers in more direct and meaningful ways, it is clear to see how feminine stereotypes and slender physiques are capturing the interests of children.

The consequence of this movement towards broadening consumer interest and extending marketing campaigns to include younger consumers is the sexualization of childhood as they attempt to emulate the desired advertised aesthetic which in turn results in their increasing dissatisfaction with their existing bodies and the development of body sensitivity in respect of size and shape. This developing awareness of "beauty" trends is fed by the television content of skinny and scantily clad celebrities, dancing and singing about mature, usually sex and relationship-related, themes.[74] If you are in any doubt of the validity of my statement, I invite you to turn on your television and select one of the many music channels sure to be at your disposal. Within the space of a few minutes, at any time of the day, there will be "risky" content which includes at least one of the previous themes. It is worrying and becoming increasingly common to see young children desiring to be smaller in an environment where they are encouraged by peers, celebrities and marketing influences to purchase "sexy" bikinis and flesh revealing clothes to emulate their favourite pop star role models; when playing 'lovely little games in high heels, strip-teasing, flouncing and jutting their chests out'[75] is increasingly understood as constituting innocent and without risk playtime as if they are testing their boundaries instead of exaggerating the mainstream female ideal. It is within this environment that we see primary school-aged children dressing up as naughty witches and scatterings of mini sexy fairies running playfully through the streets on Halloween. Instead of stepping back and considering the consequences of such behaviour, many parents are buying the costumes and chalking it down as a part of mainstream childhood, a "phase" that children pass through.

By and large the sexualization of childhood reinforces the message that a girl's primary worth resides in her ability to be a sexual object whilst teaching boys that sex and violence are synonymous and that 'women should be valued primarily for their ability to give them sexual pleasure'.[76] It also assumes that children are sexually mature due to the outward appearance of makeup, clothes and advanced puberty, and it allows 'corporations to use materials or methods of production that release endocrine-disturbing chemicals into the environment, contributing to early puberty'.[77] Taught to please others, to constantly strive to meet the cultural ideal for women whilst being systematically objectified and sexualized 'creates constant self-doubt and insecurity, problems that the rituals and obsessions of eating disorders can temporarily mask'.[78] This culture produces generations of either young women with 'damaged self-esteem and an eating disorder or young men who cannot experience sexual pleasure with a woman whose body has not been surgically altered to reflect pornographic images'.[79] The education system is lacking in providing the sexual education that teenagers need for healthy development and as such, information is gleaned from our highly sexualized media which serves to perpetuate those expectations. Boys and men are not impervious to the destructive force of gender stereotypes and the sexualization of childhood. Cultural mythology about all men being potential rapists, paedophiles and wife-batterers can be just as pernicious;[80] both sexes live in this culture and both are susceptible to the pervasiveness of cultural ideology and images; however, it is clear that women bear the brunt of our sexualized culture.

Female stereotypes and the sexualization of childhood alongside the objectification of women are all contributing factors to creating dis-ease amongst women regarding their worth in society and send the message that they are always evaluated and assigned worth in relation to men and male desire. This industry targets consumers at a younger age with denigrating images of female sexuality that causes psychological damage for many young women and teenagers. This becomes the breeding ground for body insecurity, the development of low self-esteem and body confidence that can subsequently lead to the development of a more serious disorder, namely anorexia. In the context of this literature it is clear to see how these aesthetic values have taken root within the collective female consciousness.

Dieting and consumer capitalism

Creating a dis-ease between women and their embodiment is a big money-maker. The female diet market relies on the low self-esteem of women, as cultivated by the industries we have been discussing, to secure and guarantee their global success. As we shall explore now, Weight Watchers (for example) relies on an 84 per cent reuptake rate to secure its profit margins. The success of consumer capitalism hinges on its ability to exacerbate, on a reoccurring basis, our sense of desire. For it to succeed, it must constantly ignite within the consumer a hunger for "more", this more is constantly being reshaped and redefied, so the consumer stays engaged. The system fails when consumers become bored and detached from this constant striving to "better" their circumstance. As written by Paul Campos, a 'satisfied consumer ceases to consume, until he [sic] is no longer satisfied: Thus, a kind of institutionalized sense of recurrent dissatisfaction is critical to the health and expansion of consumer markets'.[81] In relation to the food and fat obsessed culture, broadly speaking, this all boils down to virtue and who is in possession of it. Within the Western world (locations where involuntary starving is rare), the ability to control one's food hungers and impulses has become associated with a number of highly regarded virtues.[82] The slender form has come to symbolize the ability to control and sublimate desire in general, but most specifically in areas of employment, finance and economic interests. Some social commentators such as Greg Critser have noted that being overweight for many American corporations is a sure-fire career-killer.[83] The inference here is if you cannot control your body contours, how can you control your workload, your budget and your staff? Despite the clearly absurd generalization that body weight is in some way synonymous with work ethic, intelligence or discipline, the diet industry has capitalized on this message and exacerbated the link between thinness and virtue. Surely, logic dictates that the most focused employee is not the one who is distracted by the restraints of a perpetual diet or by obsessive exercise routines, it is the employee who is focused on the work in hand, who has the physical and mental energy to be innovative, creative and dedicated. However, telling people they are accepted as they are has never been a particularly successful money-maker. Not only are women battling against sexism in the workplace, but they also have to adhere to strict body rules (much stricter than their male counterparts) if they are to approximate male success (a success often granted on the basis of their gender). The vast majority of dieters fail to maintain long-term weight-loss as once a diet results in the desired weight decrease the individual assumes the same pre-diet lifestyle that maintained the previous body size (this is elaborated on in a few moments). Weight is slowly regained and the cycle of diet-weight gain-diet is repeated. Less advertised by these various diets is the fact that weight loss takes place as part of a lifestyle change. The golden tenet is one of moderation instead of rules; black and white food polarities are unhelpful. Fat, sugar and carbohydrates are important features of a balanced diet alongside various fruits, vegetables and proteins. Losing weight is about maintaining a balance between varieties of foods. Moderation dictates that sharing a weekly pizza with a side salad as part of a balanced diet is healthier than having a full pizza or full salad to oneself but who's going to pay for that advice? A moderate lifestyle in which the individual is working towards a deep level of acceptance does not come with a guaranteed weight loss schedule or a twelve-week plan. It does not come with the satisfaction of a purchase, that euphoria which accompanies an acquisition that promises access to a happier and more successful version of yourself. The aristocracy of thinness is made up of two overlapping classes: those who have managed to control their calorie intake in order to achieve unnatural thinness, and the naturally thin. Thinness represents genetic luck, a combination of individual willpower and social privilege (those who have sufficient resources to be whatever culture desires) or an eating disorder, a psychological malady played out on human flesh. Individuals with anorexia violently cling to their virtue by refusing to surrender to contemporary humanity's most gluttonous impulses. The features of anorexia of refusing to maintain a healthy body weight, a terror of becoming "fat", engaging in compulsive food rituals and dividing food into "good" and "bad" fixed groups are actually exhibited (to varying degrees) by many of the individuals engaging in day-to-day yoyo dieting. The difference is that the anorexic woman takes this dangerous logic to deadly extremes.

Capitalism plays on female insecurities and the weight women are "permitted" to carry is a constant source of insecurity as we have been exploring. As Orbach writes: 'girls are growing up today who think that constant dieting and being frightened of food are natural states'.[84] The diet industry is a capitalist dream. It taps into a self-generating market, a widespread target audience and has an incredibly high failure rate. If dieting worked, you would only have to do it once. The simple fact of the matter is that diets do not work. As Richard Klein writes, they '[n]ever have; never will'.[85] The success of capitalism hinges on consumers consuming and the more people diet, the more they desire what they cannot or should not have, especially when it plays into one of the most universal of human needs. Diet companies rely on return custom; their profitability hinges on failure and maintaining the emotional connection between "healthy," "happy" and "slender". Fad diet books have commandeered a vast proportion of our book stores and cover a whole host of slightly varying diet schedules for those individuals desperate to achieve the culturally defined "healthy" body size. In addition to the books and magazines, came the mainstream introduction of special "diet" foods, which included but was not limited to: frozen meals, crackers, biscuits and cakes, meal replacement bars and drinks, bread, pasta, nuts, seeds and animal products etc. The only food group that remained largely untouched was fresh produce such as fruit and vegetables. In addition to these new supermarket features came the advent of weight loss clinics that were no longer reserved for the morbidly obese but now catered for anyone who, by way of nature, did not naturally embody a svelte and slender frame. Herbal weight loss products in the form of drinks, pills, supplements etc. began to feature in advertising campaigns as a means of achieving weight loss goals – a great selling tactic as they persuade consumers to repeatedly invest their resources in shedding pounds in new and innovative ways. In *Body Wars*, Margo Maine writes that:

> After all of the elaborate planning, garnering of resources, and emotional investment in weight loss, dieting still rarely works. Of those who lose 25 or more pounds, 90% will regain those pounds within two

> years, and 98% will regain the weight within five years. In fact, many regain more weight than they lose.[86]

The diet industry in the UK was worth an estimated £2bm in 2014, and between 2013 and 2014 it was estimated that 55 per cent of the Britons actively tried to lose weight whilst only 5 per cent of women claimed to never think about the weight of their bodies. The former director of Weight Watchers, Richard Samber, admitted that central to the success of the company was the fact that 84 per cent of customers cannot maintain their weight loss and so continue to attend meetings and purchase merchandise. It was estimated that only 1 in 100 "slimmers" successfully manage to maintain their weight loss for more than a year.[87] For many people, the decision to diet results in increased credit card debt and the erosion of self-esteem.

Bubbling under the surface of all this is a painful truth. People rarely feel physically better the slimmer they are (except for cases when weight gain has resulted in physical limitations) or because they feel they are a better person. Often people feel better and happier because of the responses this weight loss necessitates from family, friends, colleagues and peers as losing weight seems to result in people treating you like a more admirable person when you are "thin" rather than "fat". As Campos writes 'many of us do not have the psychic strength to resist that insidious message . . . recognizing the injustice of something does not necessarily rob that thing of its power over oneself'.[88] As we have already explored, anorexia can often begin with a decision to diet. Very quickly the young woman starts to take immense satisfaction from the psychological control she can exert over her flesh. Slowly the compulsion to shed weight and engage in gruelling exercise routines takes root within her psyche and a disembodied sustenance denying personality starts to take shape within her mind. The paralyzing intensity of this socially valued denial of food-related indulgence, reinforced by cultural distain for anyone who can be remotely identified as "fat" reinforces this compulsion and feeds her fears. There is no evidence that this situation will change anytime soon.

As we have seen, within research on eating disorders and the manifestation of anorexia, society is often cited as the underpinning ill that creates the ideology for discontent. Media imagery, the fashion and beauty industries, neurosexism, female stereotypes, the sexualization of childhood and the objectification of women are all named as pervasive societal institutions that foster certain ideas regarding bodily practices and norms of beauty.[89] I hope to have demonstrated the multifaceted nature of anorexia. It is not just the consequence of a particular action; its development is far more complex than that. As we have touched upon in these opening chapters, our dualistic heritage, the female body as a battleground for control and power and gender hierarchy alongside family life and expectations and issues surrounding the construction of identity can all play a significant part in the aetiology of disordered eating and anorexia.

Notes

1 Orbach, S. (1993) *Hunger Strike: The Anorectic's Struggle as a Metaphor for Our Age*. London: Penguin Books, 3.
2 Bordo, S. (2003) *Unbearable Weight: Feminism, Western Culture, and the Body*. London: University of California Press, 137–140.
3 Isherwood, L., Stuart, E. (1998) *Introducing Body Theology*. Sheffield: Sheffield Academic Press Ltd, 53.
4 Douglas, M. (2002) *Purity and Danger: An Analysis of Concept and Taboo*. London: Routledge, 142.
5 Metcalfe, K. (2006) *Anorexia: A Stranger in the Family*. Mid-Glamorgan: Accent Press Ltd, 8.
6 Orbach (1993: xvii).
7 Orbach (1993: 4).
8 Orbach (1993: xxii).
9 For more information on body dysmorphic disorder, see Phillips, K. A. (2005) *The Broken Mirror: Understanding and Treating Body Dysmorphic Disorder*. Oxford: Oxford University Press.
10 Bordo (2003: xvii).
11 Bordo (2003: xxi).
12 Bordo (2003: xvii).
13 Bordo (2003: 288).
14 Bordo (2003: xv).
15 Bordo (2003: xvi).
16 Chappell, K. (2008) *Celeb Workout Secrets: You Can Have a Body Like the Stars*. Ebony, 164–168 (166). Available at: http://books.google.co.uk/books?id=l9MDAAAAMBAJ&pg=PA166&dq=beyonce's+exercise&hl=en&sa=X&ei=tylqVLOuBYHeaMH4gJgJ&ved=0CCAQ6AEwAA#v=onepage&q=beyonce's%20exercise&f=false [16/11/2014].
17 Cloe, A. (2014) *Average American Women's Weight and Height*. Available at: www.livestrong.com/article/357769-weight-height-for-the-average-american-woman/ [16/11/2014].
18 As we explore later in this chapter, the diet industry is a big money-maker and whilst we could safely state that there has been an increase in public awareness surrounding these damaging slender ideals over the last ten years, very little has been done to change the rhetoric. This becomes painfully apparent when conducting a brief "Beach Body" search on Amazon as myriad book covers populate the screen, advertising book after book of hints and tips, failing to question why we are expected to go beyond the realms of health to attain this painfully narrow ideal.
19 Reel, J. J. (2013) *Eating Disorders: An Encyclopedia of Causes, Treatment, and Prevention*. Santa Barbara: Greenwood Press, 20.
20 Holmes, A. (2007) *Memo to Women's Magazine Editors: White Women Hate Themselves After Reading Your Magazines*. Available at: http://jezebal.com/248484/memo-to-womens-magazine-editors-white-women-hate-themselves-after-raeding-your-magazines [22/11/2014].
21 This article showed that the average European-American woman is 5 feet, 4 inches tall and wears a size 12. Yet, the ideal communicated through these images is of a Barbie-esque figure who 'wears a size 4 in the hips, a size 2 in the waist, and rocks a size-10 bust'. For more information, see Nelson, J. (2012) *Airbrushed Nation: The Lure and Loathing of Women's Magazines*. Berkeley: Perseus Books Group, 123.
22 Nelson (2012: 123).
23 Wallace, A. (2002) *Jamie Lee Curtis: True Thighs*. Available at: www.more.com/news/womens-issues/jamie-lee-curtis-true-thighs [23/11/2014].

24 Wallace 2002.
25 Selby, J. (2014) *Emma Watson: Noah and Harry Potter Actress 'Excited About the Aging Process.' She's Only 23*. Available at: www.independent.co.uk/news/people/emma-watson-is-excited-about-the-aging-process-aged-23-9225728.html [23/11/2014].
26 Anon. (2011) *Airbrushed Make-Up Ads Banned for 'Misleading'*. Available at: www.bbc.co.uk/news/uk-14304802 [24/11/2014].
27 Nelson (2012: xiii).
28 Anon. (2014) *The Dove Campaign for Real Beauty*. Available at: www.dove.us/Social-Mission/campaign-for-real-beauty.aspx [19/11/2014].
29 Anon 2014.
30 Crilly, L. (2012) *Hope With Eating Disorders*. London: Hay House Insights, 234.
31 Howard-Taylor, L. (2008) *Biting Anorexia*. Sydney: Finch Publishing, 77.
32 Howard-Taylor (2008: 77).
33 Bordo (2003: 159).
34 Jones, E. (1956) *Sigmund Freud: Life and Work*. London: Hogarth Press, 193.
35 Ezzell, M. B. (2008) Pornography, Lad Mags, Video Games, and Boys: Reviving the Canary in the Cultural Coal Mine. In: Olfman, S. (ed.) *The Sexualization of Childhood*. Westport: Praeger Publishers Inc., 7–32 (8).
36 Metcalfe (2006: 8).
37 Metcalfe (2006: 8).
38 Bordo (2003: xxvii).
39 Bordo (2003: xxvii). This striving towards meeting these social ideals might actually represent our failure or our lack of willing to fully engage with these surface consumerist values for fear of exclusion or social illegitimacy. For a broader discussion surrounding the idea of a legitimate subject, see Chapter 3 and discussions surrounding the work of Judith Butler and the notion of a slender performance.
40 Scientific methodologies and the methodology I have employed throughout this work (weighted towards the contemporary Western cultural construction of femininity alongside feminist liberation theology and thealogy) have very different ways of asking and answering questions. As a multidisciplinary approach, I am interested to see how we can bring different areas of academic study together in order to develop our understandings of various cultural phenomena such as anorexia. This section on neurosexism is an example of this interdisciplinary approach.
41 Sax, L. (2007) *Why Gender Matters: What Parents and Teachers Need to Know About the Emerging Science of Sex Differences*. New York: Crown Publishing Group.
42 Baron-Cohen, S. (2003) *The Essential Difference*. London: Penguin Books, 1. Author's emphasis.
43 Fine, C. (2010) *Delusions of Gender: The Real Science Behind Sex Differences*. London: Icon books, xix.
44 Fine (2010: xix).
45 This view is the consequence of his ongoing research following a large group of children pre-and-post birth. Sixteen weeks into the gestation period, amniocentesis tests were carried out which involved measuring levels of testosterone in the amniotic fluid and subsequently linking those levels to behaviour. For more information, see Baron-Cohen (2003).
46 Hogan, M. (2014) *Horizon: Is Your Brain Male or Female?, BBC Two, Review: 'Thought-Provoking'*. Available at: www.telegraph.co.uk/culture/tvandradio/tv-and-radio-reviews/11129004/Horizon-Is-Your-Brain-Male-or-Female-BBC-Two-review-thought-provoking.html [09/12/2014].

47 Hogan (2014).
48 Hogan (2014).
49 Mosley, M. (2014) *Is Your Brain Male or Female?* Available at: www.bbc.co.uk/news/science-environment-29405467 [13/12/2014].
50 Hogan (2014).
51 Hogan 2014.
52 Hogan (2014).
53 Hogan (2014).
54 Mosley (2014).
55 Fine (2010: 5).
56 Fine (2010: 5).
57 Asgari, S., Dasgupta, N., Stout, J. G. (2012) When Do Counterstereotypic Ingroup Members Inspire Versus Deflate? The Effect of Successful Professional Women on Young Women's Leadership Self-Concept. In: *Personality and Social Psychology Bulletin* 38: 370–383.
58 Fine (2010: 7).
59 Fine (2010: 236).
60 Fine (2010: 236).
61 Fine (2010: 236).
62 Goldenberg, N. (1993) *Resurrecting the Body: Feminism, Religion, and Psychoanalysis*. New York: Crossroads, 61.
63 Behar, R. (2007) Gender-Related Aspects of Eating Disorders: A Psychosocial View. In: Rubin, J. S. (ed.) *Eating Disorders and Weight Loss Research*. New York: Nova Science Publishers, 39–65 (54).
64 For a scathing examination of the culture of dolls that has infiltrated the female psyche, see Walter, N. (2010) *Living Dolls: The Return of Sexism*. London: Virago, 1–15.
65 Here I refer to Walt Disney World in Orlando, Florida, and their offering to 'step inside an enchanted beauty salon that offers magical makeovers for young princesses and knights 3 to 12'. The picture accompanying this shows a room full of little girls immaculately dressed as Disney princesses (make-up and hair-spray carefully in place) and their accompanying 'Fairy Godmothers' on hand for 'almost any magical wish'. This is clearly tailored to the Disney princess with packages ranging from $59.99 to $199.95 whilst the knight package consists of hairstyling with gel, a 'mighty sword and shield' and confetti for $19.99. For more information, see Disney (2017) *Bibbidi Bobbidi Boutique-Disney Springs*. Available at: https://disneyworld.disney.go.com/shops/disney-springs/bibbidi-bobbidi-boutique-marketplace/ [25/01/2017].
66 Many feminist scholars have detailed extensive evidence to attest to the fact that we live in a patriarchal society. For a selection of examples, see Faludi, S. (1993) *Backlash: The Undeclared War Against Women*. London: Vintage; Greer, G. (2006) *The Female Eunuch*. London: Harper Perennial; Banyard, K. (2010) *The Equality Illusion: The Truth About Women and Men Today*. London: Faber and Faber; and Oakley, A. (2015) *Sex, Gender and Society*. New York: Routledge. Evidence of the patriarchal society we live in is evident in online articles such as the following from the Guardian website. This article discusses the gender-based pay gap and shows images of everyday sexism. See: Bates, L. (2017) *The Pocket Money Gap – and 10 Other Ways Girls Are Taught They're Worth Less*. Available at: www.theguardian.com/commentisfree/2017/jan/24/gender-pay-gap-boys-girls-pocket-money?CMP=fb_gu [25/01/2017].
67 Bidisha (2013) The Red Room. In: Appignanesi, L., Holmes, R., Orbach, S. (eds.) *Fifty Shades of Feminism*. London: Hachette Digital, 38–44 (39).
68 Anam, T. (2013) Things Your Mother Never Told You (for fear you would demand a sex change). In: Appignanesi, L., Holmes, R., Orbach, S. (eds.) *Fifty Shades of Feminism*. London: Hachette Digital, 17–23 (21–22).

69 One such scholar and social commentator is Naomi Wolf who writes that for her, adolescent starvation was a 'prolonged reluctance to be born into womanhood if that meant assuming a station of beauty.' As we have seen throughout this chapter and we go onto explore in Chapter 4, this idea resonates throughout literature surrounding the development of anorexia. For more information, see Wolf, N. (1994) Hunger. In: Fallon, P., Katzman, M. A., Wooley, S. C. (eds.) *Feminist Perspectives on Eating Disorders*. New York: The Guildford Press, 103; and Wolf, N. (1990) *The Beauty Myth: How Images of Beauty Are Used Against Women*. London: Vintage Books.

70 For more information, see Bruch, H. (1973) *Eating Disorders*. New York: Basic Books; and Bruch, H. (2001) *The Golden Cage: The Enigma of Anorexia Nervosa*. London: Harvard University Press.

71 Heywood, L. (1996) *Dedication to Hunger: The Anorexia Aesthetic in Modern Culture*. Berkeley: University of California Press, 68.

72 Isherwood, I. (2008) Will You Slim for Him or Bake Cakes for the Queen of Heaven? In: Isherwood, L., Althaus-Reid, M. (eds.) *Controversies in Body Theology*. London: SCM Press, 176.

73 De Beauvoir, S. (1997) *The Second Sex*. London: Vintage Classics, 1.

74 Richard Gordon writes that 'reports suggest that the disorder [anorexia] is emerging with greater frequency in younger, preadolescent children . . . has been attributed to increasing degrees of weight preoccupation and dieting among younger children, as well as to earlier emergence of the physical signs of puberty in females'. For more information, see: Gordon 2000: 21.

75 Lamb, S. (2003) *The Secret Lives of Girls: What Good Girls Really Do – Sex Play, Aggression, and Their Guilt*. London: Simon and Schuster, 43.

76 Olfman, S. (2008) *The Sexualisation of Childhood*. Westport: Praeger Publishers Inc., 2.

77 Olfman (2008: 2).

78 Olfman (2008: 71).

79 Olfman (2008: 3).

80 In a Guardian article promoting her new film, Anne Hathaway was quoted discussing the difference between toxic masculinity and male energy. She said that 'Male energy is beautiful. Male energy is welcome. Male energy is necessary. . . . That said, there has been a perversion of the beauty of male energy into this macho ideal that I don't think services anybody'. I cite this because I believe we are seeing more well-known names using their public platforms to discuss issues that feminist commentators have been mulling over for decades. Today, an increase in public recognition of the difference between creative male energy and toxic masculinity and the danger it poses to life on this planet is paramount. For more information, see Anon. (2017) *Anne Hathaway Has Psychic Connection to Giant Monster in Colossal Trailer*. Available at: www.theguardian.com/film/2017/jan/19/anne-hathaway-colossal-trailer [23/01/2017].

81 Campos, P. (2004) *The Obesity Myth: Why America's Obsession With Weight Is Hazardous to Your Health*. London: Penguin Books, 231.

82 This correlation between food and the virtues of reducing its consumption can also be found within the Christian diet industry, which has grown in prominence within the southern states of America over the last twenty years. Expanding out of particular Protestant values, this religious framework for weight loss draws upon the idea that dieting behaviours embody a hunger for a deep spiritual connection to contextualize life and provide an additional layer of meaning and authenticity than is offered within contemporary society. On the surface, this seems harmless. However, further probing shows us that at the heart of this diet industry is a morally questionable rhetoric as the size, shape and weight of

people (historically women) comes to represent their commitment to Christ and the purity of their soul. Here the attainment of a slender physique becomes synonymous with eternal glory alongside Christ in heaven. Whilst these diet groups have existed in many guises over the years, it was famously brought to mass media attention in 2000 with the diet movement of Gwen Shamblin. Drawing upon a specific form of Christianity (Protestant thinking associated with white, middle class Christian groups within the United States) and dualistic diet logic, her philosophy focused on producing stringent guidelines for the "proper" Christian body size, arguing that the high American obesity levels represented a spiritual crisis and that the overconsumption of food was the consequence of spiritual malnourishment. Her answer, an "eat thin" agenda with a core belief that the human body's state of fitness affects the individual's relationship with sacred figures such as God and Jesus in direct and indirect ways. The supposition was that there is a direct correlation between weight and religious dedication; here people can literally weigh their sin and anyone falling outside the "acceptable" weight, as defined by Shamblin, came to represent a lack of spiritual purity. A damning statement for those participating in her Church, the Remnant Fellowship. Shamblin's Weight Down Workshop was adopted by 30,000 groups throughout the United States and has inspired many contemporary Christian diet groups such as: The Eden Diet; The Makers Diet; The Hallelujah Diet; Faith and Fat Loss; Weight Loss God's Way; Take Back Your Temple; and, my personal favourite for witty titles, Bod4God. All superficially seem to play on the same message of utilizing a closer connection with God through prayer to shed the pounds and fill that previously undiagnosed spiritual hunger. For a detailed analysis of the Christian diet industry, see Griffin, R. M. (2004) *Born Again Bodies: Flesh and Spirit in American Christianity*. London: University of California Press; and Isherwood, L. (2007a) *The Fat Jesus: Feminist Explorations in Boundaries and Transgressions*. London: Darton, Longman and Todd Ltd.

83 For more information, see Critser, G. (2003) *Fat Land: How Americans Became the Fattest People in the World*. New York: Houghton Mifflin Company.

84 Orbach, S. (2009) *Bodies*. London: Profile Books Ltd, 96.

85 Klein, R. (2001) Fat Beauty. In: Braziel, J. E., LeBesco, K. (eds.) *Bodies Out of Bounds: Fatness and Transgression*. London: University of California Press, 19–37 (36).

86 Maine, M. (2000) *Body Wars: Making Peace With Women's Bodies*. Carlsbad: Gurze Books, 45.

87 For more information, see Goldhill, O. (2014) *A Nation of Weight Watchers: Is Our Obsession With Thin Making Us Fat?* Available at: www.telegraph.co.uk/women/womens-health/11003614/A-nation-of-weight-watchers-Is-our-obsession-with-thin-making-us-fat.html [15/10/2016].

88 Campos (2004: 243).

89 The influence of culture on the development of anorexia is developed by Susan Bordo in her "axis of continuity". These "axes" refer to cultural "currents" or "streams" which she cited as contributing factors to the development of anorexia. The three axes she explores in her work are: 1) dualist axis; 2) control axis; and, 3) gender/power axis. In so doing, she analyses anorexia as a social formation resulting from various historical and contemporary currents within our society. For more information, see Bordo (2003: 142–147).

3 The female body as a politically mediated form

The body politic refers to the people living in a politically organized society and is a term predominantly used in reference to the policies and practices implemented by the powers of society to regulate the human body, to control its movements and gestures. These disciplines include institutional power communicated through government and laws, disciplinary power exercised in consumption, and personal power negotiated in intimate relationships. Like all political processes, 'the social construction of women's bodies develops through battles between groups with competing political interests and with differential access to power and resources'[1] and can often serve as a 'powerful tool for controlling women's lives by fostering material changes in women's lives and bodies'.[2]

The following chapter examines how ideas about the female body affect women's lives and how these ideas develop within the psyche of women and manifest themselves in destructive ways, namely through the development of anorexia. In the previous section, I examined how ideas about women's bodies are socially constructed, now it's time to look at how these social constructions can be used to control women's lives, and how women can resist these forces. I will do this through carrying out an examination of the "docile", watched body taken from the writings of Michael Foucault, gender as performative (and what I believe to be the slender performance) from Judith Butler's thesis, an examination of Marion Woodman's ritual of transformation and Naomi Goldenberg's conceptualization of myth and fantasy as we search to find the lost goddess in both the female body and in society. Through an examination of these theories and discussions surrounding them, I hope to show how society's stereotypes and idealizations have been questioned but not quite displaced.

Foucault and the body politic

In 1979 Foucault argued that the rise of 'parliamentary institutions and of new conceptions of political liberty was accompanied by a darker countermovement, by the emergence of a new and unprecedented discipline directed against the body'.[3] Foucault described how the classical age discovered the body as a target of power that may be 'subjected, used, transformed and improved'.[4] He argued that across all societies, the body is in the grip of strict disciplinary powers, which impose constrictions, prohibitions and obligations on it. These forces culminated to create, what he described as the "docile body"; the product of the disciplined, subjected and practiced body. Three features were cited as creating this environment of disciplinary power; 1) the scale of control; 2) the object of control; and, 3) the modality of control. In these three features we see the body being insulated through segregation and isolation, treated coercively through control of its movements, gestures and attitudes and taught to monitor these behaviours through control of time throughout the life of the subject. Foucault argues that these disciplines became general formulas of domination in the seventeenth and eighteenth centuries. That they were 'meticulous, often minute, techniques, but they had their importance: because they defined a certain mode of detailed political investment of the body, a "new micro-physics" of power . . . as if they tended to cover the entire social body'.[5] He believed that governments (through organizations such as schools, hospitals, prisons) organize people and create around them a mechanism of power that allows them to see the smallest event that occurs in the state. In so doing, the state was able to

> establish presences and absences, to know where and how to locate individuals, to set up useful communications, to interrupt others, to be able at each moment to supervise the conduct of each individual, to assess it, to judge it, to calculate its qualities or merits. It was a procedure, therefore, aimed at knowing, mastering and using.[6]

He described these institutions in terms of living organisms and machines as he argued that this form of discipline is organic, genetic and cellular. Through fixing the individuals in space and time (a central element of Foucault's thesis), the institutions regulate the way in which people act and think and so the disciplined subject is controlled absolutely through power and technology. Of course, this is a very simplistic overview of Foucault's comprehensive thesis on the "docile body", but it does help emphasize the degree to which societies are able to regulate and police individuals. In reading Foucault's work, it's interesting to note that distinctions are not made between gendered bodies. Women, like men, are subjected to the same disciplinary forces described by Foucault but he appears to be blind to the disciplines that produce a type of embodiment that is specifically feminine. Sandra Lee Bartky argues that overlooking the forms of subjection that engender the female body 'is to perpetuate the silence and powerlessness of those upon whom these disciplines have been imposed'[7] and therefore reproduce the sexism that is endemic throughout Western political theory. She identifies three categories of disciplinary practices that produce a body in which appearance and gesture are recognizably feminine; 1) the practices that aim to produce a body of a certain size; 2) those that encourage a specific range of gestures, postures and movements; and, 3) those that are directed towards displaying these ideals on an ornamented surface. She writes:

> the woman who checks her make-up half a dozen times a day . . . who worries that the wind or the rain may spoil her hairdo . . . or who, feeling fat, monitors everything she eats, has become . . . a self-policing subject, a self-committed to a relentless self-surveillance . . . a form of obedience to patriarchy.[8]

Bartky noted that the "docile bodies" of women are constructed through disciplinary practices which communicate a perpetual and exhaustive regulation of the body's size and shape, its appetite, gestures and postures and general bearing in space alongside the appearance of each of its visible parts.[9] This culminates in women being unable to begin re-visioning their bodies until they learn to read the cultural messages that are inscribed upon them daily and until they 'come to see that even when the mastery of the disciplines of femininity produces a triumphant result . . . [they] are still only women'.[10]

As styles of the female figure reflect cultural preoccupations and obsessions, they vary over time and across cultures. The introduction of Twiggy in the mid-1960s marked a shift towards a slender ideal that bordered on emaciation and caught women in a perpetual preadolescent state. Advertising campaigns, magazine and newspaper articles, medicine etc. have all promoted this ideal and recommend dieting and exercise as a means of achieving it. Dieting disciplines the body's hungers as 'appetite must be monitored at all times and governed by an iron will'.[11] The body becomes an enemy, as food and nourishment are a basic human need promoting a dualistic approach to the body and mind. The difference between the approach men and women take when it comes to food is mirrored in other aspects of public and private life as captured by German photographer Marianne Wex in 1979. In a series of over 5,000 photographs and media images Wex captured significant differences in male and female movements, gestures and posture.[12] She found that women make themselves 'small and narrow, harmless; they seem tense; they take up little space'[13] whilst men, assume what is referred to as a "proffering position", as they expand into the available spaces, legs thrown wide, crotch visible, arms open, palms out. It was also found that a man's stride is longer and has more spring and rhythm to it; 'he walks with toes pointed outward, holds his arms at a greater distance from his body, and swings them further'.[14] In contrast, women were found to hold their arms closer to their bodies, palms to the side, walk guarded and with the additional constraint of high-heeled shoes, the 'body is thrown forward and off balance'[15] resulting in a shorter stride as she attempts to walk under these difficult conditions. Finer disciplines are evident through women's taught expressions of deference as under male scrutiny 'women . . . avert their eyes or cast them downward; the female gaze is trained to abandon its claim to the sovereign status of seer'.[16] Women are also taught to smile more than men,[17] be gracious, exercise deference and be expected to have a readiness to serve, basic prerequisites for many women's jobs.[18] Not only are women's bodies expected to exhibit these restrictions but they are also expected to demonstrate grace and eroticism (albeit restrained by modesty). All this should be displayed in the right way and there is discipline involved in this process too. From the application of make-up and fashion to adhering to male desires that a woman's body be soft, supple, hairless and smooth whilst betraying the years and appearing line-ness showing no signs of age, deep thought or the wisdom of experience. These practices reinforce Foucault's position and can be understood in 'light of the modernization of patriarchal domination, a modernization that unfolds historically'.[19]

The body as a "site" of "disciplinary power" was further developed by Post-Structuralism which contributed two additional elements. In drawing on the theories of Foucault, the movement encouraged recognition of the fact that configurations of power are never seamless; however comprehensive and far-reaching, there are always new opportunities for resistance. Post-Structuralism also encouraged us to acknowledge and recognize that the body is not only shaped by social norms and habitual practices of prescribed gender norms, but is also mediated by language: by metaphors, for instance, microbes as "invading", and an egg as "waiting" for sperm, alongside the use of binary oppositions such as male/female and inner/outer which ultimately organize and animate our experience and perception. Therefore, we have 'no direct, innocent, or unconstructed knowledge of our bodies; rather, we are always reading our bodies according to various interpretive schemes'.[20] These insights have informed and influenced the later writings on the politics of the body; a notable case of this is with the work of Judith Butler.

Gender performativity

Drawing on the work of Foucault and emerging from her readings of Derrida and Post-Structuralism, Butler asserted that feminism exhibits 'juridical systems of power'[21] that '*produce* subjects they subsequently come to represent'.[22] She sought to demonstrate how the classification of women had been deployed in feminism in order to show how feminism's uses of that term 'far from being neutral, are deeply implicated in power relations'.[23] In *Gender Trouble*, Butler set out to critique and disrupt the categories of sex, gender, identity and desire and argued that femininity is 'a mode of enacting and reenacting received gender norms which surface as so many styles of the flesh'.[24] She sought, therefore, to challenge the way in which feminism attempted to represent women, both politically (in protecting their interests) and linguistically (to challenge and change the definitions of the terms in use). Butler argued that 'far from feminist representations of women . . . being simple reflections of what women are . . . they are, in fact mechanisms of power through which women are themselves constructed as particular kinds of subject'.[25] She argued that feminism made a mistake in asserting that "women" shared common interests and characteristics, which created 'an unwitting regulation and reification of gender relations'[26] that reinforced a binary understanding of gender in which women and men were divided into two separate and distinct groups. Therefore, feminism limited the possibilities for women and men to choose and form their own individual identities. She wrote that whilst feminism dismissed the notion that our biology is our destiny, it created an understanding of culture that assumed that feminine and masculine genders would unavoidably be inscribed, by culture, upon "female" and "male" bodies; any alternative destiny was rendered inaccessible. She responds to this with her theorization of gender as performative and her support of a political practice based on 'subverting compulsory heterosexuality, [and through offering] . . . a radical critique of sex as natural and innate, she . . . contests the viability of woman as a unitary category'.[27] In so doing, Butler had a considerable impact on feminist debate and significantly structured the early writings on Queer Theory.[28] However, it is within the heterosexual matrix and her notion of gender performativity that I am most interested.

The "heterosexual matrix" (a means of understanding sex, gender and desire that later became heterosexual hegemony in *Bodies That Matter*) was conceptualized by Butler as the mechanism that generates ideal relations between sex, gender and desire and which understands gender as resulting naturally from sex and desire (or sexuality) as understood to follow naturally from gender. The consequence of this conceptualization is that ultimately sex determines how we perform desire and sexuality and creates a right/wrong dichotomy that labels heterosexuality as the norm. Butler argued that to live a livable life (one recognized as having legitimacy and value), individuals must first be recognized as viable subjects (those that do not deviate from the norm). Therefore, she concluded that any regime of cultural intelligibility hinges on normative violence (violence created by the norms in the generation of livable lives). It is the concept of intelligible genders[29] that reinforces and maintains the matrix. If an individual deviates from these prescribed norms, they are considered to be unintelligible and therefore, not a viable subject. Thus, if according to heteronormativity, 'to be human is to be heterosexual, then consequently anyone who is not . . . is not fully human'[30] and as such they forgo social, legal and political validity. A central element of gender politics is the act of exposing the regulatory and fictitious nature of compulsory heterosexuality whilst seeking legitimation for non-normative sexual minorities. Butler's primary political aim therefore, was to broaden the parameters of heteronormativity and to make life possible for those who were considered unintelligible. It was upon this that gender performativity was expanded.

The concept of gender performativity asserted that gender is the result of reiterated acting which produces a normal or static gender whilst masking the contradiction and volatile nature of any individual's gender act. This produces a "true gender", a narrative sustained by the collective commitment to perform, sustain and produce polar and discrete genders as a cultural fiction and punishments resulted from not "playing your part" and agreeing with these fictions. The drag performance was an example used by Butler as it offered a basic understanding of binarism in its emphasis on the performative nature of gender. The inference being that the subject[31] could don, at will, the gender they wish to embody at any given time, but this was not what Butler intended. She wrote that drag should not be considered to be an honest expression of the performer's intent but rather the performance can only be fully understood through reference to what is excluded from the subject within the domain of bodily reality. She argued that drag highlights the disjunction 'between the body of the performer and the gender that is being performed . . . [and] effectively reveals the imitative nature of *all* gender identities'.[32] In other words, it exposes the artificial nature of our gender identity and reinforces her argument that gender is a series of repetitive acts, a "strategy" which has 'cultural survival as its end . . . it is a repetition, a copy of a copy'.[33] However, the subject is not free to choose which gender he or she is going to enact. The "performance" is always determined within the limited regulatory framework and the subject is required to participate in this performance if s/he is to be considered viable and legitimate in our society. The performativity of gender is a repetition, often of painful and oppressive gender norms developed, informed and sustained by and throughout history. Thus, the performance is not a 'freedom, but a question of how to work the trap that one is inevitably in'.[34] When we perform our genders we do so by strictly adhering to our society's idealizations of what it means to fully embody femininity (and masculinity) at any given time. The performance is not merely limited to our gestures and mannerisms but also is created through speech and language. For example, speech act theory is the belief that our words not only *represent* what we endeavour to communicate but in certain circumstances they actively *do* something. This is true when a vicar pronounces a couple husband and wife in the marriage ceremony; their status as a couple changes. Butler explains that 'within speech act theory, a performative is that discursive practice that enacts or produces that which it names'.[35] She takes this further by exploring the ways that language creates our reality through everyday speech acts. As, from the moment we gender a foetus we inscribe upon that unborn child a performance that from the moment of birth is enacted by that child as s/he learns what is and is not acceptable. Butler writes:

> To the extent that the naming of the "girl" is transitive, that is, initiates the process by which a certain "girling" is compelled, the term or, rather, its symbolic power, governs the formation of a corporeally

> enacted femininity that never fully approximates the norm. This is a "girl", however, who is compelled to "cite" the norm in order to qualify and remain a viable subject. Femininity is thus not the product of choice, but the forcible citation of norm, one whose complex historicity is indissociable from relations of discipline, regulation, punishment.[36]

Butler argues that there is no sex that is not already gendered, that all bodies are gendered at the beginning of their social existence and there is no existence that is not social.[37] Ultimately this means that there is no "natural body" that exists prior to social inscription. She takes this concept further in her claim that there is no identity, no "I" that exists separately or prior to gender performativity; 'that identity is performatively constituted by the very "expressions" that are said to be its results'.[38] It is here that a distinction between performance and performativity needs to be explained. Butler does not assert that gender is a performance; rather she argues that performance assumes a preexisting subject whilst performativity contests the notion of the subject.[39] She asserts that gender is performative to the extent that it creates the identity that it is claimed to be; for Butler there is no 'doer behind the deed, no volitional agent that knowingly "does" its gender, since the gendered body is inseparable from the acts that constitute it'.[40] She is clear in her assertion that our gender acts are the effect of discourse, that there is no pre-linguistic essence or inner core. It is within the very idea of performativity that Butler seeks liberation from this oppressive structure, through re-inscription (what she terms re-citation).

Central to Butler's conceptualization of re-citation is the concept of agency, the subject's compulsion to repeat acts and their ability to repeat these acts differently. It is here that re-citation has the possibility to become a subversive act through the use of "parodic styles" such as drag and acts 'that denaturalize what they are performing by demonstrating explicitly the ways in which the natural is produced'.[41] For Butler, drag illuminates the fictitious nature of gender performativity and it is from this revealing that the subversive repetition of acts can take its form. A repetition can be subversive if 'it exposes what is taken to be natural or authentic to a particular sex, when it compels us to question what is real'.[42] In so doing, these norms cannot only be resisted but also re-worked. It's through this that we have a means of contesting the naturalization of heteronormativity and thus, produce alternative domains of cultural intelligibility. Therefore, Butler's subversive gender politics can be broken down and summarized as follows: 1) the individual's ability to identify those potentially oppressive norms that need to be interrogated and challenged; 2) denaturalization (to question what we consider to be natural); and, 3) agency (the subjects ability to repeat acts differently, to change the "rules" by which we live). However, before I explore the ways in which Butler conceives of her subversive politics, I would like to take a step back and reflect upon the ways in which femininity is produced in society in light of the slender ideal, gender inequalities and female stereotypes.

The slender performance

We live in a food-and-body obsessed culture as we are encouraged to over consume by the marketing techniques of multimillion-dollar corporations before being reprimanded by both governmental and medical establishments. Alongside these pressures we are bombarded with images in the media of computer-enhanced size 0 models[43] who are airbrushed to perfection, as it seems to have become an unspoken rule that you must adhere to if you are to be classified as beautiful, successful and desired. Appearance is being taken as a 'reflex of the self and the penalties of bodily neglect are a lowering of one's acceptability as a person, as well as an indication of laziness, low self-esteem and even moral failure'.[44] And so, the twentieth and twenty-first centuries have seen the thin woman become society's legitimate subject as she meets the damaging and debilitating standards of society; she has succeeded where the overweight woman has not. Furthermore, as the slim form becomes mandatory 'almost every conceivable consumer product is discovered to have slimming properties'[45] which is further drawn upon by Kim Chernin who writes:

> When we see another calorie counter on the stand, or read of another miracle diet in a woman's magazine, or pick up another container of low-calorie cottage cheese, we must begin to understand these trivial items symbolically and realize that what we are purchasing is the covert advice not to grow too large and too powerful for our culture.[46]

Naomi Wolf expands upon this cultural fixation with thinness and writes that it is not an obsession with female beauty but an obsession with female control and obedience. She argues that if our 'culture's fixation on female fatness or thinness were about sex, it would be a private issue between a woman and her lover; if it were about health, between a woman and herself'.[47] This led Wolf to conclude that the attention afforded to the size, weight and shape of women in our society is actually 'about how much social freedom women are going to get away with or concede'.[48] The media's analysis and attention towards female fat and the elimination of it is actually bulletins of the sex war: 'what women are gaining or losing in it, and how fast'.[49] The patriarchal family is a key player in this political positioning as it reinforces passivity and produces an environment where it is difficult for the girl or young woman to establish a clear personal identity. It creates a crisis of the self that is "resolved" by turning on the self. The fashion industry and media influences are also central to this development.[50]

We are taught to judge our bodies by the standards set on the front cover of magazines. These are created according to the "norms" and stereotypes taught, reinforced and sustained by society and emerge out of a history of control over the female body and as a consequence of living in a patriarchy and consumer culture which creates a problem and then sells us the solution, encouraging us to "let go", to feed our fantasies and desires that they have created. We have all seen those magazine pictures that chastise female celebrities for gaining weight or for the folds of flesh that escape tight clothing. The rhetoric underlying these comments is pervasive, far-reaching and never ending as perfection can never be fully realized. There are always new ways to alter and change the body, new fashions to keep women on their toes. Perfection for women caught up in this discourse is never fully achievable. Images objectifying women and weight stereotyping display dangerous and deeply destructive rhetoric for women of all shapes and sizes and send the message that the only women who will "have it all" are those that can conform to these narrowly defined ideals.

Using Butler's argument, if sex determines gender, desire and the effect of identity (acts, gestures, clothes, corporeality etc.), it also can be said to determine what aesthetic individuals in that society desire and therefore, what aesthetic they seek to project. The message projected to women in society is that to be successful, desired, to be part of the elite, they must exhibit all those desirable attributes which are considered to be exclusive to those individuals that conform most successfully to the slender ideal. Therefore, taking a step back from Butler's thesis and when considered alongside what we know of the cultural situation of women today, I believe that a "slender performance" is taking place through the mannerisms, gestures, language and actions of women in our society which is most evident in the extreme aestheticism of the anorexic individual. This performance is an extension of enacting our gender norms and adhering to society's female idealizations that inevitably take place within a framework of normative violence. As Marion Woodman notes:

> Fat in our culture is taboo, so the neurosis hits where it hurts most – at the heart of the female ego. The fat girl is not one of her peers: she cannot eat the junk foods, she is not invited to the adolescent parties, she cannot wear jeans, she is not attractive sexually. In short, in our society she is not female, and no one knows it as well as she.[51]

In other words, the fat girl is not a viable or legitimate subject in our culture. She is relegated to the margins of society by her peers who fear her wholesome, powerful, womanly body and all that it is understood to represent by the men and women who have internalized masculine goals 'that are in themselves a parody of what masculinity really is'.[52] I understand the "embodiment" of the slender ideal, along with gender identity, to be 'a performative accomplishment compelled by social sanction and taboo'.[53] The slender performance does not just refer to the slender ideal in our society but is a symptom of the general female stereotypes that inform the female standing in society; those stereotypes that value attributes of vulnerability, weakness and frailty as attractive and desirable. For me the slender performance, the extreme manifestation of which is anorexia, is a physical reflection of the situation of women today and embodies the search for wholeness, for substance and meaning in a consumer-driven world in which material products have replaced spiritual fulfilment.[54] However, unlike Butler's gender *performativity*, I believe there is a slender *performance* taking place. I draw this distinction because I am uncomfortable with Butler's assertion that there is no pre-discursive subject.

In distinguishing between performance and performativity, Butler has been accused of reducing agency to a 'doing without the doer'[55] and therefore putting an end to feminism's emancipatory politics and of causing the 'death of the subject'.[56] If we are no more than the sum total of the gender expressions we perform, do we have the authority to identify and change our own situation, of enacting the performance differently? There appears to be a problem with Butler's conceptualization of agency and therefore with a subversive politics built solely upon the actions of a fully discursive subject. An obvious question to ask, for example, is how might a performative subject, one solely produced through doing certain acts, contest heteronormativity as everything known by the subject exists within this oppressive framework? Some readers of Butler's work regard her as proposing a voluntarist politics in which subversive identities can be fabricated and reshaped at will, where the subject can intentionally make "gender trouble". Others argue that performativity is a form of determinism where subjects are locked into oppressive relations of power that they are unable to change.[57] Allison Weir argues that 'feminist politics requires a subject with the ability to act deliberately and consciously to change its situation'[58] and states that Butler's account of agency fails to provide this. Instead she provides us with a performative subject fully determined who has no scope for autonomous action. Thus, Weir concludes that Butler's subversive politics lacks a meaningful concept of agency.

However, does the lack of an autonomous and reflective human have to put an end to Butler's subversive politics? Butler appears to argue that the practices that produce gendered subjects are the 'material of social transformation'[59] instead of activities that need to be overcome or eliminated. For her, subversion does not take place in a 'site or quality prior to or outside of discourse',[60] that the practices that produce gendered subjects can be identified and subverted from within the very discourses that bind us. In drawing upon Foucault and the idea that power relations not only limit but also enable possibilities for political action, that configurations of power are never seamless however comprehensive and far-reaching, Butler argues that whilst there may not be a pre-discursive subject, agency still exists. There are always new opportunities for resistance. Agency here is located within the subject's compulsion to repeat and subversion becomes possible through the subject's ability to repeat acts differently. Agency is therefore not an innate quality of the subject, but simply an element of signification (the process through which we assign meaning or intelligibility) and repetition. However, as Moya Lloyd notes, the rest (at least in *Gender Trouble*) becomes unclear. Butler is vague on how the subject can navigate between norms and acts to subvert or transform heteronormativity. She does not provide an example of a parodic act that can challenge and rework the norms that make up the subject's performance within the heterosexual matrix.[61]

For me, Butler's response to these criticisms, framed by a revised definition of agency, fails to adequately explain how the discursive subject is capable of changing their circumstance and instead I favour a model of agency that relies on a pre-discursive subject. I use the term *performance* as opposed to *performativity* as I understand there to be some aspect of the individual that escapes this cultural conditioning and it is from here that agency arises. This is the position from which we can change our circumstance and create incremental changes to ourselves that permeate and slowly change the environments in which we live. Liberation or subversion of the slender performance is located in a "realm" that exists outside of culture that needs to be engaged with, a calling back to our matriarchal lineage, a theme that resonates throughout the work of Marion Woodman. If, as I have argued, slenderness is a performance based upon the repetition of societal norms and idealizations, then how is this to be broken down and re-imaged? What form would this reiteration or re-citation take? And what does our society look like once these boundaries are broken down? In order to examine these points, I would like to turn to the work of Woodman and her use of ritual, specifically the creation of a ritual of transformation.

Ritual of transformation

Central to Woodman's work is the suggestion that for centuries women have been living in a male-orientated culture that has kept them at a dis-ease with their bodies and their own feminine principles. In struggling to find their way in this environment they have unknowingly accepted male-orientated values and goals, 'compulsive drivenness, and concrete bread which fails to nourish their feminine mystery'.[62] In other words, women with eating disorders, such as anorexia, are expressing a disconnection between their bodies and souls as a direct consequence of what Woodman perceives to be a trap between masculine and feminine aspects of the self. She writes that many women are 'caught between two conflicting points of view: the rational, goal-oriented and just, versus the irrational, cyclic, relating'.[63] She writes that these girls and young women are disconnected from their own bodies, anxious and self-hating as a consequence of chasing after their "fathers dreams". By this she means that women engaged in this behaviour – in this striving to accomplish achievement after achievement, presenting fathers with good grades and school reports, whilst excelling in sports etc. – are seeking to earn love through perfection.[64] Reflecting on the work of Woodman, Courtney Martin writes that '[w]hen we dwell only in our "dad's mind," we become alienated from the irrational and fantastic cravings of our "mother's body" . . . [e]ven when we neglect one, try to starve it or bury it, both are always there'.[65]

Writing about perfectionism and achievement, a central concern within her work is to deepen the understanding of the embodied soul and conscious feminine.[66] In such environments, where "authentic" female nourishment is replaced with masculine, goal-oriented values, their unconscious femininity can rebel and manifest in a somatic form, in the development of anorexia or obesity (believed to be counter-poles of the same neurosis). She writes:

> In the Western cultures threatened by these syndromes, the feminine has been devalued for centuries and is now profoundly distorted. In the individual suffering from these syndromes, the feminine is feared and rejected. . . . Her . . . body epitomizes the present-day alienation from the feminine, and her obsession with her "daily bread" is only one manifestation of the desperate search for spiritual meaning.[67]

For me, anorexia and obesity are the extreme outcome of this somatic manifestation but it's the slender performance that becomes, arguably, a more pervasive and damaging activity as it is far-reaching as an act that every woman becomes engaged in to a more or lesser extent, be it calorie counting, watching what you eat, moderate to excessive exercise that goes beyond the realms of "healthy". Woodman herself experienced a 'near-fatal battle with anorexia'[68] and her work draws upon powerful female symbols, such as a Great Mother archetype[69] within which to spark a reconnection between women and their feminine principles. She does not advocate the rejection of masculine values (as male energy is creative and good) but the development of methods within which we can better balance the tensions between masculine and feminine drives and motivations whilst recognizing and displacing the aspects of masculinity that are destructive to female embodiment. She sees the loss of authentic rites of passage, to take us from one life phase to the next, as the reason why we develop somatic disorders such as anorexia. She argues that many of us are caught in a chrysalis-like state that we struggle to transcend. No longer confident we are valued for who we are, we seek to make improvements, to change into those attributes that are desired, those attributes that make up an intelligible subject to borrow Butler's terminology. Woodman writes that children are programmed to perform from birth and so 'rather than living from their own needs and feelings, they learn to assess situations in order to please others'.[70] What is lost in this cyclical process is a core of inner certainty and the resources to stand alone. Add to this peer group pressures and mass media influences and you have a generation of children developing with identities absorbed by collective stereotypes. She writes that rites of passage created opportunities for individuals to test their boundaries and provided meanings that transcended their survival. They enabled those in the community to move through life's stages without dread of old age or death as each phase was grounded within a meaningful appreciation of the life cycle in all its manifestations. The consequence of the imbalance between feminine and masculine qualities and the idea that progress is synonymous with accomplishments, has led women to reject their bodies; it has cut them off from their souls. Woodman argues that women are lacking spiritual substance; that they are suffering from a genuine hunger and thirst. She writes that we are not truly resilient, partly because we have little faith. Women caught in this state are constantly waiting for evidence of their worth and are consequently being driven to addictions and empty desires because there is no collective container for their spiritual needs – 'their natural propensity for transcendent experience, for ritual, for connection to some energy greater than their own, is being distorted into addictive behavior'[71] (anorexia, bingeing, shopping, alcohol, gambling etc.). As this distance from spirituality and religion takes its form, objects and personal possessions are invested with sacred powers and bestowed with additional meanings. The individuals living within this society create their own rituals that are facilitated by the gods of consumerism and mass capitalism; they are 'trapped by becoming what they worship'.[72] As Woodman writes:

> They create their own rituals, but because they don't realize what they are doing they may invoke the wrong god, and be subject to that power whether they like it or not.[73]

In striving to become what they perceive as the perfect human being in terms of the size of their bodies, these women go to the gym religiously, strive to transcend the need for food and sculpt the body into the image of perfection to which they have become emotionally attached. Martin writes:

> These empty substitute rituals, this misguided worship, intellectualization, addiction to moving fast has led my generation to a dark and lonely place . . . she must ask herself not *What is the size of my stomach?* but *What is the quality of my soul?. . . . Is there something solid, like resilience, instead of something hollow, like perfection?*[74]

Women are spending so much time obsessing about their bodies that they have lost the concept of a deeper and richer connection. Woodman thus explores avenues for reigniting a connection between these conflicting aspects of life. She writes that within religion, ritual is recognized as a transformative practice and so our everyday rituals are located within a larger framework whereby the individual is part of a journey through society or from one level of awareness to another. No matter what the individual does within these movements, there is an archetypal force, a God or Goddess at the centre that is invoked by the individual that sets a context for the lived life. Without those rituals to draw a distinction between the 'profane and the sacred, between what is us and what is not us, we tend to identify with archetypal patterns of being hero, father, mother'.[75] We become distanced from a sense of ourselves as human beings and instead identify with archetypes when we should remain detached from them. We attempt to emulate those figures that carry archetypal projections (political figures, celebrities etc.) and turn life into a theatre, ourselves into actors on a stage. Whatever vice we turn to within this framework, it becomes clear that the devaluation of the feminine in our society, coupled with our yearning for meaning, significance and value is tearing us apart.

There are several elements that appear to be integral to Woodman's transformative potential of ritual and perhaps, most importantly, a reconnection to a Great Mother archetype that can help women bridge the gap between herself and femininity. This is a process of enclosure, metamorphosis and emergence as women work towards transformation and self-knowledge as well as a reconnection to a repressed femininity which takes place around a central figure, an archetypal force of the Goddess. This ritual can be conceptualized as a symbolic death and rebirth, a breaking down, in this instance, of the slender performance that conceals the developing person within. Thus, resonating throughout her work is the desire to break down the mind/body dualisms that still permeate society as these rituals involve the unity of the mind and body of the participant and therefore, she argues, the mind and femininity (as the "chaotic" body has historically resided within the realm of the feminine). As the outer, symbolic actions involve and communicate to the unconscious, ceremony becomes a powerful agent for change and transformation. This transformative ritual marks a reconnection between the woman and her ancestral roots (as the biological reality of her ancestors is within her genetic code) whereby all aspects of her psyche are located within the symbolic action and the denied feminine principle can be welcomed (in all aspects of maiden, mother, crone). I see it as a challenge to the patriarchal value systems to which we belong, but the ritual involved is not a static or singular act; it is a change in the underpinning of all rituals, on all levels. This ritual healing can be like sleep or rest, a search for insight, dreaming and dissociation as long as these elements take place within a larger system conceptualized by the individual woman, actions that are bestowed with additional meaning. They have direction and a powerful urgency that comes from knowing that those elements that make up your life are destructive and need to change. It is within this framework that the slender performance can be re-conceptualized and transformed into a creative outlet.

For women to reconnect with their female mystery, to recombine their spirit and their bodies, they must acknowledge the symptom for what it is and find their authentic and forgotten voice, the Goddess lost within her rejected body. This takes place on two levels, within the psyche of the individual woman and also in society as both must rediscover their feminine roots and find the lost Goddess. As a Jungian analyst, Woodman's work is significantly influenced by the work of Carl Jung, which emphasizes the importance of dreams as an access point for the psyche. In the Association Experiment, Jung worked on the psychological responses of intense emotions to prove the existence of two systems in the individual, one voluntary and one autonomous. He eventually concluded that 'the various bodily symptoms were messages from the psyche itself'[76] and that they could therefore be given a symbolic meaning. The key to these messages, he argued, lies within the individual's dreams.[77] For Jung:

> the healing power resided in a conscious awareness of the symbolic nature of the dream, which provided the psychic meaning of those bodily symptoms by which the spirit struggled to communicate its condition and its needs. The body via the dream images was yoked to spirit. To become conscious of the body and its operations was to become conscious of the spirit.[78]

Tying in with Woodman's emphasis on a feminine reconnection to displace the dualisms at the heart of these somatic manifestations, the importance of dreams in their revealing of unconscious motivations and the potential of ritual to be transformative, is the work of Goldenberg and her focus on the importance of myth and fantasy. Her earlier work in *Changing of the Gods: Feminism and the End of Traditional Religions*[79] was heavily influenced by the work of Jung as she explored the influence our unconscious world has on our conscious decisions. A central theme in the work of Goldenberg is her passionate desire to put us in touch with our bodies and to do so she employs the use of myth, specifically a matriarchal myth as she draws upon the psychological benefit of a matriarchal prehistory or a divine women's myth for women today. She employs the use of psychoanalysis (in particular, object relations theory) to draw upon the unconscious as embodied in our daily actions. Goldenberg examines the Goddess movement from the perspective of psychoanalytic theory whilst addressing how analytic thought can be utilized in the analysis of discourses on the Goddess. In so doing she discusses four commonalities between the two models of thought. These identify the importance placed on exploring the past as a source of meaning for the present, deconstructing symbols of patriarchal power, the individual in the context of the community and the importance of fantasy and myth for the individual psyche and "rational" thought. We will discuss these commonalities later in this work but as we shall see, she places a central importance on how our understanding of fantasy and myth shape our conceptualizations of self in the context of our environments.

A constant focus throughout Goldenberg's work is the idea that the most important feature of religion is its myth. Drawing on the work of Jung and his desire for psychoanalysis to take on the revivification of myth she writes: 'Jung suggested that psychoanalysis set itself up as a new sort of religion – that psychoanalysis teach people how to live by "myth." This was the only way . . . that psychoanalysis could effectively combat 2,000 years of Christianity'.[80] In the early seventies when her work was firmly grounded within the life and work of Jung she argued that psychoanalysis is capable of replacing or revitalizing religion due to its belief in the influence of transcendent "archetypes" – immaterial forms wholly outside any human context that motivate human behaviour – in a person's life and in the necessity of myth in providing meaning and divine connection for people. Despite later rejecting the work of Jung, not simply for the inherent sexism within his development of psychoanalysis, but for the importance placed on disembodied archetypes as directly influencing an individual's psyche, she still maintains the importance of myth in religion and the necessity of the divine women's myth. She argues that the ancient myth of the superiority of the Goddess in all forms of life is of paramount importance for women as it gives them a higher place within both societal and religious structures of power. Furthermore, the terminology of myth means much more than story or illusion. Jung employed the term to refer to the deepest form of experience in human life believing that mythic images and pictures 'involve us both physiologically in our bodily reactions to them and spiritually in our higher thoughts about them'.[81] Here, when a person is conscious of the mythical underpinnings of their psychology, they are living intensely and reflectively. These people experience life as meaningful (meaning here is understood as a subjective state). The divine woman's myth within her work draws upon the idea of a matriarchal prehistory not as historic fact, but as a psychological beneficial framework for both subverting traditional patriarchal religious thought and ideologies and thus, strengthening women's conceptualizations of self.

Elaborating on meaningfulness, Goldenberg clarifies that "meaning" here can be understood as a feeling or sensation resulting from 'a sense of reality or tangibility about the life one was leading'.[82] Meaning cannot be identified in any absolute way but can be seen as operating in people's lives. The inference here is that a meaningless life is a life of disconnection and inauthenticity in which the individual is driven by subconscious acts that are not in some way correct or authentic for them. Here we touch upon the same themes that we see resonate throughout the work of Woodman. The idea of a meaningful or authentic life is also touched upon within the work of Christ who writes that women 'live out inauthentic stories provided by a culture they did not create'.[83] A direct connection is made between inauthenticity and living within the constraints of patriarchy. Within the context of this thesis, I would suggest that the social discourses that lend themselves to the development of the anorexic expression are inauthentic and meaningless in the sense that the discourses create a disjunction between the individual's mind and body, reinforcing the dualisms of our patriarchal past.[84] To counter this, adjustments are needed to bridge the gap between the individual and their bodies. Goldenberg writes: '[m]yths function as the building materials of reality. They connect the mind and body, matter and spirit, people and their experience. This connection is vivid and palpable. The value of myth is judged by the quality of the interior feeling it generates in individuals'.[85] Jung understood the main purpose of religion was to provide people with mythic structures to live their lives by. He said that this was becoming less and less of a reality in modern times and he saw psychology filling this developing void. For Jung and Goldenberg, true religion has to be alive. By this, Goldenberg writes that it has to be able to nurture a 'mythic understanding in its followers'.[86] She argued that some religions provide this in diluted forms, but as the focus in Abrahamic religions is a male divine construct (for example, Catholicism has the Jesus story, Muslims have the story of Mohammed to provide the structures for their lives) women are always at a disadvantage, as their embodiment will never fully approximate His life. For Jung, the individual needed to be able to depart from these myths and create their own which held meaning for their lives. Many religions make people feel guilty and sinful for departing from these myths. These people were understood as heretics. Reflecting on this, Goldenberg writes that religion as understood here leaves no room for heretics – no room for people to develop and live by their own myths – that 'Catholicism is fine for obedient souls'.[87]

Many women have become aware of the sexism inherent to Christianity and wise to the mythic structures that revolve around the lives of men. These structures will never be sufficient to feed their souls.[88] In displacing collective androcentric myths we need alternative structures to support the development of individual female psychologies. Goldenberg argues that it is the process of discovering the myth that is most important for the individual. Thus, when we consider the religious mythic symbols created by disciples surrounding the life and experiences of Christ, Buddha, Mohammed and all other founders of traditions, we understand that there are important elements of the original myth that only these beings could experience. Goldenberg elaborates with the following story:

> A wise woman went into a cave to meditate. She stayed there for many years, drawing all sorts of diagrams on the walls to solve the mystery of life. Finally, she drew an elliptical shape with purple chalk and added a yellow triangle in the middle. "I have solved the mystery of life," she said and left the cave to resume her previous way of life. People from all parts of the district flocked to the cave. They saw the yellow triangle inside the purple ellipse and copied it down. "Now I have the answer to life," each one exclaimed. This, of course, was not true. In fact, the purple and yellow design had come to the old woman only after years of scrutiny of her own soul. It was the process that she had undergone to discover the figure that has made it the symbol of her solution. The purple ellipse was a myth of great power for the old woman. For her disciples, it was merely a purple ellipse.[89]

Power is lost when people collectively create mythic systems based on the life of others. The uncompromising loyalty these leaders had to their visions – their myths – cannot be replicated in full by their disciplines. Jung understood that power and understanding comes from creating your own symbolic structures in the context of your life. Goldenberg writes that unless 'the disciple discovered his or her own vision, pale imitation of the leader was all that was possible'.[90] She therefore urged us to understand that what binds us together is not the contents of our religious and psychic imagery but the process of producing and reflecting upon imagery. Through this she believed we could build communities around the sharing and observing of each other's imaginal processes. The focus for Goldenberg was the creation of "living" religions, first for women (whose initial need was greatest) and then for men. Goldenberg cited Goddess feminism as a "living" religion. We will explore this further in Chapter 5.

Jung proposed psychology as the replacement to the religious myths that preceded it. He set out to develop a new strand of psychology that would function like a religion for anyone who had outgrown the religion to which they had previously ascribed, for people who had sickness of the soul. He understood psychology as a means of filling greater spiritual needs than had previously been imagined. The central focus was reviving myth within people's lives. If he could not re-establish a link between the individual and their native religion, he tried to guide them to develop a religious process within the self. His goal, from the perspective of Goldenberg, was to cure religious alienation. This is important when understood from a feminist liberation theology position as it provides avenues for challenging the patriarchy at the heart of Judeo-Christian tradition. For Goldenberg, Jung's work was pivotal as he encouraged people to look inwards to understand the forces at work in their lives. However, there are clearly issues here. The central one for me is the loss of community as psychoanalysis and therapy focuses on the relationship between the individual and the therapist. Myth here would be constructed on an individual level. Goldenberg raises this concern writing that 'one of the valuable functions the great religious traditions serve is the unification of large groups of people around a given set of symbols'.[91] Myth unites people through ritual and acts that bring people together at set times to celebrate, meditate, share in joy and grief and this happens because the participants have a shared respect, belief and reverence for the same myths, symbols and images. Thus, in the movement away from collective myths, we would lose important community ties as once we displace them, we are also displacing the communities of people who ascribe to these belief systems, whose experiences and embodiment are underpinned by these mythic constructions. However, Goldenberg argues it is not important for us to share the same myth, images and symbols, what is important is that we share the process of *creating* those systems.

What Goldenberg (utilizing the work of Jung) is emphasizing is the individual creation of myths specific to the individual's experiences and within a thealogical and thus, female empowering framework. What we do not need is new collective stereotypes or restrictive myths and images that contribute to the limiting of human existence.[92] Here we are encouraged to find our own dignity and to pursue our own truth. Goldenberg demonstrates that the process of symbol creation can build a sense of community through sharing in the process of creating myth and symbols that relate directly to our experiences, to our lives. We could experience even closer community ties when incorporating this with the work of Starhawk on large group rituals. In terms of collectively creating rituals, she writes that the organization of each event 'begin[s with discussion,] by going around the circle asking people what the time and season mean to them, and what they need or want from the ritual'.[93] It is from these answers and the common themes and images they inspire that a symbolic act is identified and focused upon eventually by the participants of the ritual. Individual and meaningful themes here come together to create a common symbolic thread that unites people, to strengthen community ties and create new community narratives. Thus, we see how Goldenberg (in her early work) utilizes the work of Jung to construct an argument that focuses on a movement towards psychologically powerful myths which focus on female experience.

In recent years, Goldenberg has focused on the use of language and words to penetrate 'sufficiently deep – in both a psychological and collective sense – that they will sound intoxicating, transformative, crazy, scary and, above all, powerful'.[94] No doubt her work has been influenced by the pioneering work of Mary Daly and her attention to the power underlying the words we use daily, as we will explore later in this book. Goldenberg's purpose here was to reconnect women with their bodies, to work towards female embodiment, and she saw this happening as a movement away from traditional patriarchal religions. This reconnection happens within the context of discourses on the Goddess and thealogy as, like Woodman, she believes that women need to be reconnected to a psychologically healing female past and powerfully symbolic female divine construct. She sees this as the means towards a "meaningful" and "authentic" life. Thealogy, and discourses on the Goddess, here are understood as providing women with reconnection to a repressed femininity, drawing on the same themes as Woodman. This reconnection is visualized within a "living" religion whereby the individual has access, and a growing appreciation, of the psychological and healing benefit of locating their existence within a broader network of connections. For both Woodman and Goldenberg, this reconnection to a deep-seated femininity happens within the context of the Goddess; however, as we will explore in Chapter 5, Goldenberg takes a more provoking and retaliatory approach in her adoption of "witchy" words with teeth and claws to subvert patriarchal power.

Bringing together the work of Butler and her concept of recitation, with the work of Woodman and a change of consciousness to underpin daily rituals, alongside Goldenberg's desire for us to develop mythic structures that hold meaning for our lives, we start to construct a framework for addressing some of the themes and motifs lying at the heart of both the anorexic expression and the slender performance. As we have explored, a central theme within the work of Goldenberg and Woodman is the idea that in utilizing female symbols of the divine, located within a broader social context, and in light of a connection to a wealthy female heritage,[95] we are provided with a psychologically beneficial framework for women in the present. Taken alongside the work of Butler and the concept of recitation, we start to conceive of a framework for subversion of the slender ideal that currently traps – in the anorexic expression and the culture of dieting – so many women. This subversion takes its form from women collectively incorporating a female divine construct into their daily lives and daily rituals. The idea is that over time, this repetition of female empowering psychologies can change the way women experience their embodiment. Incorporating the work of Woodman and Goldenberg, we see that central to any ritual is a connection to past experiences and a past history in order to re-conceptualize life in the present. There are stark differences between how psychoanalysis and thealogy conceptualize this change, as we will explore in the final chapters.

The anorexic woman needs a safe environment to reconnect and rediscover her own feminine core, to work herself free from the slenderness ideal that shackles[96] and politically sedates[97] her. For Woodman, any ritual of transformation is rooted within a search for the Great Mother buried within the individual's body. She is found when we address the frozen places within ourselves – our 'undigested pockets of pain – that need to be recognized and welcomed'.[98] As we fight to resist the emptiness and hide from our feelings, as we try and try 'again to lose the same twenty, fifty, eighty pounds, we ignore what could utterly transform us . . . and when we welcome what we most want to avoid we evoke divinity'.[99] Developed from the work of Jung, Woodman advocates an approach towards healing and liberation that utilizes the individual's unconscious world as an access point to the psyche as it is here that we can interpret messages, understandings and motivations before integrating them into rituals and work towards transformation. Ricki Tanner writes that

> [r]itual and ceremony serve to create a sacred environment for women to embody aspects of the archetypal Feminine in the multiple qualities of the ancient image of the Triple Goddess, the aspects of Maiden-Mother-Crone which assists women's understanding of the transformation phases and their experiences of change.[100]

These ritual performances lie in everyday practices that can be understood to hold symbolic meaning, and not always the kind of ritual that people may be familiar with in religious observance. These rituals are not limited to religious practice (an example provided is that of a rock concert and how these can be ritual performance spaces where transformation occurs). The path to physical and psychological integration comes from a willingness to value and interact with memory as those that repress it are doomed to repeat it over and over again. Ultimately, the ritual is to re-balance patriarchy with a matriarchal lineage where female principles are given space and freedom to develop, and it is within these ritual performances that transformation occurs.

I see it as a connection to a powerful, strong female symbol that provides the grounding for a new perspective/a new understanding of the underpinning of our acts. It is here that we can locate subversive resistance and rework those acts and behaviours that reinforce the performance. For some, this ritual can take place within a guided religious setting or through daily acts, as simply reflecting on everyday activities which, once bestowed with additional meaning can allow for the development of new subversive possibilities as subversive acts. These acts have the power to destabilize the slender performance and the individual's utilization of the anorexic expression. In this sense, eating food is a powerful transformative ritual when located within a larger system of meaning which understands the beauty of its origins and how, through it, we are part of a larger cosmic order. Woodman discusses one of her experiences of eating pineapple in a similar way 'with laughter and thanksgiving we ate the sweet flesh of the . . . pineapple, and felt a new connection to the earth, to the Goddess, to the transpersonal in ourselves and each other'.[101]

In challenging the collective use of the term "woman" and identifying and re-working the ways in which gender binaries are sustained though a model of deconstruction and recitation, Butler provides us with a model in which to identify and break down the slender performance. As discussed, I see the liberation from an obsession or compulsion with maintaining the slender ideal as involving a reconnection to a repressed femininity and a reassurance that in allowing and trusting your body to talk we start to break down these oppressive "performances" and conceive of ways to liberate ourselves from such constrained environments. The task is to identify those acts that make up the slender performance and conceive of rituals that seek to disrupt and "trouble" these binaries. Here liberation and reconnection must be grounded within an individual's search for her femininity; women must actively seek and choose to redefine these constraints.

I hope to have demonstrated how our bodies, desires and psychologies are inseparable from the influences of social power and norms and how these external acts destroy our capacity to act and decide independently of these norms. Since everything we know takes place within these frameworks that we have no power to evade, it is difficult and almost impossible to conceive of an alternative and therefore, any form of social change or reform must take place within these boundaries that bind us. Having said that, our power to identify a means for change and to locate subversive resistance is found when we reconnect to something forgotten and thought to be lost. It's a calling back to our matriarchal lineage to connect again with the cosmos and find the lost voice of our bodies. I believe that many women in our society feel compelled to put on an act, to create a fiction that is inscribed, sustained and reinforced by and through the environments in which we live. A woman engaged in the slender performance, according to the literature referred to earlier, is disconnected from her femininity, from her environment and a grounded connection to the interrelated world in which we live. For me, this highlights just how important it is for women to stop focusing on the weight of their bodies, to consider the consequences of allowing their bodies to relax, to listen to their hungers and desires and not to fear the consequences. This ritual becomes an act that places critical agency back in our hands, something removed as we are shepherded by consumerism and mass capitalism. If, as Butler says, our behaviour creates our reality, then we must change our behaviour!

Notes

1 Weitz, R. (2003) *The Politics of Women's Bodies: Sexuality, Appearance, and Behaviour*. Oxford: Oxford University Press, ix.
2 Weitz (2003: ix).
3 Bartky, S. L. (2003) Foucault, Femininity, and the Modernization of Patriarchal Power. In: Weitz, R. (ed.) *The Politics of Women's Bodies: Sexuality, Appearance, and behaviour*. Oxford: Oxford University Press, 25–45 (25).
4 Foucault, M. (1991) *Discipline and Punish: The Birth of the Prison*. London: Penguin Books, 136.
5 Foucault (1991: 139).
6 Foucault (1991: 143).
7 Bartky (2003: 27).
8 Bartky (2003: 43–44).
9 Bartky (2003: 41).
10 Bartky (2003: 44).
11 Bartky (2003: 28).
12 These pictures are a little dated now having been collected between 1974 and 1977 but nevertheless, her conclusions are very much valid and illuminating even when considered in the context of contemporary society. Alongside her examination of the sculptures of the last 3,000 to 4,000 years, Wex concluded that ideals of body language and body forms between the sexes are more different today (1979) than they have been at any other point in history. Wex, M. (1984) *Let's Take Back Our Space: "Female" and "Male" Body Language as a Result of Patriarchal Structures*. Munich, Germany: Frauenliteratur Verlag.
13 Bartky (2003: 30).
14 Bartky (2003: 30).
15 Bartky (2003: 30).
16 Bartky (2003: 30).
17 A smile elicitation study found that the rate of smile return by women was significantly higher than found with men. Women are also encouraged to stand with their stomachs pulled in, shoulders thrown back and chest out in order to display their breasts to the best advantage. For more information, see Henley, N. (1977) *Body Politics: Power, Sex, and Non-Verbal Communication*. Englewood Cliffs: Prentice Hall.
18 For more information, see Hochschild, A. R. (2012) *The Managed Heart*. Berkeley: University of California Press.
19 Bartky (2003: 27).
20 Bordo, S. (2003) *Unbearable Weight: Feminism, Western Culture, and the Body*. London: University of California Press, 298.
21 Butler, J. (1990, 2007) *Gender Troubles*. London: Routledge, 2.

22 Butler (2007: 2, author's emphasis).
23 Lloyd, M. (2007) *Judith Butler*. Cambridge: Polity Press, 26.
24 Bartky (2003: 27); quoted in Butler, J. (1985) *Embodied Identity in De Beauvoir's the Second Sex*. Paper presented at the American Philosophical Association, Pacific Division, March 22, 1985.
25 Lloyd (2007: 26).
26 Butler (2007: 8).
27 Lloyd (2007: 25).
28 Queer Theory developed out of Butler's book, *Gender Troubles*, and challenged the assumptions made by feminism that "male" and "female" binaries are fixed which both assumed and reinforced heterosexuality as the norm (this saw everything else as *Other* and therefore not viable). One of the key questions posed was why do some bodies matter more than others? It was intended to open up new possibilities for feminism but instead marked the start of a new discipline, that of Queer Theory.
29 "Intelligible" genders are those that 'institute and maintain relations of coherence and continuity among sex, gender, sexual practice, and desire'. See Butler (2007: 23).
30 Lloyd (2007: 35).
31 Butler's use of the term "subject" as opposed to "individual" or "person" draws upon the work of Jacques Lacan and refers to the underlying linguistic nature of our position within the "symbolic order". She uses this term to stress her argument that our identity is an illusion which is retroactively created through our performances.
32 Salih, S. (2007) On Judith Butler and Performativity. In: Lovaas, K. E., Jenkins, M. M. (eds.) *Sexualities and Communication in Everyday Life*. Thousand Oaks: Sage Publications, 55–68 (57), author's emphasis.
33 Salih 2007: 58.
34 Kotz, L. (1992) The Body You Want: Liz Kotz Interviews Judith Butler. In: *Artforum* 31, no. 3: 82–89. Available at: www.mariabuszek.com/kcai/PoMo Seminar/Readings/KotzButler.pdf [05/06/2014].
35 Butler, J. (1993, 2011) *Bodies That Matter: On the Discursive Limits of "Sex"*. New York: Routledge, 13.
36 Butler (2011: 232).
37 Salih (2007: 55).
38 Butler (2007: 34).
39 Salih (2007: 56).
40 Salih (2007: 56).
41 Lloyd (2007: 54).
42 Lloyd (2007: 56).
43 There are times when an alternative body size and shape sits alongside the hyper-slender ideal. Here I refer to the body shape (large(r) and toned bottoms) of women such as Jennifer Lopez, Beyonce and Kim Kardashian. These bodies are no less constructed and no less damaging. They still demand that women adhere to a very specific embodiment of femininity in the interest of cultural legitimacy.
44 Featherstone, M. (1996) *The Body: Social Process and Cultural Theory*. London: Sage Publications, 186.
45 Featherstone, M. (2001) The Body in Consumer Society. In: Banks, D., Purdy, M. (eds.) *The Sociology and Politics of Health: A Reader*. London: Routledge, 228–237 (233).
46 Chernin, K. (1994) *The Obsession: Reflections on the Tyranny of Slenderness*. New York: Harper Perennial, 96.
47 Wolf, N. (1990) *The Beauty Myth: How Images of Beauty Are Used Against Women*. London: Vintage Books, 186.

48 Wolf (1990: 187).
49 Wolf (1990: 187).
50 Studies have shown that exposure to ultra-thin models, in the media and advertising, leads to increased body dissatisfaction amongst a large proportion of women. For example, studies on the effect that thin media images have on body satisfaction (in women) have shown that body image is significantly more negative following the viewing of thin media images as opposed to viewing images of inanimate objects, plus-sized models or average-sized models. Furthermore, the studies showed that the effect was stronger for those participants less than 19 years of age. For more information, see Groesz, L. M., Levine, M. P., Murnen, S. K. (2002) The Effects of Experimental Presentation on Thin Media Images on Body Satisfaction: A Meta-Analytic Review. In: *International Journal of Eating Disorders* 31, no. 1: 1–16.
51 Woodman, M. (1982) *Addicted to Perfection: The Still Unravished Bride*. Toronto, Canada: Inner City Books, 7.
52 Woodman (1982: 7).
53 Butler, J. (1990) Performative Acts and Gender Constitution: An Essay in Phenomenology and Feminist Theory. In: Case, S. E. (ed.) *Performing Feminisms: Feminist Critical Theory and Theatre*. Baltimore: The Johns Hopkins University Press, 270–283 (271).
54 A theme I will discuss in further detail in Chapter 5.
55 Benhabib, S. (1995) Feminism and Post Modernism. In: Benhabib, S., Butler, J., Cornell, D., Fraser, N. (eds.) *Feminist Contentions: A Philosophical Exchange*. London: Routledge, 17–35 (22).
56 Flax, J. (1990) *Thinking Fragments: Psychoanalysis, Feminism and Postmodernism in the Contemporary West*. Oxford: University of California Press Ltd, 32.
57 Lloyd (2007: 57).
58 Lloyd (2007: 57).
59 Lloyd (2007: 60).
60 Lloyd (2007: 60).
61 Lloyd (2007: 61).
62 Woodman, M. (1980) *The Owl Was a Baker's Daughter: Obesity, Anorexia Nervosa and the Repressed Feminine*. Toronto, Canada: Inner City Books, 9–10.
63 Woodman, M. (1985) *The Pregnant Virgin: A Process of Psychological Transformation*. Toronto, Canada: Inner City Books, 51.
64 Woodman frames her discussion within the story of Athena – the Greek goddess of wisdom, efficiency, achievement, justice – 'If we look at the modern Athenas sprung from their father's foreheads, we do not necessarily see liberated women'. Athena here is framed as the perfect girl, marching on and making her dad proud with her good grades and wide range of achievements. Here the focus is entirely applied to meeting what she perceives to be her father's expectations. For more information, see Woodman (1982: 9).
65 Martin, C. E. (2007) *Perfect Girls, Starving Daughters: The Frightening New Normalcy of Hating Your Body*. London: Piatkus Books Ltd, 77.
66 A drive towards a feminine consciousness is a theme which features heavily throughout the remainder of Chapter 3 and Chapter 5.
67 Woodman (1980: 102).
68 Martin (2007: 77).
69 Woodman describes archetypes as eternal. She believes that each society, each generation, people of different ages, will develop individual metaphors for the same archetypal energy. For her, an archetype 'is an energy field, like that of a magnet, onto which we project images. . . . The archetype is more than everyday human energy. It is energy that bursts through us from some sacred place. . . . It bursts into flame from someplace within us, someplace that manifests imagery

shared by human beings from many cultures and many eras. . . . An archetypal image that does not change becomes a stereotype-dead energy'. Archetypes here are needed to make cultural shifts, like a shift towards female principles as we rebalance masculine and feminine attributes. The metaphor Woodman utilizes for archetype within this work is that of the Great Mother. For more information, see Bly, R., Woodman, M. (1998) *The Maiden King: The Reunion of Masculine and Feminine*. New York: Henry Holt and Company Inc, 150; and Fox, M. (2009) *The Hidden Spirituality of Men: The Metaphors to Awaken the Sacred Masculine*. Novato: New World Library, xxiv.

70 Woodman (1985: 16).
71 Woodman (1982: 29).
72 Woodman (1982: 30–31).
73 Woodman (1982: 30).
74 Martin (2007: 251, author's emphasis).
75 Woodman (1985: 19).
76 Woodman (1980: 60).
77 Woodman's work emphasizes the importance that dreams have in understanding our subconscious desires and pains. She found that the unconscious world of her female patients were characterized by images of concentration camps and enclosed spaces where the anorexic women viewed themselves as caged and trapped victims – often in terrible pain. For more information, see Woodman (1982 and 1985).
78 Woodman (1980: 60).
79 Goldenberg, N. (1979) *Changing of the Gods: Feminism and the End of Traditional Religions*. Boston: Beacon Press, 47.
80 Goldenberg (1979: 47).
81 Goldenberg (1979: 47).
82 Goldenberg (1979: 48).
83 Christ, C. P. (1995) *Diving Deep and Surfacing: Women Writers on Spiritual Quest*. Boston: Beacon Press, 1.
84 A connection between mind/body dualisms, traditional Christianity and anorexia is broached by Michelle Lelwica in her book *Starving for Salvation*. She writes that some anorexic and bulimic women 'use the language of Christianity, most notably asceticism, to articulate their search for an otherworldly order of existence'. She cites accounts of anorexic women who dualistically claim: 'I believed the mind should control the body completely. . . . I was very aesthetic' and as another woman commented: 'if I have to suffer pain. . . . I should be able with my mind to disconnect this pain from my mind's activity'. Another female patient said: 'the corporeal didn't really matter' and another: '[m]y soul was free. My soul sort of flew. It was tied down by this big bag of rocks that was my body'. Lelwica's aim in providing these examples is to demonstrate how the contemporary anorexic experience is underscored by dualistic logic which in turn is underpinned by the 'patriarchal tactics of traditional religion'. The anorexic body within her writings embodies the radical separation of dualistic logic as manifested within Christian doctrine. She writes about how the writings of Christian authors prior to Descartes have been historically misperceived and misinterpreted. She argues that the body and soul were implicitly understood as interdependent, an idea that was later lost as understandings of the soul and body as radically separated took root within the Christian tradition. Lelwica notes that one of the main difficulties facing her patients in therapy is interrogating this dualistic mind-set to establish where the "psyche" ends and the "body" begins. She argues that the medical professionals, therapists and individuals caught up in this dualistic thinking need to interrogate the dualistic logic and challenge the language and symbols lying at its foundation. Talking about the mind/body split that does not actually exist allows for a breaking

down of this mind-set and removes them from utilizing this strategy as a means of giving their imaginative world meaning and escaping the daily challenges that they struggle to face as a unified body. For more information, see Lelwica, M. M. (1999) *Starving for Salvation: The Spiritual Dimensions of Eating Problems Among American Girls and Women*. New York: Oxford University Press, 114–115.

85 Goldenberg (1979: 48).

86 Goldenberg (1979: 49).

87 Goldenberg (1979: 50).

88 Goldenberg found that these and other issues remained present in most religious structures. For more information, see Goldenberg (1979: 49–52).

89 Goldenberg (1979: 52).

90 Goldenberg (1979: 52).

91 Goldenberg (1979: 53).

92 Naomi Wolf writes about destructive and restrictive myths in *The Beauty Myth*. She argues that there exists an elusive and powerful quality called "beauty" which is imperative for female embodiment (but not for male). She writes that women seek to embody it whilst men seek to possess the women who embody it. Here she is drawing attention to the fact that women all over the world are "buying" into the belief that life success is contingent on meeting various beauty prerequisites. Discussions surrounding the "beauty myth" form the undercurrent which runs throughout this book. For more information on *The Beauty Myth*, see Wolf, N. (1990) *The Beauty Myth: How Images of Beauty Are Used Against Women*. London: Vintage Books; Wolf, N. (1994) Hunger. In: Fallon, P., Katzman, M. A., Wooley, S. C. (eds.) *Feminist Perspectives on Eating Disorders*. New York: The Guildford Press; and Weiss, S. I. (2002) *Coping With the Beauty Myth: A Guide for Real Girls*. New York: Rosen Publishing Group.

93 Starhawk (1982a) *Dreaming the Dark: Magic, Sex & Politics*. Boston: Beacon Press, 159.

94 Goldenberg, N. (2004) Witches and Words. In: *Feminist Theology* 12, no. 2: 203–211 (205).

95 Resonating throughout psychoanalysis and Goddess feminism is the idea that the present is a fiction of the past. Whilst the Goddess movement draws upon the notion of a collective prehistory, object relations theory and psychotherapy emphasize the importance of the individual's earliest experiences and how these influence actions and feelings in the present. These are themes that we explore in greater detail in Chapter 5.

96 Vandereycken, W. (1994) *From Fasting Saints to Anorexic Girls: The History of Self-Starvation*. New York: New York University Press.

97 For more information, see Wolf (1990 and 1994).

98 Roth, G. (2010) *Women, Food and God: An Unexpected Path to Almost Everything*. London: Simon and Schuster UK LTD, 5.

99 Roth (2010: 33).

100 Tanner, R. S. (2007) *The Female Trickster: The Mask That Reveals, Post-Jungian and Postmodern Psychological Perspectives on Women in Contemporary Culture*. London: Routledge, 73.

101 Woodman, M. (1987) From Concrete to Consciousness: The Emergence of the Feminine. In: Mahdi, L. C., Foster, S., Little, M. (eds.) *Betwixt and Between: Patterns of Masculine and Feminine Initiation*. Chicago: Open Court Publishing Company, 201–223 (207).

4 The female body as a historically mediated form

Having examined the political discourses that inform our understandings of gender and power in contemporary society, let us now consider alternative approaches to starving the body throughout the years and the difference between these as forms of protest. From ethnic disorders and culture-bound syndromes to self-starvation and hunger strikes as a political tool, each of these brought with them a different understanding of the female body and of the societies in which they emerged. As such, this chapter will begin with a focus on the female body as a historically mediated form. I will examine theories which suggest that anorexia takes its place following hysteria and agoraphobia as a device aimed at keeping women at a dis-ease with both their bodies and their position within society. Following this I will focus on the broader political dimensions of anorexia and self-starvation as I examine the work of Naomi Wolf, Sarah Sceats, Lauren Slater, Paula Saukko and Helen Gremillion. The latter two add a therapeutic context to these discussions as we continue to develop an appreciation of the complexity of healing and therapy for women with anorexia.

The second half of this chapter will focus on the question of whether there is any psychological benefit or spirituality to result from the anorexic experience in the context of "cutting" and other self-harm practices. In this we look at human responses to pain alongside the religious emphasis on suffering for our sins and the attributes associated with aestheticism. I will also touch upon the understandings of pain as a medical "problem", something that necessitates a solution. As Ariel Glucklich writes in *Sacred Pain*:

> Pain is not a simple matter: There is an enormous difference between the unwanted pain of a cancer patient or victim of a car crash, and the voluntary and modulated self-hurting of a religious practitioner. Religious pain produces states of consciousness, and cognitive-emotional changes, that affect the identity of the individual subject and her state of belonging to a larger community or to a more fundamental state of being.[1]

I will consider whether anorexia can be considered within this religious sacred pain framework providing the same bonds with her community and the environment in which she lives.

Anorexia as a culture-bound syndrome

In *Eating Disorders* by Richard Gordon, the concept of an ethic disorder, also known as a culture-bound syndrome, is unpacked in reference to the development of anorexia within our culture. This concept arises from the work of George Devereux and is understood as an individual's protest against prevailing ideals and cultural expectations. Devereux suggested that demonstrations of such unusual behaviour may be secretly respected and revered as 'others within the culture secretly identify with the symptomatic person's dilemma'.[2] This is often because the types of conflicts that manifest in the development of a culture-bound syndrome are significantly more widespread 'than the actual number of individuals who manifest symptoms'.[3] Thus, the responses of peers are usually ambivalent with a mixture of admiration, hostility and sometimes fear. He argues that these syndromes are not usually consciously acknowledged and they reflect the efforts of individuals of a culturally defined inferior status – often defined by sex, age or colour – to escape from or protest against their oppression by the more powerful.[4] They reflected what Victor Turner called the "power of the weak".[5] Even though the behaviour is ultimately self-destructive, through this syndrome, the individual is able to gain some degree of control or to indirectly punish those who are more powerful. However, as such actions are unarticulated and indirect, they rarely result in a fundamental change but rather reinforce the status quo as explored in earlier chapters.

Self-starvation has a long history and was typically employed by women as a tool of control. Anorexia, of course, is a contemporary example of this. There are many accounts throughout the fourteenth and fifteenth centuries of self-starvation among women in Europe and the church later sanctified many of these.[6] Rudolph Bell called these women "holy anorexics" and noted that in many ways these women 'resembled contemporary anorexics, despite the vast cultural divide between the medieval and the modern world'.[7] Like contemporary anorexics, many of these women began their fasting in adolescence and it was typically deployed to resolve a sense of unworthiness and acute self-doubt, as a solitary quest for a sense of moral and spiritual perfection and as a form of protest against the prevailing role for women. It was in reducing their bodies to a non-reproductive and asexual state that they were able to avoid arranged marriages or the conventional life of the period. Caroline Bynum suggested that this unconventional behaviour served as a reproach to their families, many of whom 'were part of a secular and materialistic mercantile class and were embarrassed by their daughters' fanatical asceticism and religiosity'.[8] Furthermore, she points out that fasting went far beyond conventional religious practices of the time that were limited to a philosophy of moderation. Self-starvation as a form of protest allowed many women to convey their dissatisfaction and unwillingness to accept the limitations of the female role; they aspired to something higher (themes we explored in Chapter 1 with the story of Ellen West). This took place in an environment in which the notion of spiritual authority or autonomy for women in the church was absolutely unacceptable. Whilst parallels can most certainly be drawn between the early instances of self-starvation and modern diagnoses of anorexia, there are clear distinctions to be drawn between the two behaviours. One of the most striking differences is that contemporary anorexics starve themselves for a specific body shape which is driven by cultural expectations, norms and stereotypes and has very little to do, in most cases, with moral and spiritual ideals.

Hunger strikes[9] and fasting as modes of political protest were historically employed by the socially oppressed and were used as a means of humiliating those in control and obtaining concessions from them. Gender marked a significant difference in the ways these activities were perceived and understood. The hunger strike was a powerful symbolic tool that was typically implemented by men (a notable exception was the protests of the suffragettes), whilst female fasting, permissible predominantly in psychiatric or religious contexts, is a protest which remains veiled in a symptomatic and mystic language (anorexia, of course, falls into this category). The inference here is that even when they are downtrodden, 'it is more acceptable for males to engage in direct aggression – even when it takes a passive form'.[10] With the introduction of the hunger striker in the twentieth century and their public and political feats of asceticism, fasting became secularized in Europe and the United States and quickly became distanced from a moral or religious agenda. Their food refusal 'was a sheer act of will and self-control for its own sake, a public spectacle devoid of moral content'.[11] It was in this context that anorexia emerged as a recognized disease (however it would be years before a full understanding of this disease was developed and interrogated).

In the nineteenth and twentieth centuries increasing interest with hunger artists alongside the contemporary awareness of anorexia accompanied a developing societal appreciation of the increasing dis-ease people were feeling towards the social stratum. With self-starvation, women and men protested against the inequalities and fixed social roles that were so abhorrent to them. As a political protest, anorexia expresses a contest between the individual and other people in their environment over control of the individual's body; the statement she is making is political despite being unconsciously undertaken.

Reinforcing this, Philip Barker in *Assessment in Psychiatric and Mental Health Nursing: In Search of the Whole Person*, draws upon the work of Thomas Szasz in 1974 and his assertion that starvation is not a psychiatric problem; it's political. Barker writes that the very nature of psychology often assumes that individuals operate in a vacuum as opposed to being malleable subjects influenced by their environments. We act as if 'pathology always lies within the person, rather than within the person's relationships with his [or her] world'.[12] He draws upon Szasz's argument that "mental illness" and "psychiatric disorder" may be understood as little more than a reflection of a sense of oppression imposed by the environment that represents the "real" problem. We are not born with a starvation gene; people do not suddenly become mentally ill. Quoting Szasz, Barker writes: '[a]ddiction, obesity, starvation (anorexia nervosa) are political problems, not psychiatric: each condenses and expresses a contest between the individual and some other person or persons in his [sic] environment over the control of the individual's body'.[13] One of Barker's central concerns was in respect of therapy and his belief that treatments which failed to acknowledge the political and social undercurrents that contribute towards these psychological expressions would ultimately prove unsuccessful. He therefore encourages those in the field to find the social and material resources within the environment to work towards genuine well-being. He advocates the examination of the environment – its institutions, the family etc. – to look at individual restrictions, influences and freedoms whilst measuring the potential for individual growth and development. Exploring the elements of our surroundings which contribute towards these destructive psychological maladies is central here. These themes are further drawn out when considering the relationship between hysteria, agoraphobia and anorexia as responses to the environments in which they emerged. We will explore this relationship now.

Hysteria, agoraphobia and anorexia

The commonalities between hysteria, agoraphobia and anorexia indicative of the latter half of the nineteenth and twentieth centuries respectively[14] have been drawn upon within literature on the development of anorexia. We find an example of this within the writings of Bordo.[15] She argues that the central mechanism of these three social phenomena involve a transformation of meaning 'through which conditions that are objectively (and, on one level, experientially) constraining, enslaving, and even murderous, come to be experienced as liberating, transforming, and life giving'.[16] These make up a group of gender-related and historically localized disorders that have historically been understood as class- and race-based, occurring predominantly amongst white middle- and upper middle-class women. Bordo offers her analysis of hysteria, agoraphobia and anorexia as an example of how 'various contemporary critical discourses may be joined to yield an understanding of the subtle and often unwitting role played by our bodies in the symbolization and reproduction of gender'.[17] These disorders display a disturbingly concrete construction of femininity that is an extremely literal and exaggerated interpretation of the ruling feminine mystique. Within this ideological construction of femininity, we see the markings of homogenizing and normalizing principles at play as all racial, class and other differences are erased as one standardized and coercive model is marketed as the ideal, something that all women should aspire towards. Bordo writes:

> The symptomatology of these disorders reveals itself textuality. Loss of mobility, loss of voice, inability to leave the home, feeding others whilst

> starving oneself, taking up space, and whittling down the space one's body takes up-all have symbolic meaning, all have *political* meaning under the varying rules governing the historical construction of gender. Working within this framework, we see that whether we look at hysteria, agoraphobia, or anorexia, we find the body of the sufferer deeply inscribed with an ideological construction of femininity emblematic of the period in question.[18]

The difference between these female disorders and "normal" female practices are thrown into sharp relief when unpacking these three maladies to which women have been particularly vulnerable throughout history, as we will go on to explore now.

Hysteria embodies an exaggerated form of stereotypically female and feminine traits that included attributes of delicacy and vulnerability, dreaminess and sexual passivity and repression alongside capricious emotionality and a labile constitution. On the surface, the woman with hysteria becomes a male construction to complement his attributes and designated role of protector, boss, controller and breadwinner. Drawing upon the work of Freud, Bordo writes that this construction was scientized and formalized by Freud (amongst others) who described "normal" femininity in these terms. The dissociations, the nervous tremors, faints and fogging of perception all associated with this condition were produced because of the prevailing construction of femininity but also go so much deeper in describing the incapability of women whilst reinforcing the gender status quo. As Orbach discusses in *Hunger Strike*: '[t]he nineteenth century feminine ideal of frailty and romance which found such marked expression in the literature and the illnesses of Victorian women, rests on a view of women as the inherently inferior and weaker sex'.[19] However, a feminist reading of hysteria shows us that within this exaggeration of idealized womanliness and its caricature of femininity, hysteria contained an implicit indictment of female worthlessness within the environment in which it emerged. Gordon writes that hysteria 'represented a strategy of coming to grips with the socially prescribed dependency and passivity that was central to the nineteenth-century female sex role: through becoming hysterical, a woman both rebelled against, and yet exaggerated, this stereotype'.[20] This illness might have also served to represent an escape from her female obligations, using her body as a form of protest against the social order that kept her existence limited to the household, childcare and looking after her husband. Although, as with anorexia, any form of rebellion or challenge to this ideology is likely to have been unconscious. The term hysteria was singularly associated with women and is to this day. However, the subtleties of hysteria pale in comparison to the exaggerated literalism of agoraphobia and anorexia.

The rules of femininity are communicated through the culturally transmitted visual images. It is through these that we have been taught how to construct the appropriate surface for the presentation of the self as we learn the rules through body discourse: 'through images that tell us what clothes, body shape, facial expression, movements, and behavior are required'.[21] Agoraphobia first began to escalate among women during the 1950s and early 1960s as there developed a resurgence in the female ideals of domesticity and dependency. It is commonly linked with the post-World War Two pressure on women to leave their employment (having entered the "male" working sphere throughout the war years) and again enter the safe confines of the family home embodying attributes of vulnerability, childlike passivity and neediness for male protection. The perfect personification of these ideals is the housebound agoraphobic who lives this female ideal to the letter through her literal living of the rules. This is a condition that involves 'a phobic avoidance of public spaces, public transportation, and crowds, can in many instances be seen as a metaphoric encapsulation of the situation of the dependent and unassertive wife'.[22] However, as Gordon suggests, this expression/behaviour could also be understood as a 'strategy by which a woman could effectively dominate her husband, by commanding his presence and aid, whilst simultaneously conforming to role expectations of dependency'.[23] Agoraphobia comes to represent the logical, if not extreme, extension of society's sex-role stereotype for women.

In the wake of hysteria and agoraphobia, anorexia can be understood as the most recent in a long tradition of stereotyped expressions of "female distress". It is arguably the most literal and caricatured personification of the cultural female idealization. The embodiment of this expression requires the interpretation of multiple readings, some of which are related to gender and these are the ones I shall focus on.[24] In anorexia we see a dangerously accurate inscription of the rules (symbolic and literal) underpinning the contemporary construction of femininity that need to be adhered to if she is to approximate the "norm". It requires that the woman feeds others whilst denying herself and to think of her own desires for self-nurturance and satiation as greedy with any "indulgence" rendering her physically and morally weak and out-of-control. There is a great pressure for her to develop an 'other-oriented emotional economy'.[25] This construction of femininity yields a powerful message, 'that female hunger – for public power, for independence, for sexual gratification – be contained'.[26] Her space must be limited. These rules and pressures are deeply and dangerously etched on the female anorexic body. In addition to these feminine pressures we have seen in the twentieth century an introduction of women to "masculine" ideals and the requirement of women to embody both "feminine" and "masculine" attributes to survive personal, public and professional spheres. It is at this intersection, between these contrasting attributes that the female anorexia body resides. She is in a double bind of a duel embodiment, none of which was her making. Devoid of the depth required to create a new sustaining and empowering ethic or culture – a "new man" or a "new woman" – she instead creates a parody – a dangerous game as this image and consumer-driven environment increasingly struggles to distinguish between parodies and possibilities of self. As Bordo writes 'the "androgynous" ideal ultimately exposes its internal contradiction and becomes a war that tears the subject in two – a war explicitly thematized by many anorexics as a battle between male and female sides of the self'.[27] The expression embodies a desire to meet the female idealizations of society whilst meeting the prerequisites for success within patriarchal institutions. These are the undercurrents of the "superwoman" ideology which has become a symbol of contemporary womanhood.[28]

In hysteria, agoraphobia and anorexia, the female body can be understood as a surface upon which conventional constructions of femininity are exposed in an extremely literal way. This should act as a warning of what is waiting just around the corner of feminine norms and beauty necessities. In the context of revealing the hidden and often dangerous nature of the construction of femininity, it is easy to see how the bodies of women embodying these maladies can be interpreted by feminist scholars as embodied protest despite them being 'unconscious, inchoate, and counterproductive protest[s] without an effective language, voice, or politics';[29] they are a protest nonetheless in the challenging of the mainstream female ideal. It is also clear to see how female embodiment is damaged by societal constructions of femininity and communicated through social institutions and through family, friends and peers whilst being visually reinforced by the media and advertising campaigns. An understanding of anorexia in the context of the maladies which preceded it demonstrates that anorexia takes its place as part of a milieu of psychological expressions within which we find political currents. Anorexia is about slenderness as a citadel of historical and contemporary meaning. By this I mean that to analyze the anorexic expression we need to examine the interpretation of slenderness as offering multiple readings on the body, some of which are gender related, some of which are not. My focus here, when considering the political undercurrents of such an expression, is a gendered reading. Hence my focus has been on the construction of femininity (symbolic and literal) which encourages the feeding of others (husband and children) before the self and which encourages feelings of guilt and distain (greedy and excessive) in relation to desires of self-feeding and self-nurturance as we have touched upon throughout this body of work. As has been documented at length by Bordo, Chernin and Orbach – to name a few social commentators – women are taught in myriad ways to control their bodies, space and sexuality. These restrictions are deeply etched on the anorexic body and take their place next to hysteria and agoraphobia as ideological constructions of femininity emblematic of the periods in which they developed. As Bordo writes of anorexia: 'The ideal of slenderness . . . and the diet and exercise regimens that have become inseparable from it, offer the illusion of meeting, through the body, the contradictory demands of the contemporary ideology of femininity'.[30] Touching upon the relationship between anorexia, hysteria and agoraphobia helps to demonstrate the nature of anorexia as being very much culturally situated. It reinforces the argument that anorexia is a form of political protest, on the part of women, to displace the social expectations rife in our society. Only, it fails to elicit any real change and instead ultimately proves to be a self-destructive expression of female struggle for reconciliation with these environments representing her dissatisfaction with gender limitations and the developing female role. This is all expressed through utilizing contemporary beauty ideals which value the slender form. We will explore this construction alongside the political undercurrents of diet rhetoric now as we examine the work of Wolf.

The politics of female self-starvation

In 1994 Wolf wrote that 'women do not eat or starve within a public social order that has a material vested interest in their troubles with eating'.[31] Elaborating on this, she writes that it was between 1918 and 1925, the same time that Western women received the right to vote, that dieting and thinness became a female preoccupation. Before this 'women's natural amplitude was their beauty'[32] with representations of the female nude portraying lush fertility and sexual fat. The female form went through a transformation from this curvaceous, full and ripe figure to a new linear and streamlined aesthetic.[33] She writes that the movement of women into traditional male-defined spheres marked a shift in the desired female aesthetic and introduced what she describes as the One Stone Solution. Wolf's premise is that 14 pounds (a UK stone) 'is roughly what stands between 50% of women who are not overweight but believe they are and their ideal selves'.[34] Once lost, that stone is regained as the individual returns to pre-diet eating habits and the body restores itself to the weight that is natural to it, and so the cycle of weight loss and weight gain continues. This reductionist rhetoric redefined women's understandings regarding loss of control, bodily shame and low self-esteem and created a deep-seated anxiety about being "too fat" which culminated in generations of women who loathed their bodies and set in motion the mass conviction of female failure which was 'defined as implicit to womanhood itself'.[35] For Wolf, this desire for a slender aesthetic is political. This is evidenced by the guilt experienced by women when they eat "too much". She writes:

> The great weight shift must be understood as one of the major historical developments of the century, a direct solution to the dangers posed by the women's movement and by economic and reproductive freedom. Women's advances had begun to give them high self-esteem, a sense of effectiveness, activity, courage, and clarity of mind. Prolonged and periodic caloric restriction is a means to take the teeth out of this revolution. The great weight shift . . . followed the birth of feminism so that women just reaching for power would become weak, preoccupied, and (as it evolved) mentally ill in useful ways and in astonishing proportions.[36]

Wolf argues that there is increasing evidence that dieting is one of the main causes of eating disorders such as anorexia[37] and that this desire to diet has been created by the thinness "ideal" which she sees as a political solution to women's increased presence and power within society. She argues that:

> [t]he anorexic may begin her journey defiant, but from the point of view of a male-dominated society, she ends up as the perfect woman: she is weak, sexless, and voiceless, and can only with difficulty focus on the world beyond her plate.[38]

Many social commentators, Wolf included, argue that gender roles have doubled for this generation of women as the pressure to conform to the masculine atmosphere has created the expectation for them to look like "real women" whilst behaving like "real men".[39] Women must compete like men whilst retaining their femininity.[40] The anorexic woman causes no trouble; in the words of Wolf, she is politically castrated with just enough energy to finish her work neatly and jump back on the treadmill, she has no energy to get angry, to storm and shout and change her social position, nor does she want to because she has bought into the slender ideal like everyone else. She wants to radiate that rigorously disciplined and controlled "beauty" that is so desired and coveted by everyone around her.[41] Wolf argues that the beauty myth does not just neutralize the achievements of women – reminding the audience of graduations and future bosses that beauty and slenderness speaks of acceptance of the prerequisites necessary to participate in male-defined institutions, reminding everyone that she knows how to play the game – but it also distracts women from redefining the playing field and challenging the destructive rhetoric which seeks to reinforce the status quo. The Women's Movement might have forced education systems and the workplace to accept women, but it was not successful in challenging the maleness of power itself. Where is the next generation of women activists to push the revolution forward? Wolf wrote in 1994 that one fifth of well-educated American young women are starving to death and may be too physically weak to do much more than cope with immediate personal demands.[42] Fast forward twenty-two years and it is not uncommon to see daily and weekly newspaper, blog or magazine articles about university women in the UK struggling with some form of disordered eating.[43] It may not be a stretch to argue that many woman, as a direct consequence of society's idealization of the slender female form, have expressed concerns about the weight they carry (despite their size) and spent a considerable amount of time thinking about what their bodies say about them and how they can change that perception. What is so distressing is there is no obvious villain to point a finger at. The work looks like it has been carried out by the young woman's own hands. It's her choice. It's her body. Yes? *No!* Being accepted, fitting-in and meeting external expectations are desires that are too strong to be ignored. The performance of the slender ideal secures certain advantages in school and later in the workplace as it communicates attributes of strength, discipline and control. This is not just discipline and control over her body but also about the discipline and control that can be exerted on her as this slender body is seen as something that can be more easily manipulated into conformity within the workplace. This is a body the institutions can work with. Wolf writes that until our culture tells girls and young women that they are valued for who they are – 'that women are valuable to it with or without the excuse of "beauty"'[44] – girls and women will continue to starve.

Sarah Sceats tells us that our relationship with food is of central importance to an understanding of human society. This is evident in psychoanalytic theory, which tells us that our formative feeding experiences are inscribed on our psyches and therefore, that food and eating play a crucial part in the development of our identity and our understanding of family, ethnicity and class. She argues that the prevalence of eating disorders in Western culture indicates 'an insecurity about embodiment, the nature of being and the boundaries between the self and the world'.[45] As is the case with sexuality, the significance of eating is socially, psychologically and politically constructed and customs, behaviours and symbolisms are indicators and the results of cultural conditioning. An obvious, and yet paradoxical example of this, is bingeing and self-starvation which develop within a context of consumerism in which consumption is promoted as desirable, yet overweight women are portrayed as joke figures and stigmatized as sexually promiscuous, stupid or coarse.

In a memoir reflecting her experiences working as a therapist, Lauren Slater comments on her own and other women's history as victims of 'cultures' fear of the feminine, unable to lay down our system of weapons and spread our legs open to life because we learned that in this posture we would be shamed, not invigorated'.[46] She comments that a culture that fosters within us a fear of fat, floppy, soft, dimpled flesh, is a culture that kills us. In examining similar themes, Kim Chernin discusses our culture's lost notion that the body holds meaning. She argues that this loss reflects significantly on our society that is 'seriously divided within itself, splitting itself off from nature, dividing the mind from the body, dividing thought from feeling, dividing one race against another, dividing the supposed nature of woman from the supposed nature of man'.[47] As part of this process of self-division we have been taught to ascribe worth and serious regard only to things that concern the soul and the spirit, the mind and its creations. However, when we probe below the surface and examine our obsession with size and weight, we begin to realize that 'a woman obsessed with her body is also obsessed with the limitations of her emotional life . . . she is expressing a serious concern about the state of her soul'.[48] In a series of books about women and their bodies,[49] Chernin writes about women's 'veiled and often disguised'[50] obsession with their right to grow, develop and ultimately to be accepted by a culture that ceases to damage them. A woman obsessed with the size and weight of her body is expressing the fact that she feels uncomfortable being female in this culture. In examining the relationship between women and their bodies and the control to placate hungers and urges, she demonstrates women's alienation from a 'natural source of female power'[51] and as such, women's inability to 'develop a reverential feeling for her body'.[52] However, as written by Paula Saukko[53] 'there are other stories being told and other voices to be heard about eating disorders'.[54] Central to her analysis of anorexia is a breaking down of gendered, normative notions of being whilst moving away from explanations limited to the effects of media and fashion advertising. She draws upon the experiences of women, placing their "authentic voices" central to her scholarship and analysis. Her aim is to work away from arguments which focus on the concept of these women as "victims" of social discourse as she seeks to promote a more self-reflective and less judgmental framework for working with anorexic women. Here the concept of "victim" is broken down and the use of "woman" is reestablished, as she becomes the reliable witness to her own experiences. The symptoms are no longer reserved simply for the analysis and deciphering of medical experts, psychologists or feminist scholars but her understanding of the underlying issues and her utilization of this particular expression is unpacked. From inactive and powerless, she becomes an active participant in the recovery process. In her work, Saukko calls for the scholars, medical experts, psychologists and women with anorexia to continue to interrogate all discourses that suggest 'what we should be or what the world should be'[55] leading to a 'positive, productive ability to see that our personal lives and politics are more complex than they seem and therefore require more complex therapeutic and political strategies'.[56] In this, the young woman with anorexia plays a central role in the process of healing. This is something also discussed by Helen Gremillion in the context of narrative-based therapy.

In her work looking at the benefits of narrative-based therapy, Gremillion writes that treatment centre therapies can often unwittingly participate in culturally dominant norms and ideals surrounding gender, physical fitness, individualism and family life that do not aid in helping women to find a way out of the disordered eating patterns. Whilst participating and unknowingly reinforcing social norms and ideals, these influences also structure the nature of the therapy provided as practitioners and therapists focus on combatting social focuses whilst neglecting the individual's life experiences that contribute to the development of anorexic tendencies in their particular case.[57] Remembering that anorexia is multifaceted and that many cultural "streams" converge in the development of this expression, consideration throughout therapy must be given to all the strands that make up the anorexic web so we can fully untangle the participant. In focusing on narrative-based therapies which place analysis of the anorexic experience (and thus some level of control) into both the individual's hands as well as the therapists, she argues we can erode dangerous assumptions about the underlying causes and triggers and work towards a mutually based relational therapy which does not reinforce normative notions of being. She writes that 'therapeutic practices are never culturally neutral, because they help reconfigure persons' lives and relationships in particular social contexts'[58] but through narrative therapy which works to 'identify and decenter the truth claims of psychiatric objectivity and the dominant cultural discourses that support these claims',[59] therapists can participate in reconfiguring dominant social forms and therefore, dismantle some of the identified underlying triggers and risk factors. Gremillion's research led her to conclude that '[y]oung women and girls who struggle with anorexia both appropriate powerful social norms about feminine autonomy and self-control and challenge these norms by enacting them through illness'.[60] As such, therapy needs to both displace the social norms and create new opportunities. She writes that narrative therapies[61] work with clients 'collaboratively to construct (or "coauthor") new stories about the self, the body, and relationships by drawing on aspects of patients' experiences that do not fit neatly into a given problem story'.[62]

The work referred to above reinforces the argument that anorexia is far from a unique and individual construction created by girls and women to deal with internal conflicts. Its influences are far more varied and far-reaching than that. According to these academics, anorexia is at the same time a response to the inequality of the sexes, the normative construction of the feminine, a coping mechanism for surviving these demands and a clever strategy aimed at keeping women preoccupied with female prerequisites before they can challenge the gender status quo and re-level the working sphere. We have discussed the political aspects surrounding the development of anorexia and how we might start to construct a response to the underlying pressures utilizing the voices of women and the collaboration of narrative-based therapies.[63] This approach also opens the path for developing understandings of the underpinning pressures which lead to the development of anorexia. Following the reading of Saukko and Gremillion, whilst there may be other stories being told and often more forces outside the social at play, my conceptualization of anorexia is that its development is heavily influenced by the normative construction of femininity in contemporary society and importance should be placed on how these ideals are communicated to the female sex.

Is there any spirituality to be gleaned from the anorexic experience?

Having considered some of the finer details of anorexia as a disorder, an illness to be eradicated, what I have not touched upon is the idea that there is any benefit to be gleaned from this expression. Therefore, the second half of this chapter is dedicated to the question of whether there can be any positive outcome to the experience of anorexia for women within society today. With this in mind, I will explore the work of Ariel Glucklich on Sacred Pain, followed by Elizabeth Baxter's analysis of "cutting" as a healing rite of passage.

In *Sacred Pain*, Ariel Glucklich discusses different types of religious pain and suffering and the difference between the perspective of the participant and the onlooker. Glucklich writes: '[a]mong the oldest form of the religious life around the world are rituals of self-hurting and even a theological glorification of suffering that seems entirely inconsistent with common sense'.[64] The premise of the book is to find the causes of religious self-hurting and explore the often-hidden rationality behind the depiction of pain as a good and positive experience. Ultimately, Glucklich demonstrates that a ritually controlled regiment of pain can have a transformative effect on the participant's consciousness in which personal identity gives way to a broader identification with God, truth or other spiritual ideals. He argues that the idea of pain as good and transforming for the individual was negated by modern medicine's development of anesthesia and the concept of pain as a bad thing, something to be avoided. This advancement undermined the idea that pain can be good. What was particularly interesting for the context of my study was the idea of the transformative nature of collective painful rites of passage. Glucklich discusses rituals of possession and exorcism, tortures of the inquisition and rites of passage from around the globe. Although he discusses pain rituals in a religious context, for me this raises the question of whether there exists a transformative spiritual element to the individual's experience of anorexic behaviours.

The self-proclaimed central task of *Sacred Pain* is to 'transform destructive or disintegrated suffering into a positive religious-psychological mechanism for reintegration within a more deeply valued level of reality than individual experience'.[65] To me this speaks of transcending the body and the attainment of a higher level of existence. In his book, Glucklich quotes Fakir Mufasar who documents his experiences of various body modification practices in the journal *Body Play*. One of the experiences shared with the reader is Mufasar's experience of the O-KEE-PA ritual which is traditionally practiced by Mandan tribes on the banks of the Missouri River. Hanging himself on hooks inserted into his chest, Mufasar writes:

> spirit and body co-exist now. Aware of each other but separate. It's an ecstasy state where no matter what happens in the body, no matter how much more intense the physical sensation become, I feel no more. Sensations just "are".[66]

This experience is referred to as a healing pain, one of two fundamental pain types. Glucklich writes that the various models of pain[67] boil down to two fundamental types, disintegrative and integrative pain. The former is likely to be identified as punitive or as an enemy. In relation to the Biblical story of Job, he writes: '[t]he pain Job experienced was disintegrative: It entirely disrupted his life, isolated him from the world, devastated his sense of well-being, his very desire to live'.[68] In contrast, the latter integrative pain is exampled as similar to the woman's experience of childbirth as an experience that strengthens 'the woman's sense of identity'[69] and allows her to 'situate herself within nature and within her social and spiritual world'.[70] This pain is more commonly described as healing or personally transforming as opposed to punitive. The difference here is not the intensity of the pain and suffering, but the end result and the potential for liberation.

The identification and classification of these two types helps Glucklich to demonstrate the difference between damaging and liberating experiences of pain. Clearly, for example, there is a difference between the experience of a victim of a car crash or a cancer patient and the voluntary and modulated self-hurting of a religious practitioner. In the latter understanding, the individual is described as undergoing different states of consciousness and cognitive-emotional changes that affect them whilst strengthening their state of belonging to a larger community and to a more fundamental state of being. The pain strengthens the individual's bond with a higher being and with others within the broader community. Pain is also context sensitive; the same pain in different contexts can be either punitive or transforming and can shift between the two; disintegrative pain can be transformed into integrative pain and vice versa. The two pain types 'are two ways of talking about pain from the (shifting) perspective of the ego in pain'.[71]

The question for me is whether anorexia should be included in the former or latter understanding, and you can see how it might fall into both categories. As a religious experience by way of spiritual transformation, female mystics and women employed fasting as a means of attaining spiritual perfection and a closer relationship with the divine. This certainly has the trademarks of Glucklich's description of integrative pain, but what about the contemporary experience of women with anorexia? If the end goal of the self-starving of fasting saints was a religious transformation and deeper relationship with the divine, and the end goal of contemporary anorexia is the slender feminine ideal for social acceptance and legitimacy, in which box are we to neatly store the contemporary anorexic experience? Can anorexia be a rite of passage at all? Before answering these points, I would like to take a look at the work of Elizabeth Baxter.

Baxter discusses "cutting" rituals as healing rites of passage that young people might enact following an earlier trauma. For Baxter, the ritual and ritualization of self-harming itself can take place within a healing framework that allows the individual woman[72] to establish her own personal identity separate from her earlier abuse or trauma. In her discussions, the witnessing of "cutting" and seeing the young woman's pain and wounds can play an important part in the healing process. For the "cutter", this dramatic ritual is her way of proving she is the survivor of her past; she is reclaiming and re-being. As Baxter writes:

> [t]he *I am not* creates a loss of sacrality, a loss of real presence, a dismembering. For effective re-membering, the community is required to be real and safe enough to hold and witness the pain and to heal the brokenhearted, by re-establishing real presence, the *I am*.[73]

Commonalties exist throughout her description of the self-harming process and the ritualization of the anorexic. However, as discussed earlier in this book, anorexia is more commonly connected to the contemporary construction of the feminine as opposed to the experience of abuse or earlier childhood trauma. For Baxter, cutting can be a carefully set-out, ordered, obsessively prepared and disciplined ritual which allows the individual to connect with some sort of fractured upbringing to express her pain and terror and find some release from these pressures. In this she creates her own initiation rites that get jumbled up alongside 'Western society's initiation structures, such as legal ages for behavior, confirmation and senior school'.[74] Ritualized cutting as a rite of passage provides the young woman with both a temporary relief from anxiety, desperation and depersonalization whilst also touching upon human experiences of salvation, orderliness and healing. In this physical storytelling – carved into her very skin – we see her struggle to reconcile past experiences with her environment. In performing this act, she reminds herself that she is an alive and active agent. Other elements at play include purification, as the "sickness" is bled from her body (in a similar way the anorexic woman might avoid "dirty" food and revel in the purity and lightness of emaciation) and control, taking back her body that has been denigrated and manipulated by different pressures. Again, these themes are common across these two expressions.

When constructing a liberation framework to contextualize these rites of passage, Baxter locates healing within community practices and more precisely, a witnessing ritual that she has drawn upon herself to help young women heal within her therapeutic community in Yorkshire. Self-harming in the form of cutting here takes place within a healing framework as it provides the opportunity for the individual to 'parade her innerwear as outerwear'[75] and to take control of her pain whilst redefining, re-creating and re-being. Witnessing this expression by the community (represented by the presence of a therapist or friend) becomes part of this process of healing and re-creation. Through witnessing and 'gently bathing the wounds together'[76] or simply staying to witness the pain and hurt, the witness can transform the "cutting" ritual into a healing rite of passage that can, over time, develop into an act of liberation from her earlier trauma. Listening is essential, 'for in mid-journey a self-harmer cannot hear our words of comfort, she needs to be heard through our witness of her actions'.[77] In most therapeutic work, Baxter has found that the individual slowly overcomes her feelings of being out-of-control. This instead gives way to feelings of being in control of the healing process and her life. Through witnessing the rite of passage, a role reversal takes place as the witness becomes part of the pain and subsequent healing. It is this witnessing which, over time, results in the completion of the rite and hopefully, in liberation from the trauma that emotionally hinders her development. Within her Christian Religious framework Baxter concludes that:

> witnessing to the compassionate love of Christ/Christa, and acting it out in and through community, helps towards the healing of those who fear their 'demons', those abusive powers projected onto them by others, making them feel as if those powers completely possess their body and soul.[78]

Many parallels can be drawn between the experience of the "cutter" and the anorexic (a struggle for control, issues surrounding identity and understanding personal boundaries and the creation of new and constructive ways of being within their environments), but there are clear differences (the link between "cutting" and previous physical or emotional trauma and the anorexic's reaction to the pressures and contradictions of contemporary society). There are a couple of themes that have presented themselves following my reading of Baxter and Glucklich when considering the anorexic expression: 1) the idea of self-harming as a healing rite of passage; and, 2) whether anorexia can be understood in the same frame of reference and if so, what part is played by the witness and community in the healing process?

Anorexia as a healing rite of passage

The idea that anorexia can be a healing expression is a troubling one for me. As we start to explore anorexia within the integrative/disintegrative framework of Glucklich and the healing ritual of Baxter, it is worth reminding ourselves that anorexia is a multifaceted expression that becomes manifest for manifold reasons. Catherine Garrett writes in *Beyond Anorexia* about the construction of the false body image the woman with anorexia has about herself and her use of this addiction or compulsion as a mask to cover underlying issues of identity, control and power. This approach indicates that anorexia is a front and that the true self is waiting to be discovered. As a common theme throughout literature on anorexia, healing might then involve the identification and destruction of the layers of damaging discourses that overlay the life of a woman with anorexic symptoms. There are several reasons why this might be the case as elaborated by Garrett. First, and as we discussed in the earlier chapters, 'anorexia may be described as a watershed in the development of identity: since it has most often (though not invariably) manifested itself in adolescence; it is often interpreted as part of the individuals struggle for autonomy from parents'[79] (historically the mother as the primary caregiver). Second, this might arise when a 'child's earliest needs are not appropriately met by the caregiver'[80] which subsequently gives way to the child's construction of an alternative internal world in which the caregiver becomes both a "bad object" (the rejecting object) and the "good object" (the object of desire). Within this alternative and dichotomous space, the individual withdraws into a fantasy life that subsequently gives way to the creation of a false self. This is a self 'without needs (since these cannot be met) and who attempts to meet the projections of others. . . . The 'real self' is thereby split off and rejected'.[81] These two reasons for the development of anorexia fall into Object Relations Theory. For Susie Orbach the false body created through anorexia – a malleable and controlled body – is her defence mechanism against the unacceptable real body that becomes the "bad object" because it represents the negative aspects of the mother as caregiver (and her struggle to emotionally distance herself from her mother) whilst visually representing her failure to meet the cultural slender idealizations. Orbach writes:

> [w]e can begin to see, then, that the cause she has taken on is a precious one: the creation of a safe place in the world. She is trying to legitimate herself, to eke out a space, to bring dignity where dismissal and indignity were rife. Her cause is no less imperative than that of an overtly political hunger striker. The resolve of her commitment is equally intense. The political prisoner who embarks upon a hunger strike does so to draw attention to the injustice of her or his incarceration and the righteousness of her or his cause. The anorexic woman on hunger strike echoes these themes. Her self-denial is in effect a protest against the rules that circumscribe a woman's life, a demand that she has an absolute right to exist.[82]

In an internal balancing act, the anorexic woman attempts to turn unacceptability into acceptability through the implementation of internal judges who she tries to placate (as Glucklich may conceptualize it; disintegrative into integrative pain). The woman might feel 'empty inside, void of feelings, fearful of initiating, and lacking an internal sense of continuity and security'.[83] Anorexic behaviour is the process of simultaneously protecting and denying that aspect of her psyche. This might suggest that anorexia is the woman's coping mechanism for internal feelings that she struggles to reconcile. Here, we see that the experience is not just about thinness but reinforces the diversity and political nature of the expression reinforcing notions of control and managing developmental challenges. However, even within this framework, slenderness and society's ideals still play a major role. It is the slender body that gets praised for its control, discipline, purity and transcendence. Achieving 'slenderness is an important factor. It is a visible proof of the woman's success'.[84] The success is a fantastic achievement for her psychologically in the context of experiencing herself as unsuccessful. This helps to placate the internal judges that police her actions.

Another advocate of the object relations theory is Catherine Steiner-Adair[85] who argues that anorexia results from a failure to acknowledge the importance of relationships in the development of a feminine identity. She treats herself as an island, invulnerable, removed and transcendent. Therefore, the goal for the woman expressing anorexic tendencies is to reconnect with her body and environment (and thereby, reconnect to the broader community) and to remember how to live beyond the compulsion to control her body. Her work highlights the 'importance of human connection in recovery'[86] and thus, with reference to Baxter, the broader role of the witness to see, understand and aid in the transformation process. The transition to a state beyond anorexia is the desired outcome. In this, the symbolic self is consciously integrated into the self that is experienced as "real", "whole" and "autonomous". This is often referred to as a sense of 'inner connection'.[87] To work towards recovery, 'the self must be understood as made up of many interconnected parts and recovery must be conceptualized as transcendence, not of the self, but of ego'.[88] This is an ongoing process of transformation, of becoming whole in an environment where our relationship with our contemporary bodies is dualistic, helped no doubt by the diet rhetoric reinforced at every turn. This is more extremely displayed on the body of the anorexic and it's the woman with anorexia who is forced to deal with this dualism head on by way of her mortality, as the anorexic symptoms threaten her life. This begs the questions of whether the experience and survival of anorexia would create in the young woman a deep-seated connection to her body that is uncommon today, thus opening more possibilities for life outside such dualistic demands.

Reflecting on the work of Garrett and the creation of the false self and fantasy life, anorexia may present (through making the unconscious conscious) the opportunity, which might not otherwise present itself, to identify the damaging and destructive social discourses that contribute to the development of anorexia and conceive of ways to break them down through changing the female performance. Put another way, are we only now discussing the damaging slender ideal because of the development of anorexia and the lives it claims year-on-year? Through the existence of anorexia, could we transform the construction of the feminine altogether and create an inclusive space away from normative ideals? In this space, the fantasy and false self are destroyed, allowing the denied and denigrated aspects of her personality full expression and a safe space to flourish. Maybe the role of the witness here is to help the unconscious become conscious. To see in the witnesses' reflection, her-own entrapment and to become aware of the social discourses that contribute towards this manifestation, the anorexic individual can take her first step in a long journey towards recovery.

In terms of Glucklich and distinguishing between integrative and disintegrative pain, Garrett writes that contemporary anorexia is likely to be about '*individual* redemption from guilt and salvation through self-preservation'.[89] Maybe this is a misguided act implemented by the young woman and aimed at helping her reconcile these internal struggles. For her, this may be an integrative ritual that she utilizes as a means of reconciling herself with these feelings of guilt (of not being perfect enough) and tries to reach a level of purity and perfection that would be impossible, to her, through another medium. This however would be a misguided endeavour, as there is little to be gained from starving the body so aggressively. This brings us back to the central questions of this examination and analysis: can self-harm be understood in an integrative pain framework? Can anorexia be understood as a self-harm practice and if so, in the same way as Baxter uses the "cutting" and "witnessing" ritual as a model of therapeutic healing, can anorexia be understood as a healing ritual or rite of passage? Ultimately is there anything positive to result from the anorexic experience – could anorexia be conceptualized as subversive?

Baxter clearly argues that self-harm behaviours such as "cutting" within the right environment and in the presence of a witness can be part of an integrative pain type. Within her Christian framework, the process of cutting is understood as the individual's coping mechanism and communication of her pain and betrayal. Through this exposure, over time and in conjunction with the right therapeutic setting, this can become an act of liberation and healing a previous trauma. I do not believe we can reach the same conclusions when discussing anorexia. First of all, I believe the distinction of anorexia as a self-harming practice is correct when considering the following definition: 'self-injurious behavior (SIB) is defined as those behaviors that involve the deliberate infliction of direct physical harm to one's own body without the intent to die as a result of the behavior itself'.[90] This definition is further divided into three classification types. Briefly speaking these are: major self-mutilation (understood as severe acts such as castration or eye enucleation – acts typically associated with psychotic disorders), stereotypical self-mutilation (for example, repeated acts such as head-banging or self-biting) and moderate/superficial self-mutilation (this includes acts such as cutting, hair pulling, scratching, picking or burning, and other similar forms of superficial self-injury). I would include anorexia and other eating disorders within the third category as a behaviour which harms the body through a severe restriction of nutrition leading to a host of physical and psychological dangerous ramifications (as discussed in Chapter 1). The clinical phenomenology of eating disorders and self-injurious behaviour share important overlaps in that they both take place predominantly within females at the onset of adolescence. Moderate and superficial self-injurious behaviours can be impulsive or compulsive. The compulsive subtype can be understood as habitual, repetitive and "automatic"; there is not usually any conscious intent and involves a build-up of pressure and mounting anxiety prior to the act followed by relief after the behaviour has been performed. The impulsive subtype on the other hand is defined as 'usually episodic, involves little conscious resistance, and provides some form of gratification beyond reduction of tension or anxiety'.[91] Reports from the individuals engaging in such activities usually state that the behaviour helps them to deal with negative emotions such as loneliness, depression and depersonalization. This behaviour also satisfies the individual's need for 'self-punishment and the manipulation of others'.[92] This classification of impulsive behaviours overlaps with what we know of the anorexic experience. Both behaviour patterns can be linked with 'body dissatisfaction, asceticism, or a pervading sense of ineffectiveness which often implies an element of self-punishment (e.g. self-starvation, other body mortification practices such as self-flagellation)'.[93] They are also ways for the individual to take possession and control of their body. Many women with anorexia identify their behaviour as self-injurious[94] but as a focused activity aimed at cultural acceptability (as this is the framework we are working in), a coping mechanism to deal with feelings of loneliness, low self-esteem, depression and depersonalization and a struggle for control and power over ownership of the female body, I do not see how anorexia can legitimately be understood within an integrative pain framework or as a healing ritual. The reason for this is unpacked further in the answer to the remaining question: can anorexia be considered a subversive act?

In the same way that Butler drew on the drag performance as a parody of our gender acts and therefore, an opportunity for awareness (in demonstrating the exaggerated nature of our gender performance) and resistance (an opportunity to change the performance), can anorexia be understood as a pathway to liberation from these slender constraints in its revealing of our culture's demands for the self-eradication and arguably (according to some of the academics above), the disempowerment of women? This might be problematic for a few reasons.

For example, for many scholars, as demonstrated through this work, anorexia as a political protest is rarely acknowledged as such by the women under its spell whilst the drag performance is consciously enacted by the performer. Although the anorexic body presents itself as a caricature of the contemporary hyper-slender ideal, it is using the body, an area traditionally assigned to women, to express her displeasure and disdain. Despite being unaware of the political statement, as Bordo notes, 'employing the language of femininity to protest the conditions of the female world . . . will always involve ambiguities'.[95] Even as she becomes aware of the political protest she is making, she ends up being the "perfect"[96] woman, weak, sexless, vulnerable and delicate, distracted from anything beyond the boundaries of her regimented plate. Coupled with her extreme pain and distress, those who maintain the lithe, slender body with such apparent ease, models and the small percentage that embody a figure naturally endowed with this wafer frame, keep the slender wish alive for so many young women. In this, any political statement she is consciously or subconsciously making is lost. As such, I cannot help but disagree with the idea that anorexia is an unconscious opportunity to subvert and deconstruct the culturally idealized female body. I do not see how anorexia can be understood as an affront to patriarchy, as an expression of liberation from its social constraints and as a rejection of the social manipulation of the female body. For me, anorexia is not an effective means of challenging or undermining contemporary society's female idealizations and norms.

I do however agree with Bordo when she argues that eating disorders begin as sane and mentally healthy responses to these insane cultural pressures, that it is not a sign of mental health to try and fight for the control of your own body amongst these narrowly and powerfully defined social expectations. For some, eating disorders seem like the only escape, the only way to get "out of the game" but eating disorders will never be a forceful enough statement to oppose these powerful ideals. Using thinness as a weapon to expose the ludicrousness of the thinness paradigm will always present a paradox of patriarchal influence and liberation from those constraints. Maybe, instead of discussing the perceived conformity or rebellious nature of anorexia, we should be discussing the naturalized gender role that is in need of deconstruction. Given Wolf's argument that women may gravitate towards eating disorders as a distorted effort to escape the confines of femininity and take back some control of their bodies, we surely need to address the link between gender ideals and anorexia and explore new creative ways of resisting these constraints. Attention needs to be spent on gender inequalities and creating a "gender-neutral" or "gender-fluid" space as we work to break down the social barriers between male and female and create an inclusive environment for both sexes and thus, undo this dangerous and disembodied ideology. In turn, this might be enough to deconstruct the damaging ideology underpinning the slender ideal and disable the need for such a dangerous expression for women to reclaim control of their bodies.

As I wrote earlier, the idea that anorexia can be a healing expression is a troubling one for me. I do not think that contemporary anorexia, arising from the constructions of femininity (as we explored when we discussed the relationship between hysteria, agoraphobia and anorexia) and the social pressures which teach us that cultural acceptability is contingent on certain beauty prerequisites, can be understood within an integrative pain framework. Fundamentally anorexia is not a form of religious self-hurting and the aim is not a broader identification with divinity. I feel that any transformative element is limited to its revealing of the dangerous nature of the contemporary construction of femininity and beauty necessities in its extreme embodiment of these ideals and normalizing discourses. I also think that anorexia, as we have been discussing it, is far removed from the rites of passage as discussed within the context of "cutting" and other self-harm practices discussed by Baxter. Self-harm and "cutting" practices here are a response to earlier trauma and are implemented by the individual as a means of communicating their pain, the end goal being reconciliation, healing and release.

In this chapter we have examined the female body as a historically mediated form, the commonalities between hysteria, agoraphobia and anorexia as reactions to the construction of the feminine indicative of the nineteenth, twentieth and twenty-first centuries and the political dimensions of female self-starvation; we started to examine pathways from these damaging expressions through narrative therapy. The second half of this chapter focused on whether there is any psychological benefit or spirituality to result from the anorexic experience in the context of "cutting" and other self-harm practices/self-injurious behaviour. An obvious conclusion arising from these discussions surrounding the political dimensions of anorexia in the context of hysteria and agoraphobia is that the social construction of the feminine and beauty necessities that loiter over the lives of women are dangerous. My conclusion: subversive resistance comes from challenging this construction and the gender inequalities that determine our roles, responsibilities, appearance and value in society.

Notes

1 Glucklich, A. (2001) *Sacred Pain: Hurting the Body for the Sake of the Soul*. New York: Oxford University Press, 6.
2 Gordon, R. A. (2000) *Eating Disorders: Anatomy of a Social Epidemic*. Oxford: Blackwell Publishers, 189.
3 Gordon (2000: 189).
4 For more information on the anthropological study of psychiatric disorders and society and psychiatry, see Lipsedge, M., Littlewood, R. (1997) *Aliens and Alienists: Ethnic Minorities and Psychiatry*. London: Routledge.
5 In his development of the concept of liminality (to be betwixt and between positions designated by society's laws, customs, conventions etc.) Turner conceptualized what he believed to be a place where the socially oppressed could reverse established social structures and express their cultural oppositions. This could be achieved through the ritual "power of the weak" (thought to be embodied by shamans, mediums, magicians, jesters and other marginal groups). Psychiatric disorders can be thought to exist in this same liminal space and thus serve as a medium for protest against society's norms and values. For more information on the concept of liminality and the ritual "power of the weak", see Turner, V. (2008) *The Ritual Process: Structure and Anti-Structure*. Piscataway: Aldine Transaction.
6 For more information, see Bell, R. M. (1987) *Holy Anorexia*. London: The University of Chicago Press; Bynum, C. W. (1987) *Holy Feast and Holy Fast: The Religious Significance of Food to Medieval Women*. London: University of California Press.
7 Gordon (2000: 192).
8 Gordon (2000: 192).
9 Hunger strikes can be understood as a method of non-violent resistance in which participants fast as an act of political protest with a goal of gaining political advantage or policy change. Usually participants consume liquids but not food. Within a feminist context, the most widely recognized hunger strikes were carried out by the suffragettes in the early twentieth century. Marion Wallace-Dunlop was the first suffragette to hunger strike and following her arrest in 1909 for militancy she refused to eat until her status as a political prisoner was recognized. She refused food for ninety-one hours. For more information on the political use of hunger strikes, including its utilization by the suffragettes, see Wilson, L. (2015) Starvation and Self-Mutilation in Religious Traditions. In: Juergensmeyer, M., Kitts, M., Jerryson, M. (eds.) *The Oxford Handbook of Religion and Violence*. Oxford: Oxford University Press, 242–250; and Vernon, J. (2007) *Hunger: A Modern History*. London: The Belknap Press of Harvard University Press.
10 Gordon (2000: 194).
11 Gordon (2000: 195).
12 Barker, P. J. (2004) *Assessment in Psychiatric and Mental Health Nursing: In Search of the Whole Person*. Cheltenham: Nelson Thornes Ltd, 261.

13 Barker (2004: 261).
14 That is not to say that hysterical symptoms do not occur in the twentieth and twenty-first centuries or that symptoms of anorexia where not experienced in the nineteenth century (they were typically recorded in relation to a diagnosis of hysteria).
15 For more information, see Bordo, S. (2003) *Unbearable Weight: Feminism, Western Culture, and the Body*. London: University of California Press.
16 Bordo (2003: 168).
17 Bordo (2003: 168).
18 Bordo (2003: 168, author's emphasis).
19 Orbach, S. (1993) *Hunger Strike: The Anorectic's Struggle as a Metaphor for Our Age*. London: Penguin Books, 6.
20 Gordon (2000: 191).
21 Bordo (2003: 170).
22 Gordon (2000: 191).
23 Gordon (2000: 191).
24 Other readings cover economic, psychosocial, historical and racial considerations of the dimensions of anorexia as we have already explored.
25 Bordo (2003: 171).
26 Bordo (2003: 171).
27 Bordo (2003: 174).
28 "Superwoman" ideology features heavily within the work of Wolf and is the idea that women could "have it all" at the same time. It is an unrealistic and idealistic feminine construction which served to further fracture female self-esteem by setting a damaging ideal as "norm". For more information, see Wolf, N. (1990) *The Beauty Myth: How Images of Beauty Are Used Against Women*. London: Vintage Books; and Wolf, N. (1994) Hunger. In: Fallon, P., Katzman, M. A., Wooley, S. C. (eds.) *Feminist Perspectives on Eating Disorders*. New York: The Guildford Press.
29 Bordo (2003: 175).
30 Bordo (2003: 18).
31 Wolf (1994: 97).
32 Wolf (1994: 96).
33 Changing representations of women in the Western world is a subject discussed at length by Susan Bordo. In her book *Twilight* Zones she critically analyses contemporary cultural images for their often-unrealistic standards whilst providing a history of their development and political underpinnings. For more information, see Bordo (1999).
34 Wolf (1994: 96).
35 Wolf (1994: 97).
36 Wolf (1994: 97).
37 Many scholars and academic writing in the field argue that whilst dieting itself is not sufficient to cause anorexia, that the mind-sets, attitudes and behaviours associated with dieting may predispose individuals to develop these eating habits. For more information, see Wolf (1994); Dwyer, J. (1985) Nutritional Aspects of Anorexia Nervosa and Bulimia. In: Emmett, S. W. (ed.) *Theory and Treatment of Anorexia Nervosa and Bulimia: Biomedical Sociocultural, and Psychological Perspectives*. New York: Brunner/Mazel Inc, 20–51 (29); and Lawrence, M. (2008) *The Anorexic Mind*. London: Karnac Books, 19.
38 Wolf (1994: 100).
39 Richard Gordon discusses anorexia in the context of relevant cultural factors such as conflicts in the contemporary female role. Focusing on changing social expectations for women, he writes that women are increasingly expected to retain all aspects of femininity whilst progressing the feminist cause by gaining access to traditionally male-defined working spheres. The contradictions of this

dichotomy are cited as contributing to the anorexic expression within contemporary society. For more information, see Gordon (2000). The idea that women are expected to ascribe to certain beauty prerequisites when entering traditionally male domains (such as politics) is drawn upon by Shelia Jefferys in *Women and Misogyny* and also by Deborah Rhodes in *The Beauty Bias*. Jefferys writes that women are increasingly making their mark on traditionally male domains, but they are required to 'show deference to men in their appearance, with high heels, make-up and restrictive clothing' which are inappropriate to the seriousness of their positions. She argues that women are required to self-objectify and enact harmful beauty practices if they are to avoid rebuke. This is further reinforced by Rhodes, a legal scholar who, when elected chair of the American Bar Association's Commission on Women in the Profession, was pressured to adopt these beauty practices. For more information, see Jefferys, S. (2005, 2015) *Women and Misogyny: Harmful Cultural Practices in the West*. London: Routledge; and Rhode, D. (2011) *The Beauty Bias: The Injustice of Appearance in Life and Law*. Oxford: Oxford University Press. The idea that success is contingent on meeting certain beauty prerequisites is also touched upon by economist Daniel Hamermesh who argues that ugliness is no different from discrimination based on race or a disability. Hamermesh suggests that unattractive people need legal protection. Having investigated the financial benefits of beauty, Hamermesh found that the best-looking workers earn, on average, 10–15 per cent more per year. For more information, see Hamermesh, D. S. (2011) *Beauty Pays: Why Attractive People Are More Successful*. Oxford: Princeton University Press.

40 This calls to mind the work of Joan Riviere and her conceptualization of *Womanliness as a Masquerade* back in 1929. The premise of her argument is that womanliness can be worn as a form of mask or performance enacted by women as they display intelligence. This performance is understood as a way of subconsciously reassuring men that they still possess the phallic power, that her intelligence is not a threat to their security. Thus, this masquerade results from an unconscious attempt to avoid the retribution feared from men in response to an appropriation of the masculine role by the female. This masquerade is not portrayed as a joyful or life-affirming, embodied experience. Rather, it comes across as an anxiety-ridden gesture that is uncomfortable, disturbing and psychologically damaging for the woman who performs according to what is desirable to the male gaze. Riviere, J. (1986) Womanliness as a Masquerade. In: Burgin, V., Donald, J., Kaplan, C. (eds.) *Formations of Fantasy*. London: Methuen.

41 Kamille Gentles-Peart discusses American beauty discourses that instil the message that the ultimate beauty in the Euro-American beauty regime is the thin, white body. She challenges the dominant cultural discourses that appear to reinforce the message that 'thinness as well as whiteness are the central components and prerequisites of beauty'. For more information, see Gentles-Peart, K. (2016) *Romance With Voluptuousness: Caribbean Women and Thick Bodies in the United States*. Lincoln: University of Nebraska Press.

42 Whilst many women continue to negotiate the demands of "the beauty myth", many are still taking political stands to continue the fight for equality. For example, in the opening weeks of 2017 we saw large (many female-driven) protests against the inauguration of the Trump administration in the United States. Globally, women and men have been coming together to protest against the presidency of Donald Trump as a consequence of his divisive policies, racist rhetoric and clear (and often jovially discussed) misogyny. For more information, see Anon. (2017) *Global Protests on Donald Trump Inauguration Day*. Available at: www.bbc.co.uk/news/world-us-canada-38699844 [24/01/2017].

43 An example of this is found within a 2014 article by the *Independent* online newspaper. Drawing upon information provided by B-eat, it was claimed that out of 200 students surveyed, 32 per cent were diagnosed as having an eating

disorder whilst more than 50 per cent believed there was not enough university support for those suffering from eating disordered behaviour. Whilst this was not subdivided by sex, the only voices quoted in the article were female (with one example, where no gender was mentioned). The article did not mention the scope of this survey but suggested that this was indicative of UK universities in general. For more information, see O'Connor, M. (2014) *Eating Disorders Awareness Week Shows that Student Hunger for Greater University Support Still Exists*. Available at: www.independent.co.uk/student/student-life/eating-disorders-awareness-week-shows-that-student-hunger-for-greater-university-support-still-9160524.html [22/10/2016].

44 Wolf (1994: 104).

45 Sceats, S. (2005) *Food, Consumption and the Body in Contemporary Women's Fiction*. Cambridge: Cambridge University Press, 1.

46 Slater, L. (1997) *Welcome to My Country*. London: Penguin Books, 50.

47 Chernin, K. (1994) *The Obsession: Reflections on the Tyranny of Slenderness*. New York: Harper Perennial, 2.

48 Chernin (1994: 2).

49 Chernin (1994); Chernin, K. (1985) *The Hungry Self: Women, Eating and Identity*. New York: HarperCollins Publishers; and Chernin, K. (1987) *Reinventing Eve: Modern Woman in Search of Herself*. New York: HarperCollins Publishers, Inc.

50 Chernin (1994: 2).

51 Chernin (1994: 3).

52 Chernin (1994: 3).

53 Saukko, P. (2008) *The Anorexic Self: A Personnel, Political Analysis of Diagnostic Discourse*. New York: State of New York Press.

54 Saukko (2008: 78).

55 Saukko (2008: 113).

56 Saukko (2008: 113).

57 There are scholars who argue that there is an element of healing or something sacred to be found within certain self-harm contexts. I refer here to the work of Ariel Glucklich in *Sacred Pain: Hurting the Body for the Sake of the Soul* and Elizabeth Baxter's article *Cutting Edge*. In the final section of this chapter I draw upon these texts and address the question of whether there is any spirituality to be gleaned from the anorexic experience.

58 Gremillion, H. (2003) *Feeding Anorexia: Gender and Power at a Treatment Centre*. London: Duke University Press, 193.

59 Gremillion (2003: 194).

60 Gremillion (2003: 194–195).

61 Narrative-based therapy is also touched upon by Richard and Ann Treadgold, who used an approach which externalized and ultimately isolated the anorexic personality from Diana, their daughter. In blaming the anorexic identity, they were able to discuss the issues at play without isolating their daughter further. Over time, Diana took the same approach and by externalizing these destructive behaviours, she slowly recovered from her obsession with starving her body. For more information, see Treadgold, R., Treadgold, A., Treadgold, D. (2009) Rediscovering a Daughter. In: Malson, H., Burns, M. (eds.) *Critical Feminist Approaches to Eating Disorders*. London: Routledge, 233–245.

62 Gremillion (2003: 195).

63 Discussed in more detail in the following chapter and conclusion.

64 Glucklich (2001: 3).

65 Glucklich (2001: 6).

66 Fakir Mufasar quoted in Glucklich (2001: 31).

67 In turn, Glucklich takes the reader through several models of pain to demonstrate the varied nature of the pain experience. These models include juridical, medical, military, athletic, magical, psychotropic and ecstatic.
68 Glucklich (2001: 33).
69 Glucklich (2001: 33).
70 Glucklich (2001: 33).
71 Ego here should be understood as 'the conscious "steering mechanism" of the human organism' or the end goal of the individual (Glucklich 2001: 33–34).
72 Baxter points out that girls are 'four times more likely to self-harm than boys' and that, on the whole, 'woman and girls act out self-harm interiorly through eating or cutting behaviours' whilst boys may gravitate towards physical fighting with peers or family members in order to work out internal conflicts. Baxter, E. (2000) Cutting Edge: Witnessing Rites of Passage in a Therapeutic Community. In: Isherwood, L., Althaus-Reid, M. (eds.) *Controversies in Body Theology*. London: SCM Press, 48–70 (50–51).
73 Baxter (2000: 60, author's emphasis).
74 Baxter (2000: 51).
75 Baxter (2000: 57).
76 Baxter (2000: 61).
77 Baxter (2000: 62).
78 Baxter (2000: 64).
79 Garrett (1998: 54).
80 Garrett (1998: 54).
81 Garrett (1998: 54).
82 Orbach (1993: 88).
83 Orbach (1993: 90).
84 Orbach (1993: 91).
85 Steiner-Adair, C. (1990) New Maps of Development, New Models of Therapy: The Psychology of Women and the Treatment of Eating Disorders. In: Johnson, C. (ed.) *Psychodynamic Treatment of Anorexic Nervosa and Bulimia*. New York: Gilford Press, 225–245.
86 Garrett (1998: 53).
87 Garrett (1998: 53).
88 Garrett (1998: 53).
89 Garrett (1998: 122, author's emphasis).
90 Favaro, A., Ferrara, S., Santonastaso, P. (2004) Impulsive and Compulsive Self-Injurious Behaviour and Eating Disorders: An Epidemiological Study. In: Levitt, J. L., Sansone, R. A., Cohn, L. (eds.) *Self-Harm Behaviour and Eating Disorders: Dynamics, Assessment, and Treatment*. New York: Brunner-Routledge, 31–45 (31).
91 Favaro, Ferrara, Santonastaso (2004: 32).
92 Favaro, Ferrara, Santonastaso (2004: 32).
93 Favaro, Ferrara, Santonastaso (2004: 32).
94 Favaro, Ferrara, Santonastaso (2004: 32).
95 Bordo (1999: 99).
96 Working within the framework offered by Wolf.

5 The female body as a thealogically mediated form

All the work on society's contemporary construction of femininity and the inevitable rise of anorexia has led us here, to discussions surrounding thealogy and Goddess feminism. As such, within the following pages I will examine literature surrounding the development of thealogy and theorize on the idea that it is through thealogy and Goddess feminism that women can reconnect with their bodies and experience a greater sense of embodiment as women.

Taking on a broader meaning, I will demonstrate that thealogy has wider implications for contemporary society in its challenging of a singular male God, the sole creator of society as we know it today which, as we have seen, has (and continues to) legitimate the superiority of men and all things masculine. This has caused a fracture between women and their embodiment, the consequence of which, I argue, we see within the anorexic expression today.

Understood as a body of thought derived from women's experience and a broader history of emancipatory ideas and feminist reflections on the femaleness of divinity and the divinity of femaleness, thealogy can be broadly defined as 'discourse about the Goddess (or the logos of thea)'.[1] Thealogy exists in many guises for women and men and as such, the use of "the Goddess" has a multitude of meanings. For some "the Goddess" is more simply and abstractedly "Goddess", for others "the Goddess" or "Goddess" is too monotheistic and the polytheistic term "Goddesses" is favoured. For some she is a self-originating divinity, whilst others understand her as a 'liberating archetype whose power is psychological and political rather than external to and transcendent of the individual or movement'.[2] It is this element of the movement – the political and psychological aspects of Goddess feminism – that I am most interested in exploring considering the nature of this project. These motivations are most academically articulated within the discourse of thealogy, Goddess feminism and spiritual feminism (terms often used interchangeably). Existing on the margins of these discourses is Wicca, the witchcraft movement and those who identify as "witches". Broadly speaking, the Wicca and witchcraft movement 'sees itself as continuing the tradition of historical wise women down the ages who, in all societies, were healers and repositories of natural and spiritual wisdom'.[3] The Witchcraft movement focuses on the creation and performance of sacred rituals that work towards shaping and transforming energy and events into acts that benefit individuals and society. Emphasis here is placed on the female spiritual principle, into developing an intuitive wisdom and the reinforcement of the sacredness of nature and our environments. Whilst we will touch upon Wicca and the witchcraft movement later as we explore the work of Naomi Goldenberg and her conceptualization of powerful "witchy words", focus is on the discourse of thealogy and Goddess feminism as I fear the radical nature of Wicca does not allow for comfortable dissemination in society (and valuing the subversive nature of this movement, Goldenberg questions whether it should). I will argue that the broader concept of a female divinity as a political, challenging and thus subversive, myth has the potential to provide powerful psychological symbols for women that will more readily lend themselves to societal sharing.

The title of this chapter is something of a misnomer. As thealogy exists without parameters, a thealogically mediated body is quite simply a body that exists (and co-exists) alongside the rest of creation without a false sense of entitlement, without "power-over" but instead revelling in our interconnectedness and interdependence which in turn helps us to dismantle our dualistic heritage. My premise is that a society that legitimates a female divinity, in place of or alongside the male, will start to weave an alternative model of embodiment for the benefit of women within its boundaries.[4] In this chapter I will examine discussions surrounding thealogy and Goddess feminism as providing symbols, myths, traditions and rituals that invigorate and empower women. I will explore and contextualize contemporary studies and writings from a variety of sources and consider the idea that if the concepts central to Goddess feminism were incorporated into society even in small part, that women started to see their bodies as divine and valued in and of themselves, their experience of embodiment would change radically for the better. With that end in mind, drawing everything together, I break the following chapter into two sections. First, I examine the Goddess socially as I explore what She means to those who have incorporated thealogical discourses into their lives. Second, I will focus upon the Goddess as a powerful psychological symbol for women today as I make the argument that Her presence in society would displace the foundational features of anorexia whilst providing us with a framework for addressing the utilization of the anorexic expression by so many women today.

Thealogy and discourses on the Goddess

Emerging from liberation theologies and challenging what we already know of the poor position afforded to women within the Judeo-Christian tradition was thealogy, also known as Goddess feminism, which offered religious and spiritual women an opportunity to pursue alternative theologies and alternative religions. The central purpose of thealogy is the study of a female divinity. If the change of prefix *thea* (Goddess) for *theo* (God) is recognized, it is often assumed to be a mere political move by radical feminists in an attempt to draw attention to (and change) the androcentric nature of religious language and symbolism in favour of female sacrality. Melissa Raphael writes that 'Goddess feminism came into being by differentiating itself from the secular women's movement; thealogy came into being by distinguishing itself from feminist theology's attempt to reconfigure the God of Western theism in the light of women's experience and feminist theory'.[5] A central belief of Goddess feminism is the 'full humanity of women and the absolute value of all living things'.[6] Thealogy and Goddess feminism are, on the whole, made up of those individuals who identify and oppose 'patriarchal structures of religious and social power and whose religious practice is not only centred on the Goddess but also supports all women's right and access to the sacred and to autonomous religious self-expression and organization'.[7] The political dynamic of Goddess feminism marks it out from other parts of the Goddess movement as Goddess feminists strive towards the reinstatement of the Goddess as an affirmation and sign of the political and spiritual power of women, so whilst Goddess feminism is part of the Goddess movement, 'its political dynamic marks it out from other elements within the movement'.[8] In this spirit, drawing on the work of Raphael, thealogy is a 'historically and intrinsically feminist discourse and project – a prophetic attempt to name and reclaim female divinity and to use the power generated by that reclamation to the ends of the single process of personal/spiritual/political transformation'.[9] Politically, the movement is a challenge to patriarchal religious structures that support the control and subordination of women and as such, the term "female sacrality" has a close relationship with thealogical discourse and Goddess feminism in its understanding of the female body 'as a locus and medium of the sacred that informs the thealogy and practice of spiritual feminism'.[10]

Female sacrality and the Goddess are not fixed concepts owned by any one religion. They can be reflected upon within any religious framework,[11] but consideration must be given to the patriarchal structures that contribute to supporting the gendered status quo and reinforcing the inequalities of power, domination, ecological devastation and the marginalization of women both inside and outside of religion. Goddess feminism is not just about reading, studying and memorizing facts and ancient stories but is located in our experiences of the world in which we live. It respects not only written sources, but also 'oral, local, plural, particular, changing, imaginal ways of knowing that have more often been characterized as 'female''.[12] It may be experienced as monotheistic, pantheistic and polytheistic. Practice can take place on an individual level, as part of a community of like-minded practitioners in a variety of locations, at home, outside in the natural environment and/or at organized group events. Adherents to the Goddess Movement are unlikely to have a sanctified place of worship and instead favour non-constructed worship spaces making the Goddess assessable to all, allowing for flexibility and malleability as She can be incorporated into any number of settings to the benefit of those who subscribe to her symbolism. On an individual level, Goddess feminists can create their own personal altar or shrine reflecting their interpretation of divinity and the celebration of the divine elements they hold most dear. Alternatively, they can assess elements of the Goddess as a group, participating in the organization and enactment of ritual, as I will elaborate on in a few moments. Here women can cater for their own spiritual needs and structure their own spiritual development:

> [t]he Goddess is immanent in the natural environment and in women's own bodies; she does not need to be invoked and mediated in specifically sanctified places. In Goddess feminism, the female body is sacred; it incarnates the Goddess to such a degree that sacred space is simply that which the body's being there sacralizes. There is, therefore, no need of a formal boundary of brick or stone to separate the sacred from the profane.[13]

A question this raises is one of community. How do you have a community of people helping and participating in each other's lives – a support network – in what has been criticized as being an individualistic, apolitical and essentialist spirituality/religion?[14] It is also without a single founder revered for the movement's conception, a charismatic leadership hierarchy or notions of obedient authority (elements that may be lost if it is incorporated into other belief systems).[15]

As Raphael identifies above, immanentism is central to many Goddess feminist reflections on the Goddess and there are many ways that this immanence has been visualized. For example, focusing on the psychology of religion and spirituality, Goldenberg[16] proposes that we engage with our inner Goddess and mythologies and focus on the creation of personalized spiritualities whilst Starhawk[17] draws upon this immanence to reinforce our interconnectedness with our environments through which we are all divinely linked. These visions further challenge the mind/body dualisms so prominent within traditional Judeo-Christian theologies for they suggest that we are connected to divinity through the body and nature whilst also challenging traditional conceptions of transcendence which are typically associated with monotheism.[18] Transcendence is commonly criticized throughout thealogical texts due to its link with mind/body dualisms and its reinforcement of male superiority and the establishing of a divine hierarchy. It is thus suggested that an immanent earth-and-body-centred direction would be beneficial to human life on earth and would foster an interconnected reflection on nature and the life cycles which is at best overlooked by traditional theologies. However, the concept of immanentism has not been without its own criticisms. Josephine Robinson, for instance, writes that the removal of *theos* leaves a vacuum through the omission of God, the creator and instead creates a void which is filled by the study of self. Thus, Goddess feminists come to understand religious beliefs as metaphors of personal fulfilment, often with ethical overtones. In her work she seems to hint at proponents of thealogy being egotistic, self-involved and inward-looking above all else: 'most use the language of belief to reflect their pre-eminent concern with self'.[19] Robinson writes that to worship a fully immanent deity is to ultimately worship the "self" and "inner Goddess" where the "inner Goddess" becomes the personification of the imperial self. However, for many women, an immanent divinity participating in their lives is a radical statement that reinforces our interdependence and interconnection with all of humanity and the earth. As Starhawk writes:

> The Goddess is immanent, but She needs human help to realize Her fullest beauty. The harmonious balance of plant/animal/human/divine awareness is not automatic; it must constantly be renewed, and this is the true function of Craft rituals. Inner work, spiritual work, is most effective when it proceeds hand in hand with outer work.[20]

The important future purpose of thealogy and spiritual feminism is to 'generate new social and political realities'.[21] For many women and men, thealogy is a way of life grounded within the individual's experiences and relationships. These individuals might associate more with an imminent divinity than the transcendence of traditional theology. However, for many it is not a case of either/or. In the quest for dismantling mind/body dualisms, thealogians such as Christ understand the Goddess as immanent and transcendent writing:

> If there is no unchanging source or principle or God with which the mind or soul can ally itself, then there is no "transcendence" in the classical sense. This does not mean that there is only pure immediacy. There is still room for awareness of and reflection on self and world.[22]

She writes that mystical experiences happen within the finite and changing world when we are aware that we are part of a larger community, history and natural world which is more ineffable than ourselves and subject to change. For Christ the image of the Goddess is the 'catalyst that enables women to clear away the false consciousness of self-hatred, dependence, and dualistic thinking created by patriarchal religion'[23] and once this has been achieved 'the image of the Goddess is no longer necessary'.[24] Nelle Morton also challenges the polarity between transcendence and immanence writing:

> When I speak of the Goddess as metaphoric image I am in no way referring to an entity "out there" who appears miraculously as a fairy godmother and turns the pumpkin into a carriage. . . In the sense that

I am woman I see the Goddess in myself, but I need something tangible, a concrete image or a concrete event to capture my full attention and draw me into the metaphoric process'.[25]

For Morton the Goddess is a transitional figure that ushers in immanence. Here the 'Goddess works herself out of the picture'[26] and in so doing we have the opportunity to find our own path and way of life that connects us to our bodies, minds and spirits. She calls upon the connection between divinity and nature, writing that the Goddess as metaphoric image profoundly influenced her perspective on life and was necessary to sever her relationship with a masculine God within an androcentric religion. Working to displace patriarchal dualisms and reconcile the disjunction between our mind and bodies, she writes that the Goddess

> ushered in a reality that reflects the sacredness of my existence, that gives me self-esteem so I can perceive the universe and its people through my woman-self and not depend on the perception conditioned by patriarchal culture and patriarchal religion.[27]

For her the God of patriarchal religion is a dead metaphor after centuries of male "power-over" and status quo imagery. The Goddess instilled within her a new responsibility in the world, to work against oppression, discrimination, poverty and war whilst introducing her into a profound sense of community with other women dispelling the 'patriarchal fog'.[28] Drawing upon these themes, Starhawk suggests that understanding divinity as immanent and thus embodied, means that we live our spirituality through the world; that we are all manifestations of the sacred. This reinforces the idea that we are all interconnected and necessitates the development of a deep-seated ecological respect as we are drawn to 'take action to preserve the life of the earth, to live with integrity and responsibility'.[29] Goddess religion as lived in community demonstrates that the focus of this spirituality is not individual salvation or enlightenment but the growth and transformation that result because of intimate relationships and common struggles. Community here includes the earth, our friends and family in addition to global humanity.

These themes are also explored within the work of Susan Griffin and Alice Walker who experience the divine through passionate connection within sexuality and nature. Griffin weaves together her love for women with her love for nature referring to the earth as "she" and "my sister" in which the "she" being loved is understood simultaneously as mother, daughter, lover and earth. She calls for the breaking down of hierarchy as she urges us to remember our love for each other and the earth in this interconnected world. She writes:

> This earth is my sister; I love her daily grace, her silent daring and how loved I am how we admire this strength in each other, all that we have

> lost, all that we have suffered, all that we know: we are stunned by this beauty, and I do not forget: what she is to me what I am to her.[30]

In this work she evokes a deep connection between women and nature as she draws heavily upon the idea that life begins and ends in nature and that we are dependent upon this relationship throughout life. Walker, speaking through her character Shug, challenges the image of God as an old white man and instead refers to God as "It", and this "It" as being fully immanent and connected, 'inside you and inside everyone else. . . . I knew that if I cut a tree, my arm would bleed'.[31] Her relationship with divinity is located in love, compassion and connection.

In her extensive work on the Goddess, Christ distinguishes between three elements of the Goddess movement as follows: the Goddess as divine female existing in multiple cultural manifestations who can be invoked through prayer and ritual; the Goddess as a symbol of the cyclical nature of life representing life, death and rebirth as energy in culture and nature; and, the Goddess as an affirmation of 'the legitimacy and beauty of female power'.[32] The latter two points understand the Goddess as symbol as opposed to metaphysical reality. Understandings of divinity as embodied in a female form offer women a framework for self-discovery, affirmation and a connection to the divine which may be lacking for many women within Western religious traditions and is therefore helpful as we explore empowering symbols for women. As Christ elaborates:

> For me and for many others, finding the Goddess has felt like coming home to a vision of life that we had always known deeply within ourselves: that we are part of nature and that our destiny is to participate fully in the cycles of birth, death, and renewal that characterize life on this earth. We find in the Goddess a compelling image of female power, a vision of the deep connection of all beings in the web of life, and a call to create peace on earth.[33]

The Goddess for Christ is a powerful symbol of strength and unity. This conceptualization of the Goddess not only challenges the hierarchical philosophy of the Judeo-Christian tradition but provides women with a clear symbol of the sacredness of the female which reinforces its goodness, beauty and power whilst legitimating female power as independent and beneficent. She does not claim that female power is always good but reinforces the argument that 'independent female power is not always bad'.[34] The symbol of the Goddess means that female power does not need to be 'controlled or reined in by male power'.[35] She draws on the Goddess as a symbol that empowers women on personal and psychological levels to transform the institutions of culture. She writes that 'psychologically, it [the symbol of the Goddess] means the defeat of the view engendered by patriarchy that women's power is inferior and dangerous'.[36] Dispelling notions of the female body as a source of sin,[37] Christ calls us to see in the Goddess a symbol of the cycle of birth, death and rebirth and to reformulate our preconceptions of sexuality, birthing and menstruation as the central sources of this sin.[38] This image is invoked to counteract hostilities and religious taboos which have traditionally presided over the lives of women. Contextualized within current cultural misogynist trends, Christ states that the Goddess: 'calls us to transform the pornographic images of women so readily available on the internet and the advertising images of female bodies that lead women to attempt to redefine their bodies through anorexia, bulimia, and cosmetic surgery'.[39] She reinforces the message that a woman's will should be valued as much as any man's and that the bonds between mother and daughter, which have traditionally been less celebrated than that of the bond between father and son, should be celebrated and revered, that women no longer need to teach their daughters to accept subordination to men. The Goddess is raw and fierce and through Her symbolism we have the power to change the world. Reflecting on our dualistic heritage, Christ notes that it would be very tempting to turn the mind/body dualism on its head and move from devaluing women, the body, the earth and nature to devaluing the male, the spirit, rationality and the mind but for her this would be an inadequate solution. She writes that it is clear that men are just as much a part of nature as women are. Their bodies are subject to the same life cycles of birth and death as women, and they are also central to the process of procreation. Thus, what we need is not a reversal of dualist values but rather a transformation of the way we think about them and the way we think about divinity, humanity and nature. In this, Christ is not just reflecting upon the affirmation of femaleness and independent female power, but she is addressing more abstract theological questions about the nature of divine power.

Whilst the Goddess has had a profound effect on the lives of many women as a personal divinity, for some the value of the Goddess is as a psychologically meaningful mythology. This is the case for Goldenberg who writes that whilst she cannot be a witch in the orthodox sense, she does find the Goddess psychologically interesting. It appears to be in its discursive and deviant nature that thealogy and spiritual feminism can, for Goldenberg, challenge the patriarchal order for all that it occludes, namely the female. The time she spent with contemporary witches led to her belief that they use religion and ritual as psychological tools to build individual strengths in their practice of a religion that places 'divinity or supernatural power within the person'.[40] She writes: 'in a very practical sense they have turned religion into psychology'.[41] Goldenberg writes that witchcraft is the only Western religion that recognized female divinity in her own right arguing that the only remnant of a Goddess within the Christian tradition is Mary and she is solely recognized because of her son. She draws extensively on Jungian psychology in her work as she focuses on the psychological benefit of Wicca and female symbols of divinity.[42] Within the work of Goldenberg, the Goddess's value for women is as a psychologically powerful symbol for female empowerment today as we will explore in detail throughout the second half of this chapter.

Tension surrounding the incorporation of Goddess constructs into developing spiritualities surrounds issues of appropriation (Cynthia Eller refers to this as "cultural borrowing") and whether we are ethically bound to develop stories and mythologies from the cultures within which we were born or currently reside. The question posed is whether we can develop authentic stories when mining from such a broad range of traditions outside of their cultural settings. Here I refer to the incorporation of cultural and religious traditions from other continents, such as those found within Eastern, ancient Greek, Native American, and African religions into Western Goddess feminists developing personal spiritualities. Unpacking this further, Eller writes that the 'joy of feminist religions' syncretism is marred somewhat by the fact that when one borrows religiously, one is borrowing from someone (or some culture), and often without their permission'.[43] Linked with postcolonialism, this is the idea that one should not or cannot incorporate or translate elements of religious traditions from formally colonized people into their own spiritual frameworks, to think with or be inspired by. Whilst this has troubled spiritual feminists, it has not prevented the absorption of the myths, rituals and symbols of other continents into their personal spiritualities.

One of the most popular sources for feminist borrowing is the ancient traditions such as ancient African religions (for notions such as "spiritual kinship" and voodoo), Native American spirituality ("medicine woman" and "shaman"), Eastern religions (religion found east of Europe and South of Russia which includes, for example, Hinduism and Buddhism) and ancient Greek Goddess figures.[44] These ancient cultures, despite the patriarchy at their core, have provided a wealth of symbols, myths and rituals that have been incorporated into developing spiritual feminism in the West with the intention of transforming androcentric roots into avenues for female empowerment. For many women, elements of these religions and spiritualities are synonymous with growth, awareness, integration (of mind, body, nature and environment) which encourages the individual to pursue spiritual growth and development. It is predominantly the goddesses that receive the most attention from Goddess feminists despite the broad traditions from which these women are mining. Eller writes: 'in Eastern religions spiritual feminists discover the living remnants of what they believe was once a worldwide phenomenon of goddess worship',[45] that the East has retained the Goddess imagery that has been eroded by Western religion. Christ further extrapolates upon the relationship between spiritual feminists and ancient goddess symbols, writing that whilst the ancient Goddess symbols from around the world are nourishing for women constructing their spiritualities, that 'women's imagination is by no means subject to the authority of the past'.[46] Instead, many women select the elements of these traditions that most comfortably fit within their developing spiritualities. Even women who have no natural inclination towards the East have taken up an interest in its Goddess traditions.[47] However, as elements of these traditions are taken out of their geographical locations and relocated into different cultures, there is a risk here that the histories and societies that cultivated these Goddess figures will be lost and thus that these goddesses will lose their history, their context and symbolic power. On the other hand, in their dissemination into other cultures we have the power to overwrite the power dynamics that framed the development of the goddesses in these cultures. Here I refer to the misogynist heritage of many of these religions and spiritualities. This has been an area fraught with tension as we see within the work of Monica Sjoo and Barbara Mor, who write in *The Great Cosmic Mother*: 'The sexual misery and misogynists of Buddhism, practicing a secret and self-indulgence in the form of spiritual nihilism, leading to institutionalized sadism, neglect, and hatred of their fellow creatures, are very similar to the patriarchal monastic Christian world of the European Middle Ages'.[48] Here recognition is given to the patriarchal frameworks existing within these traditions from which the goddesses were created and to noting the uncomfortable discrepancy between the powerful goddess images of these cultures and their treatment of women. Very little escapes the overlay of patriarchal discourse. In the process of "cultural borrowing" themes are lovingly reproduced and retold as part of ritual, are avidly researched and artistic representations of female statues are widely available. These Goddess images (particularly European and Middle Eastern) play an important role in the reconstruction of Western history for women within their developing feminist spiritualities. Consideration however must be given to the ethics of this appropriation and whether it is ethical to pick and choose elements for our pleasure. For example, do spiritual outsiders have the right to incorporate the religious symbols and traditions indigenous to another group into their developing spiritualities without converting to the whole religion? Does selecting some elements whilst rejecting others violate the traditions from which these women are mining?

Those whose spirituality is developed within an understanding of Jungian psychology may feel that the appearance of goddesses from other cultures in their dreams or visions is as much owned by them as by those born within that particular continent.[49] Others may feel like they are reclaiming a female divine framework that has been eroded in the West by patriarchy.[50] From this perspective they are reclaiming their heritage as opposed to appropriating another culture's tradition. Alternatively, they could be seen as drawing upon elements of other traditions to argue the universality of existence and the drawing together of life. For other Western women these traditions may speak to them too powerfully to be ignored. As Rita Gross writes: 'as someone who has spent more years as a practicing Buddhist than following any Western ideology or religion',[51] the idea that it may be improper to incorporate elements into '[my practices] is a very strange claim indeed'.[52] She strongly argues that:

> One might as well claim that Africans, Chinese, or Indians should not adopt anything from Christianity or convert to Christianity because it is the religion of their former colonizers. In my own experience, I have usually observed this judgement coming from Westerners, not Asians, from people who know little about Asian religions, and from a certain kind of politically correct liberal who is trying to score political-academic capital against other scholars.[53]

Others (in respect of Native American traditions) may argue that residence in the continent permits their practice of these traditions despite not being born into them. It may be felt that as long as historical accuracy is respected, and rituals and contributions sympathetic to authentic representations are practiced, that participation of the global community is not only accepted but also encouraged. For example, Hallie Austen in *The Heart of the Goddess* writes that if you 'experience Spider Grandmother guiding you, work for Native Americans' rights to regain and keep their lands'.[54] Eller writes that in the most part

> spiritual feminists advise respect not in consideration to those they are borrowing from, but in a concern for the integrity of their own spiritual practice . . . that one may accidently invoke energies or powers that can't be readily controlled by the uninitiated.[55]

She also describes how a number of spiritual feminists seek to avoid the issue altogether by staying with the tradition that they feel is properly theirs whilst arguing that religions need to develop organically if they are to have authenticity, power and meaning. Zsuzsanna Budapest is a proponent of this perspective as she advocates the exploration of the rich traditions close to home, writing: 'We know more about Native American shamanism than our own. We have honorable spiritual roots, so let's reclaim them!'[56] It is clearly an area fraught with tensions with no right or wrong answer.

It is not just the issue of appropriation that causes fractures amongst Goddess feminists but questions surrounding a matriarchal prehistory. There are many Goddess adherents who believe that once patriarchal rule comes to its "end" (as is the cyclical nature of things), when the Goddess is celebrated once more, that in addition to the production of new values and new biophilic and egalitarian social order, that women's status will rise as female ecological generative energies will be liberated and once again celebrated. Reflecting on the Hebrew Scriptures, many Goddess feminists have maintained and reinforced the argument that Yahweh grew to power as a jealous God whose followers violently dismantled existing religious structures that focused on the worship of female divinities and their connection to nature.[57] Gradually, the annual holidays marking the seasonal cycles of "mother earth" were redefined in the context of male triumphs. Goldenberg writes that the 'Exodus story obscured tales of the goddesses and their festivals of spring. The winter solstice became identified with a military victory instead of with the birth of the child of the Goddess'.[58] As Christian symbolism became popular, Jesus replaced the sons and lovers of the Goddess and the complete female submission to male authority became the norm for women. Deities that once represented different facets of the Goddess were replaced with the Virgin Mary.[59] Goldenberg (as have many women within the Goddess movement) proposes that 'sexual politics have formed the traditional myths of Western culture'.[60]

For many Goddess feminists, Goddess worship is humanity's common religious heritage.[61] The supposition is that matrifocal or matristic (a term used to denote a non-authoritarian community that celebrates "female" characteristics and values) Goddess-worshipping cultures can be dated back to 30,000 BCE and various evidences indicate that this society understood divinity as a 'qualitatively different, pacific, egalitarian, spiritual power whose dynamics are always in harmony with those of nature'.[62] Proponents of this argument (Marija Gimbutas and Merlin Stone to name two) argue that 'in prehistoric and early historic periods of human development, religions existed in which people revered their supreme creator as female'.[63] Stone argued that historical evidence shows that Goddess worship and early Christianity existed simultaneously for thousands of years but female religion 'far from naturally fading away, was the victim of centuries of continual persecution and suppression by the advocates of the newer religions which held male deities as supreme'.[64] At this time, the creation myth of Adam and Eve took root within our collective consciousness and the divine hierarchy was established.

Debate surrounding the existence of a matriarchal heritage has historically been a highly contested area fraught with tensions and controversy not only with non-feminists but also within feminist thought and scholarship.[65] However discussions on the historical accuracy of a matriarchal prehistory are largely superfluous to my work here. The importance of a matriarchal prehistory *myth* is my focus as a mechanism for displacing social stereotypes and female damaging idealizations within the lives of women today. As Goldenberg argues, rather than focusing on a historical basis for contemporary Goddess traditions, we should be focusing on the power women are claiming today.[66] Drawing upon the work of Starhawk, Goldenberg writes:

> while the past may serve us with models and myths, we need not look to it to justify the re-emergence of the feminine principle. Whether or not women ever ruled in matriarchies, women are taking power today. Whether or not contemporary Witchcraft has its roots in the Stone Age, its branches reach into the future.[67]

For Starhawk, the importance of the past is how it is utilized in the present. She knows that her religion is based around hopes for power, influence, control and justice, as is the case for other religions. Knowing this, the power lies not only in the true fact of previous events but also in their power as myths or fictions to provide layers of additional meaning for life in the present and in the future. For Goldenberg, the importance lies not in the historical accuracy (as any matriarchal prehistory cannot be conclusively proven) but in its use in women's imagination as a drive towards fuelling political goals in the present.[68] Here we focus on the power of this matriarchal myth to heal. This is the belief that the *idea* of a matrifocal past can take women (and thealogy) a long way as we call upon conceptualizations of the past to improve the situation of women in the present,[69] arguing that utilizing a matriarchal prehistory in the form of an ancient myth of the superiority of the Goddess provides women with a higher place within social and religious structures of power. This provides new avenues for strengthening women's conceptualizations of self. Extrapolating on this, Goldenberg suggests that the image of the Goddess when merged with elements of psychoanalysis and object relations theory can provide empowering psychological frameworks for women today, as we will return to in a few moments.

For many Goddess feminists and those participating in the various Goddess movements, the symbol of a female divinity holds multiple meanings and opportunities for embodied living due to its diverse, informal and open nature. My purpose here was to provide an overview of how the Goddess has been incorporated into the lives of women, to demonstrate how She has been draw upon to empower women in society today. Not only does Goddess feminism provide the framework for dismantling the destructive discourses underpinning female disempowerment, but the concept of immanence locates divinity within the female body, promoting positive reflections on embodiment whilst its fluidity provides opportunities for multidisciplinary dialogue. At its heart, Goddess feminism is a malleable thealogy that allows for its central principles to operate in different shapes to form the most inclusive and adaptive space which is important as we explore new opportunities and new healing frameworks for female embodiment today.

Language and the construction of reality

Not only has religion played a central role in our conceptualizations of self, but the power of language and the influence it has on our reflections on embodiment and construction of identity, is highly significant. Language, culture and the human body are interconnected and the history of language as tied up in patriarchal power relations has been contentious for many women and men writing within feminist theory and thought.[70] It has been said that language 'partakes in the white-male-is-norm ideology and is used predominantly as a vehicle to circulate established power relations'.[71] As a consequence, many feminist critiques argue that '[l]anguage, for women, is not good enough'.[72] As a pervasive and deeply damaging model of communication for women and men, we are called upon to change it, to make it fitter for our use through challenging patriarchal hierarchies of power. Nowhere is this more evident than when reflecting on the revolutionary work of Mary Daly. From the very first pages of Daly's *Gyn/Ecology* we are transported into a world of spiralling Hags on intergalactic voyages, the challenging of patriarchal female constructs through "reversing the reversals" of words such as *Crone, Harpy, Fury, Glamour* (originally used to denote a spell cast by women[73] and now most commonly associated with Glamour magazines and female beauty idealizations) and redefining *Spinster* as a woman whose occupation is to spin (spinning here is used to denote the spinning of an alternative realm of existence that is as outward looking as it is inward looking). Part of this process of spinning is identifying and banishing the "ghostly gases" that have taken root in our psyches. Declaring her 'true course was and is Outercourse – moving beyond the imprisoning mental, physical, emotional, spiritual walls of the state of possession',[74] she writes that "God", "androgyny" and "homosexuality" are false words, that there is no way to remove male and masculine imagery from God which presented a problem for any woman within the Judeo-Christian tradition. Thus, she writes that 'when writing/speaking "anthropomorphically" of ultimate reality, of the divine spark of be-ing, I now choose to write/speak gynomorphically. I do so because *God* represents the necrophilia of patriarchy, whereas *Goddess* affirms the life loving be-ing of women and nature'.[75] Whilst remaining conscious that the term "Goddess" can be used to merely substitute the term "God", she gravitates towards the term as a woman-identified gendered shift away from masculine language (and divinity) and as an alternative to androgyny. Celebrating cerebral spinning, Daly describes her work as anti-academic (repelled by patriarchal institutions) but not anti-intellectual. Her redefining of language forces us to look again at the constraints and damage of language writing: 'deception is embedded in the very texture of the worlds we use, and here is where our exorcism can begin'.[76] She calls for us to become our own exorcists and expel the internalized Godhead from ourselves and our lives in His various manifestations. Daly's approach to patriarchal texts is best described as idiosyncratic as she subverts androcentric language and challenges existing beliefs about society and morality through utilizing symbols such as slashes and hyphens to draw attention to women's issues. Her textual web-spinning catches androcentric words and recreates the imagery they invoke as she re-reads, re-words and reverses the demonization of female sacrality. She writes:

> I unravelled reversals, finding the Archaic Origins of myths and symbols that had been stolen and twisted to serve the masters' purposes.[77]
>
> In order to reverse the reversals completely we must deal with the fact that patriarchal myths contain stolen mythic powers. They are something like distorting lenses through which we *can* see into the Background.

But it is necessary to break their codes in order to use them as viewers; that is, we must see their lie in order to see their truth.[78]

Her writing demonstrates how patriarchal constructions of female otherness have laid the groundwork for attributing certain stereotypes (irrationality and capricious emotionality) based on naturalistic justifications that have maintained the gender status quo. In light of this, Daly writes that the first step in reclaiming is Spiralling and Sparkling (the lighting of women's fire as a 'source and symbol of energy, of gynergy'[79]) as she urges us to start the voyage by examining all the various manifestations of 'Goddess murder on this patriarchal planet'[80] and the 'deep and universal intent to destroy the divine spark in women'.[81] She argues that we have to understand the deadly intent in order to start the process of exorcism. This is followed by the creation of a new place for women within space and time, the development of a new woman-identified environment through deep listening and speaking through experience. Here we start to move beyond the patriarchal mindset in recalling, reclaiming and remembering our witch's magical powers to bewitch and transform. This involves the weaving and crafting of new language and definitions as we are called to co-construct an alternative reality. This is not always about reversing everything valued in a patriarchal system, but searching anthropological data and the history of religions in search of female supernatural power, the power that has been alienated from women and turned sour by patriarchal discourse. This is a way of deconstructing the patriarchal construct of pseudo-feminism formulated at the inception of the Women's Movement, of welcoming back the 'real rebels/renegades [that] have been driven away from positions of patriarchally defined power, replaced by reformist and roboticised tokens'.[82] Her subversive uses of words dismantle the gendered boundaries that we have internalized whilst opening up opportunities for women and men to co-create and co-exist.[83] The Goddess within this framework is an enabling expression for reflecting on the sacred. Once the reader acclimatizes to her writing, Daly's work is wholly liberating in its open boundaries, re-creations and playful regenerations and restorations.

Employing the same subversive elements as Daly, Goldenberg draws on words such as "witch" and "Goddess" to demonstrate their power in challenging patriarchy by bringing to mind images and symbols that patriarchy has tried to eradicate. In *Witches and Words* she writes that witchy language challenges the 'performance of patriarchal grandiosity'.[84] Magically conjuring images of female carnality, deep emotion, vulnerability and the cyclical nature of the natural world she writes that they have the power to touch us deeply. Goldenberg is concerned that these benefits may be lost if the radical edge is softened by mass dissemination writing that in its marginality 'witchy words have teeth and claws'[85] making them orally aggressive whilst suggesting 'a determined hunger and a ravenous desire for survival'.[86] For her, this marks this movement as powerfully empowering for women. On the contrary Christ, whilst agreeing on the powerful and transforming benefit of the Goddess for women, writes that '[a]s long as 'Goddess' and 'God-She,' like the word 'feminist' are controversial, we still have a long way to go before we as a culture can fully accept female power as a beneficent and independent power'.[87] Through illustrating the importance between narrative, knowledge and power, she argued that the symbols and language used by religions and spiritualities have an enormous potency even for the individuals who are not directly affiliated with those belief systems. The consequence of this assertion is that until we have religions and spiritualities that use gender-neutral or humanity empowering symbols and language to reflect upon divinity, we will not experience full gender equality or develop a platform for the equal treatment of individuals regardless of race, sexual orientation, size, shape etc. She used the term "Goddess-talk" which refers to an explicitly female construction to express the sacred within her thealogy. This is a view shared by Jewish feminist theologian Judith Plaskow, who argues that we must learn to use the term "Goddess" instead of "God" when referring to divinity. She writes: 'The deep resistance called forth by her naming indicates that the needs she answered are still with us'.[88] However much Christian and Jewish practitioners and theologians reinforce that their God has no body, no gender, no age and no race, that God is neither female nor male, the argument is shattered as soon as the terms "Goddess" and "God the Mother" is proposed. Unconscious androcentrism runs deep throughout these traditional narratives. Christ refers to the "deformation of language" as a model of deconstruction when using terms from mystical traditions. She examines the creation of traditional language within a different context, one allowing for the subversion of the patriarchal social structures of consciousness that have kept women in subordinate positions. For example, in discussing the "nothingness" of women's experience, as discussed within Goddess mystical traditions, she calls attention to the 'powerful experience of finitude or limitation in which social structures and structures of consciousness which had provided meaning in a person's life are called into question and recognised as less than absolute'.[89] She argued that these experiences provide women with an opportunity to challenge and subvert patriarchal structures of power. This calls to mind the work of Judith Butler in Chapter 3 and the concept of re-citation as a platform for subverting gender narratives. Christ argues that we must continue to de-form language, deliberately changing its meaning and its context but this is an exercise fraught with tensions and danger. This new use of language could cause misunderstandings by those who are not versed in the new contexts and are instead soldered to old meanings. Despite this, Christ argues that we must broaden these understandings if we are to broaden the nature of language. Christ recognizes Morton as one of the central influences of her work on the reconfiguration of the symbols and language invoked to reflect on the nature of divinity.

Morton is commonly referred to as one of the fore-sisters of thealogy and Goddess feminism alongside Goldenberg and Christ (whilst Daly's work is of central importance to discourses on the Goddess in general, in her challenging of patriarchal structures of power, she is more of a spiritual feminist as she moves away from the Goddess and towards androcentric and gender-neutral terminologies). Arguably, she is most well known for her challenging of God language and the inception of Goddess-talk. Following her rejection of exclusively male imagery of divinity, she developed a deep-seated distrust of divinity as a transcendent male. For her, God is a redundant and dead symbol which has lost its redemptive power as a metaphor. Instead she turned towards language and symbolism of the Goddess as she explored the 'exorcizing and regenerative possibilities of Goddess-talk as metaphoric process, moving beyond any attempt to reify the divine'.[90] Morton understood Goddess-talk as a means of moving towards a meta-physical spirituality.[91] She saw the Goddess as setting in motion a metaphoric movement in which the Goddesses role was to 'make herself dispensable'.[92] She ultimately argued that Goddess religion would only result in a sex change of the head of the hierarchical structure if this metaphoric element was not recognized. In Goddess-talk we find a divine metaphor that is freeing and healing for women. It challenges God-talk and its refusal to use anything but male and masculine metaphors for divinity, seeking to broaden the parameters for inclusive gender narratives. In her chapter on *The Goddess as Metaphoric Image* she writes that understanding the Goddess as metaphoric image opens women up to women's spirituality in ways which were never conceivable or possible when working within the confines of "God the Father". It is through this that we can 'claim our bodies as ours and as ourselves and our minds as our own and ourselves'.[93] Recognizing the contentious nature of language, Marion Woodman prefers the use of music and dance as they transport her to a 'non personal dimension, a world that speaks directly to her heart, instead of her head, a world where she can experience wholeness and harmony'.[94] She writes that language can be dangerous for women because they tend to encase them in a realm of masculine ideas. She suggests that the medium of creative dance and music are more conducive to the creation of transformative rituals to bring 'consciousness into the forgotten muscles'.[95] We will explore this in more detail later in this chapter whilst exploring the use of ritual.

The ineffability of divinity will always present language difficulties, but these difficulties increase exponentially as '[w]omen are experiencing . . . in the area of spirituality that which the patriarchal language has no words to describe'.[96] Further complications overlaying the movement towards Goddess-talk and the use of female language to communicate the nature of divinity concern "Otherness" and the tensions of creating exclusions. For example, Christ has been criticized by Kathleen Sands for presenting a singular notion or ideal construct that refers to a singular experience. For her this fails to encapsulate the diverse experiences of women. Sands writes that

Christ 'still dreams of the oneness that has entranced Western rationalism'.[97] She is criticized for her lack of offering alternative models for divinity that can be invoked by individuals from different walks of life. Specifically, she has been criticized for excluding male images of God from her thealogy and thus simply reversing the status quo in favour of women. In so doing she avoids acknowledging the fact that male images of God need to be liberated too. She is still offering a singular image of divinity constructed by-and-large to cater for her individual needs. This would not be a problem if she was not offering a systematic thealogy within an academic context for Goddess studies. Having self-identified these criticisms, Christ clarifies that she is directly addressing the subordination of women in her work. Her work is concerned with affirming female power in the context of this patriarchal starting point and it must be recognized that she can only comment on the Goddess in relation to her own experiences and developments, which she identifies as such throughout her writing.

Another criticism of language as employed throughout literature on the Goddess surrounds the often-employed terminology of the Goddess in Trinitarian terms, the Goddess as maiden, mother, crone. Specifically, it is the notion of motherhood as intrinsic to female-hood that I argue is in need of deconstruction. For me this is the most controversial construct of the Goddess due to its potentially oppressive associations and limiting of the experiences of women alongside the clear exclusion of men. As described by Reid-Bowen, the Mother Goddess is: 'patterned upon biological and female capacities relating to pregnancy, birthing and breast feeding, behavioural norms associated with motherhood, such as care, nurture and support, and broader naturalistic forces or principles, such as fertility, generativity and growth'.[98] Thealogically, this model emphasizes that creation is contingent upon the female body and its presence and support in early life and as such, the model of the Goddess as mother 'is one that is felt by most Goddess feminists to present a better account of the acts and processes of creation and creativity than the patriarchal alternatives'.[99] Aside from the philosophical and metaphysical considerations (birthing of the world, universe, solar and planetary systems, tension between immanence and transcendence), there are broader consequences for the lives of women that may isolate rather than empower. The point I am addressing here is the implication that female-hood and motherhood are somehow mutually exclusive or synonymous. Despite the renewed emphasis within Goddess literature on the symbolic nature of the term (bodily realities of motherhood or childbirth[100]), it will always bring to mind associations surrounding procreation, the bringing of new life into the word. In so doing, it may obscure alternative sexual practices (such as lesbianism) and the reality of single women. It also renders motherhood the "norm" and thus excludes those women who are, by biology, unable to procreate, or who simple do not wish to have children. Pregnancy and birth are not the only forms of creativity available to women. Thealogy and Goddess feminism should remain fluid and understood in terms that make it relatable for changing audiences. For me, deconstructing this vision of the Goddess would be a step towards making Her more inclusive. I do not propose an exchange of terms, as transgressing these boundaries, on this broad scale, is a problematic task. I propose that for now we leave the Goddess of maiden, mother, crone behind us and take up Goldenberg's calling to create our own symbolisms that relate to our lived experiences.[101]

Language also presents difficulties when it comes to discussions surrounding the term "Goddess". As we touched upon in the chapter's introduction, Goddess feminists employ a varying range of terms such as "the Goddess", "Goddess", "Goddesses" or even "female/feminine divine" or "sacred feminine" unless the decision is made to opt for androgynous or monistic understandings of divine representations in lieu of anthropomorphic approaches to divinity as female or male. Contention also surrounds the classification of Goddess feminism as "spirituality" or "religion", as the movement towards a female divinity caused academics and practitioners to question the nature of the language used to describe their growing discord with the androcentric nature of the term "religion". Thus, for some adherents and writers of Goddess feminism (such as Goldenberg) "spirituality" is preferred as it is understood as an ecological, gynocentric and "radical" term in comparison to "religion" which indicates a reformation of patriarchal religions as opposed to the re-creations, re-births and matriarchal restorations that many Goddess feminists envision. Goldenberg argued that the creation of feminist spiritualities would spark the end of transcendent and patriarchal religion either by eroding them completely or by transforming them until they are unrecognizable.[102] This rings true for Daly who felt that movement away from the term "religion" reflected a movement from the Judeo-Christian tradition that is understood as irredeemably patriarchal, that "religion" is a highly 'ambivalent term connoting all the dogmatic, expansionist and authoritarian characteristics of institutionalized patriarchal religion'.[103] However, to some adherents, Goddess feminism is the only form of authentic religion and they would seek to distance themselves from the classification of the Goddess movement solely as spirituality. This is the case for Starhawk and Z. Budapest who both write about their Goddess traditions in the context of a religion although spirituality plays a central part in their religious visions. Extrapolating on Goddess and spiritual feminism as a religion, Raphael writes that whilst they are non-centralized, non-dogmatic and have no recognized and formal cannon of sacred texts, they have most of the other ingredients necessary to use the term religion. For example, even in the informal and non-authoritarian form, Goddess feminism has a sacred history, cosmology, ontology, thealogy, ethics, priestesses, favoured texts and rituals. Together, these elements become a means by which women can collectively re-call elements of their embodiment that have become distanced throughout life within patriarchal institutions. As mentioned earlier in my book, I am wary of the term religion because of its patriarchal heritage.

I favour the term spirituality[104] within which to encase my developing work although I appreciate that this is also fraught with tensions.[105]

For Goddess feminism, challenging our patriarchal heritage is a core agenda, a point solidified in our discussions surrounding God and Goddess-talk within this section of the chapter. The language used to discuss the nature of divinity will always be a contentious issue. Whether we work with Daly to "reverse the reversals", invoke Goldenberg's "witchy words" to challenge and subvert patriarchal structures of power, employing Christ's focus on dispelling damaging and destructive stereotypical notions of the Goddess to allow for mainstream application or utilizing Morton's Goddess symbolism as metaphorical, language will always present us with difficulties and limitations. I engage in discussions surrounding the nature of language to demonstrate the scope of patriarchal power and to draw attention to activities that draw upon alternative expressions as we work towards embodied reflections.

So far in this chapter, we have examined what may be described as some foundational features of Goddess feminism as we explored the Goddess as immanent, how the Goddess has been incorporated into individual thealogies, issues surrounding appropriation, the use of a prehistoric matriarchal myth to heal and the problematic nature of the language we use daily. My purpose in plotting these features is to demonstrate how the qualities central to this movement have the potential, when endowed with enough power, to disrupt the disembodiment at the heart of the anorexic expression and by extension, the slender performance. Here we are starting to establish the parameters of a thealogically mediated body whilst addressing the subjective nature of these terms and how they are shaped by personal interpretation, moods, motivations and desires. How this plays out alongside what we know of the anorexic expression and the construction of transformative ritual will be discussed now as we explore the Goddess as a psychologically valuable symbol.

The Goddess as a symbol of psychological strength

As we explored in Chapter 3, a central theme in the work of Goldenberg is her passionate desire to put us in touch with our bodies. To do so she employs the use of psychoanalysis, which she defines as 'talk that works through the body'.[106] She writes: 'I realised that what psychoanalysis was offering me was a connection with emotions and personal history'.[107] In examining the Goddess movement from the perspective of psychoanalytic theory she considers how analytic thought can be used to understand the Goddess, and it is here that we see the commonalities between discourses on the Goddess and psychoanalysis. In drawing upon her work on the harmonies between these two areas of thought, I will demonstrate the psychological benefit of the symbolism inherent to Goddess feminism and how this can be applied to the anorexic expression within contemporary society through ritual. My emphasis on the importance of ritual will be explored in the next section of this chapter. I employ the use of ritual as a new and developing consciousness that underpins daily activities which, when informed by a female empowering divine construct, becomes transformative. In the remainder of this chapter there are three features of this transformative practice that I will flesh out. At the heart of this developing consciousness is active (as anorexia has shown itself to be a passive expression in its compulsive regurgitation of the discourses underpinning its construction) reflections on embodiment, a questioning of the patriarchal discourses that underpin anorexia's manifestation, and an engagement in the creation of ritual and individually meaningful myth to inspire healing and liberation from these constraints. Before addressing these features further, an examination of the commonalities between Goddess feminism and psychoanalysis is valuable.

Goldenberg identifies four key commonalities between the Goddess movement and psychoanalytic theory in the form of objects relations theory. These are as follows: they both focus on the past as an important source of meaning; they both work towards the deconstruction of the central images of patriarchal authority; importance is placed on describing the individual as formed within the context of a community; and, they both recognize fantasy as a key structure of "rational" thought. Drawing upon object relations theory[108] and the importance it places on the reflection of past experiences (infancy and early childhood), Goldenberg writes that central to both philosophies and the individuals participating in the activity is 'a sense of connection to the past [which] is cultivated for the purpose of heightening involvement in the present'.[109] She writes that object relations theory arguably places an even greater value on the redemptive value of connection to the past than does Goddess feminism, writing that '[a]ll analytic theory aims at learning to see more about the past in the psychological structures of the present'.[110] That no event is ever seen as fully determined by present circumstances or by motives for a future end: '[i]n analysis, the present is largely a *fiction* of the past. The present is a formation or a construction of the past in the sense of the Latin root of the word "fiction" (*fingere*), meaning "to form"'.[111] Focusing on reflection of the individuals personal past, where emphasis is placed on the early relationship between the infant and mother and how presence and absence structures the infant's development, object relations theory departs from classical analytic theory by replacing the father figure with the mother, and thus places a woman at the centre of the universe whilst championing a shift from a focus on male symbols to a focus on female ones (a movement away from the sexism inherent within the work of Jung and Freud's keen interest on the father and symbol of the phallus). Turning our attention to Goddess feminism, as we have just explored, a connection to the past has been employed to legitimize contemporary women's experience in the form of a matriarchal prehistory. This may be referred to as Goddess mythology or the divine women's myth and relates to the idea that at some point in history women played a central role in the religious and social organization of human environments. Goldenberg writes that this myth can 'provide women with a compendium of female passions and sensibilities . . . [as they] are used to call attention to the complexity of female experience and to dignify that experience by revealing its ancient roots'.[112] They can therefore be understood as sources of information that confer meaning on the present by drawing on ancient stories relating to the inception of culture. Here we are drawing upon a repressed female heritage that celebrated female virtues. As we explored earlier in this chapter, Goldenberg draws upon this matriarchal prehistory, not to labour any historical accuracy but as a psychologically and politically beneficial tool for women in the present and future advocating that we focus on the benefit this image has on our psyche instead of matriarchal prehistory as historic fact. For example, rituals marking the progression of time (in celebrating seasonal changes and astrological movements) alongside the use of stories and Goddess symbolism, connect the present with the past and thus acquaint women with a deep background to underpin psychological development and locate their embodiment providing levels of meaning (I am drawing upon the terms "meaning" and "meaningful" as laid out in Chapter 3) that I have argued are absent for many women in contemporary society. This disconnection of women from a source of female wisdom was also a reoccurring theme within the work of Woodman in Chapter 3. As we explored earlier, she argues that living in a patriarchy strips from women a deep-seated female divine connection and thus, an inner core of certainty and a deep source of meaning, the manifestation of which is the development of somatic maladies such as anorexia and obesity (the latter is the focus of her work). The female in this environment is devalued in favour of masculine attributes and as a consequence, women struggle to emulate a socially acceptable model of existence whilst fostering and maintaining female empowering roots. This discomfort, even when it is not consciously acknowledged, expresses itself somatically through the body. Elaborating further on the second and third commonality, both Goddess feminism and object relations theory focus on the symbolism of the mother as a tool for displacing images of patriarchal authority and as a means of drawing people together.[113] Goldenberg argues that as every single human life begins in the body of a woman, our earliest experiences are of connectedness and interdependence, writing:

> I suggest that the mutual concern of psychoanalysis and thealogy with articulating the context of human life arises because both philosophies centre around the image of a powerful women in the past. Since every human life begins in the body of a woman, the image of women, whether thought of as mother or as Goddess, always points to an early history of connectedness. Mother-*mater*-matter-matrix.[114]

Object relations theory however limits its application of the female role to the mother and the mother-infant relationship whilst Goddess feminism extends the image to divinity and the planet as a whole.[115] In so doing, it broadens the psychological potential for a healing paradigm of female symbolism whilst working towards the erosion of male authoritarianism in Western culture. Taking these together we have a Goddess feminist framework whereby the individual woman would have access to a deep-seated female imagination that would contribute towards the subversion of patriarchal rhetoric. Taking this deconstruction of male symbols out into the world, we challenge the patriarchal power relations that underpin the anorexic construction and engage in the co-creation of embodied and contextualized Western thought.

Taking this further, I argue that this needs to be incorporated into society. This is where I depart from the work of Goldenberg as she resists the translation of this challenging on a mass scale as she fears that Goddess feminism would lose its radical edge in mass adoption. Framing her subversive psychology within what she understands to be most subversive form of thealogical thinking – that of witchcraft – she employs the terminology of "witches" and "wicca" for their deviance and power as deconstructive tools. She is drawn towards discourses on the Goddess, and in particular the application of witchcraft, because 'it is rife with magical discourse that encourages us to play with fire'.[116] For her, one of the central features of witchcraft has been its use in deconstructing traditional religious thought through the celebration of women and nature. It is through this that the mainstream religious monopoly on life has been challenged and tested. However, she is reserved about the development of academic thealogical discourse that may contribute towards the domestication of the Goddess and the witch worrying that the subversive nature would be lost through universal application. Whilst her work focuses on the radical nature of the symbolism of the witch and the subversive and challenging nature of "witchy words", I argue it is within the symbol of the Goddess that we really make advancements to challenge the patriarchal social structures within which we live. I am referring to societal dissemination through normalizing the Goddess symbol in society. Once we take Her image for granted, once referring to Her no longer raises eyebrows, shocks or surprises people, then I believe we will be closer to really disrupting the patriarchal discourses that underpin the anorexic expression. As Christ argues, as long as the "Goddess" and "God-She" are controversial, we still have a long way to go before society can accept female power as divine.[117] I take heed of Goldenberg's worries that attending to the Goddess will result in 'another of the same'[118] as a 'variant of standard theological ideologies regarding an exalted deity'.[119] However, based on my readings on the Goddess as reflected upon within the work of this chapter, I believe this to be unlikely. The core foundation of thealogical thought is profoundly different from the world view and social structures that contributed to female disembodiment at the hands of the Judeo-Christian traditions, as we have touched upon throughout this work. For example, thealogy and Goddess feminism sees life as a process rather than a system of various hierarchies whilst placing female experience central to its vision of life. I remain fervently with the Goddess as it is within Her symbolism and thealogy that I see more potential for societal dissemination. For me, this is of central importance as we address the anorexic expression and theorize on alternative subversive strategies. Through exploring the commonalities between psychoanalysis and Goddess feminism we have seen the joint respect for the female condition in society. This is clearly evident within the discourse of thealogy as the central focus is on female experience and a female divinity. A questioning of patriarchal power is endemic to thealogical explorations. Goldenberg writes that both 'the facts and the fantasies of the Goddess movement function to crack the edifice of patriarchy by encouraging the emergence of suppressed patterns of language, visions, dreams, and theories'.[120] Through raising suspicion that male institutions are not all they seem, they are not infallible, Goddess ideology loosens the grip masculine symbols have on their contemporary audiences. Up to now we have addressed commonality points one and two whilst shining some light on how this literature is located alongside what we know of the construction of anorexia. Turning our attention to the third commonality, the individual as formed in the context of community, we see the importance that both object relations theory and Goddess feminism places on connection and interdependence as individualism and self-determination are set aside.

Both models of thought teach that people are created in large part by their relationships. For object relations theory, focus is on the reliance a baby or young child has for at least one adult. A baby cannot survive as a solitary being. This state translates to adulthood as humans rely upon relations with people past and present as Joan Riviere writes:

> There is no such thing as a single human being, pure and simple, unmixed with other human beings. Each personality is a world in himself, a company of many. That self, that life of one's own . . . is a composite structure which has been and is being formed and built up since the day of our birth out of countless never-ending influences and exchanges between ourselves and others.[121]

Whilst emphasis is placed on the adult human in the context of community, focus is usually applied to the infant's immediate human environment. Feminist theory is more concerned with the larger social conditions that inform human living as we have touched upon throughout this body of work. In a similar fashion, Goddess theory is concerned with expanding awareness of conditions that underpin life in society. The idea that we are all part of a larger web-of-life, which includes the whole of nature, is central to the Goddess imagination and finds its origins within ancient pagan perceptions. Human life is reflected upon in the context of the elements of the world in which we live. Importance is placed on the state of the water, air and soil that surrounds us and maintains our life. The earth is conceptualized as part of the Goddess and is thus sacred. Everything is spiritual and nothing is profane. The mutual concern of both theories with articulating the context of human life, as drawn upon throughout this work, arises from female imagery. The whole earth is conceptualized as the body of the Goddess and is therefore sacred. This fosters respect and reverence for life in all its forms. Neither promises a utopian and radically different future (although, as we have seen, Goddess feminism has been criticized for romanticizing the Goddess and a prehistoric matriarchal past). For both discourses there is

> no redemption expected to come in the form of a saviour, or as a promise land, or from the benefits of scientific progress. For both thealogy and psychoanalysis, there is only the rather modest hope of improving life through reflection on the past.[122]

A common goal is to make the world a better place through displacing the father figure from dominance in the symbolic order.

As we turn our attention to the fourth commonality, fantasy as a key structure of "rational" thought, we return again to the contents of Chapter 3 and discussion surrounding the creation of myth and fantasy as I draw on the elements that will contribute towards dismantling the anorexic expression. Addressing discussions surrounding fantasy as central to "rational" thought, one aspect of the human context upon which many Goddess feminists and object relations analysts agree is fantasy. Namely, the recognition that fantasy, or wish constitutes the 'primary matrix for all mental processes'.[123] Fantasy or the act of wishing within witchcraft pervades almost every practice because 'it teaches women to use spells and rituals to express their hopes, ambitions, and desires'.[124] I would extend that beyond the boundaries of witchcraft as wishful thinking and the concept of sending positive, creative and loving energy into the world permeates much literature on Goddess feminism and therefore, makes it relevant for discussions within this body of work. Fantasy here is valuable in its ability to focus the mind and to mobilize willpower. The basic premise is that a goal that can be visualized in detail is more likely to be realized. They therefore concentrate on representing these goals or wishes symbolically in the form of physical objects (such as talismans or amulets) or in the movement, meditation or incantations of ritual work. Here, the idea of a matriarchal prehistory is put forward as a wish about history, expressing the desire for it to be realized in the present and the future. Quoting Monique Wittig from *Les Guerilleres*, Goldenberg writes: 'There was a time when you were not a slave, remember. Try hard to remember. Or, failing that, invent'.[125] The recognition of a matriarchal heritage is a concept that empowers the situation of women in the present especially as more and more women engage with its fantasies. Research into a matriarchal past is motivated by the desire to improve life today as we have already explored. In this quotation Wittig demonstrates that an invented past can substitute for a remembered one, and why not? After all, as Goldenberg reminds us, 'faith is simply a very strong wish'.[126] A reoccurring theme within thealogical literature is the idea that the importance of the past lies in how it informs the present as we explored earlier in discussions surrounding matriarchal prehistory. Object relations theorists share the conviction that fantasy and wish are central to human creativity and form the foundation of all thinking. What is felt to be real in the fantasy and "inner" life is understood to inform and influence actions in the "outer" or external world. The exploration of the individual's unconscious fantasy is used to explore character structure, creativity and ambition as life is based around these internal features. Whilst both object relations theory, as understood within the context of Goldenberg's work, and Goddess feminism understand the external human world as the consequence of internal fantasy, there is disagreement surrounding our ability to change these projections through willpower. Goldenberg writes that to an object relations analyst, the structure of an individual's fantasy life is established during infancy and early childhood. A person's attitude, "inner" life and fantasies are greatly influenced by their early environment and by the caregivers who shaped that environment. Thus, a small change to the expression of fantasy is only possible if something, like analysis, effects a change in psychic dynamics as it is too much the consequence of personal history to be changed by willpower, the use of spells and ritual alone.

Goldenberg writes that as important fictions, religion creates the framework for our lives. Thus, a connection to a deep past, in the form of an individual connection to this divine women's myth, whilst critically analyzing and engaging with early experiences and the effect they had on the individuals present conceptualization of self, I argue, can help women trapped by the anorexic expression to construct a meaningful framework for what appears to be an empty and fraught present circumstance based on an empty model of embodiment. This is where we can co-construct myth, fantasy (as psychological frameworks) and rituals (as we will go on to discuss in the next pages) to connect us to different parts of our physical and developmental history that are grounded within a connection to a female divine construct. Thus, in the identification of ties between the past and the present, we can take part in the creation of layers of additional meaning for life today. Within this understanding of object relations theory, the past is never surmounted, just lived out in different ways in the present. Understanding this, whilst utilizing it to draw upon a matriarchal myth, may aid in the creation of new, female-empowering models of therapeutic healing. For example, in the context of the female utilization of the anorexic expression, a female-empowering matriarchal myth, regardless of the culture that inspired its creation, may be employed to disable the patriarchal currents underpinning the anorexic expression and illuminate the path towards embodying reflections of the myriad manifestations of the female form. I argue that mass reflection on the Goddess would permeate society and slowly erode the disembodiment at the heart of the development of anorexia in its providing of a psychologically healing framework for women today and challenging of patriarchal discourse. Here we are discussing a female deep past to act as a foundation for a developing consciousness located outside the boundaries of patriarchal society or at least providing a forum for pushing against these boundaries.

Goldenberg's aim in offering an analysis between psychoanalysis and Goddess feminism is to provide new avenues for female embodiment and power through labouring the importance of a divine female heritage through myth, within which we are all connected in the web-of-life – the foundation of which is political as she seeks to disrupt patriarchal power and challenge male supremacy. My focus in this work, for the deconstruction of the anorexic expression, is to call upon the psychological benefit of a matriarchal prehistory. The benefit I see here for the anorexic expression lies in the ties it creates between women and a powerful female heritage as we locate female embodiment as part of a female celebrating and positive past. Here we invoke the Goddess as a relatable and powerfully embodied female symbol within a conceptualization of the connectedness of life. I draw upon the work of Goldenberg and the four commonalities between these two models of thought to demonstrate the potential of Goddess feminism within a therapeutic context for dismantling the anorexic expression today. This is all put into practice through the use of ritual and its potential to address the compulsive behaviours at the heart of this expression as we will explore now.

Ritual

As anorexic behaviour is ritualistic and formulaic in nature,[127] displacing its enactment through creative engagement in alternative ritual construction is central to displacing the power it holds over the individual. Here we will explore the construction of life-enhancing ritual practices and how they have been incorporated into the developing spiritualities of many women today.

Broadly speaking, ritual, within a Goddess feminist context can be understood as 'a patterned movement of energy to accomplish purpose'.[128] Rituals are part of every culture. They bind a community together, creating a heart, a centre for people. Rituals invoke the "deep self" of a group as, through participation in ritual, participants are familiar with each other's presences and joined in a common goal. Starhawk writes that the pattern of the movement of energy in a Craft ritual takes place within a very simple structure that usually has a pre-defined beginning, middle and end, beginning with grounding and connecting to the earth (through meditation), followed by a cleansing (symbolically or physically through the use of water) with a focus on releasing pain and tensions through movement and/or sound. Following these acts (and sometimes before) is the "casting" of the circle, an act of 'separating the ritual space and time from ordinary space and time, as we invoke four elements [earth, air, fire and water]. We invoke the Goddess and the God, and whatever other powers or presences we wish to greet'.[129] Power and energy is raised through group breathing, chanting, meditation and dancing whilst reflecting on individual or group images, actions or symbols. This trance-like state adds an "otherworldly" element to the ritual whilst establishing energy boundaries and protecting the individuals in the creation of this safe space. Here female power and healing energy is focused on addressing group and world concerns.[130] The flexibility of rituals allow for myriad applications. Rituals can be carried out at home, in nature or a place of special importance as determined by the individual or group/groups participating. They can take place at an established time and in a structured format or as a consciousness underpinning everyday activities.[131] Even when participants do not identify as witches, Goddess feminists subscribe to forms of magical thinking and make no absolute distinction between elements of transformation and renewal created by ritual and political action. Emphasis on the interdependence of life on earth is a common theme within ritual as employed by Goddess feminism, as Goldenberg writes: 'observing major and minor sabbaths tied to the four seasons and to the two solstices and equinoxes keeps alive a sense of connection to nature's recurring pattern of change'[132] whilst attention to the phases of the moon links us as humanity, to the monthly cycle of repetition that takes place around us on a planetary level.[133] In so doing, the participants are explicitly linked to the timelessness of seasonal and astrological movements, a powerful symbolic to underpin our actions in contemporary life. Ritual can be an act of reconnection and healing which demands the participants to consciously engage in concepts of empowerment and embodiment in the raising of energy through chanting, music and body movements.

For example, in *Daughters of the Goddess* Ruth Barrett writes about the transformative potential of ritual. She writes, that women who participate in the larger gatherings experience more concentrated feelings using words such as "life-enhancing" and "transforming" to describe their experiences. This may result as a consequence of the ritual organization as facilitators engage in 'careful, purposeful development of the ritual',[134] as a consequence of the mindfulness and mixing energies of a larger number of participants (the energy raised is greater than the numerical number of participants)[135] or the expectation attendants hold of being emotionally or physically moved. Barrett writes that the structure of the ritual can vary significantly depending on its focus, allowing for optimum creativity. She works with groups to help identify the themes and purpose they want to embed within their ritual development.[136] In this context, ritual is embodied creation of energy focused on the participants' purification, self-blessing and consecration as working towards altering 'everyday consciousness and access[ing] the magical mind'.[137]

Ritual practices can be enacted and reflected upon by women and men at joint or same sex gatherings and within any religious or spiritual tradition. Jan Berry, for example, writes about her use of ritual at times of personal distress such as her resignation from the Baptist ministry due to The Baptist Union's condemnation of gay sexuality. This ritual was 'an attempt to mark an important transition in [her] . . . life; to resist the sense of vulnerability and oppression, and to claim [her] . . . own freedom and choice in leaving'.[138] Although this was enacted in a Christian context, it demonstrates the nature of a ritual's application. Rituals can be used to mark the ending of a job, to bless a relationship, to bless a house, and the closure of a difficult or damaging period in the individual's life. They can also celebrate the seasonal cycles or themes such as loss, remembrance, desire, death and rebirth. Due to the broad application, the creation and participation can be as diverse and as broad as the individual's imagination. Berry writes that ritual 'provides a framework in which powerful emotions can be confronted and expressed'[139] allowing the individual to 'enter a space beyond words, where symbols, bodily movement, and symbolic action are the vehicles of meaning'.[140] This is where I would like to introduce ritual as an approach for deconstructing both the anorexic expression and, by extension, the slender performance. For me, as we work towards a Spirituality of Anorexia as a spiritual quest towards consciousness and reconnection, it is clear to see how ritual, in collaboration with the work of Goldenberg on the creation of myth and the use of the commonalities between Goddess feminism and object relations theory, can provide powerful resources for the deconstruction of the damaging undercurrents of the anorexic expression, and the slender performance.

There is much ritualization surrounding the life of women living out the anorexic expression and the most obvious example of this can be found within the individual's treatment of food. As we have already explored, the anorexic woman's relationship with food is fraught with tensions. Her mind is endlessly engaged in food-related thoughts. She is constantly occupied in measuring and weighing-up what she can and cannot have as she increasingly revises down the quantities and types of food she is "allowed" to consume. She is engaged in a constant obsession about the calorie contents of various foods, recipes and cooking. Some of her involvement with food is channelled into the preparation of meals for family and friends as she takes time shopping, researching recipes, cooking and discussing with them food options, dinner party menus and new restaurants despite significantly restricting her own consumption. There is a striking dichotomy here as she publically exhibits a keen – bordering on obsessive – interest in food, whilst privately and meticulously planning, down to the last calorie, what she is permitted to consume. In feeding family and friends her desire for food is projected onto others as she provides for them what she actually craves for herself. At first, the food she denies and the rituals she creates are based on conventional nutritional information for the reduction of weight. This might be expressed through engaging in the latest diets or starting to cut out known "bad" foods. Slowly she introduces new rules and regulations into this ritualized behaviour as she sets herself a series of tasks that need to be undertaken prior to, during and following the process of food consumption. A clear example of this ritualized behaviour can be found within the autobiography of Portia de Rossi in this candid reflection:

> It's time to face last night. It was yogurt night, when I get my yogurt ready for the week. It's a dangerous night because there's always a chance of disaster when I allow myself to handle a lot of food at one time. But I had no indication that I was going to be in danger. I had eaten my 60-calorie portion of tuna normally, using chopsticks and allowing each bite of canned fish to be only the height and width of the tips of the chopsticks themselves. After dinner, I smoked cigarettes to allow myself the time I needed to digest the tuna properly and to feel the satisfaction of fullness. I went to the kitchen feeling no anxiety as I took out the tools I needed to perform the weekly operation: the kitchen scale, eight small plastic containers, one blue mixing bowl, Splenda, my measuring spoon, and my fork. I took the plain yogurt out of the fridge and, using the kitchen scale, divided it among the plastic containers adding one half teaspoon of Splenda to each portion . . . hid the containers in the . . . freezer. . . . I knew that the thirty minutes it takes for the yogurt to reach the perfect consistency . . . wasn't up, and that checking on it was an abnormality, but that's exactly what I did.[141]

This excerpt demonstrates some of the weekly and daily rituals constructed by the individual for the purpose of controlling the process of food consumption. Rossi describes the inner turmoil that proceeded the weekly portioning of the yogurt. She sat, smoking four cigarettes, facing the freezer – '[s]taring at the door was the only way I could be certain that I wasn't opening it'[142] – trying to take away the urge for the 'icy-cold sweetness'.[143] Deviation from the routine is dangerous: it

> created an opening that invited in the thoughts I'm most afraid of – thoughts created by an evil force disguising it-self as logic, poised to manipulate me with common sense. *Reward yourself. You ate nothing at lunch. . . . It's only yogurt. Do it. You deserve it.*[144]

Breaking the crust of each icy serving, she consumed the entire week's worth of yogurt portions. She writes about being in a trancelike state as her fingers travelled back and forth from the container to her mouth, the repetition of which 'lulled the relentless chatter into quiet meditation'.[145] The following part of her book meticulously details the next morning's gruelling exercise regime. This is representative of many memoirs reflecting on the experience of anorexia and the ritualization of eating. The rituals and regulations that come to circumscribe her food intake increase in number until it becomes impossible for her to envision eating in a spontaneous way. She is engaged in a labyrinth of restrictive practices that prevent her from consuming the food her body so desperately needs. Eventually her will power slips, as is evidenced within the work of Rossi, and punishments, self-loathing and depression set in. The use of ritual in deconstructing the anorexic expression must address the compulsive ritualization as expressed here. We will explore this in practice in a few moments.

The use of ritual within therapeutic settings is common especially for addressing the mental health of patients but focus is rarely placed on the symbolism of the Goddess to structure its enactment. Named Goddess/ Great Mother/divine female-focused ritual is less commonly employed in psychotherapeutic settings but has been used by Woodman in her work on dream analysis[146] and Roth in relation to compulsive eating.[147] The utilization of ritual within a Goddess feminist framework, picking up on the qualities and themes of interconnection, community, freedom from patriarchal constrains through the use of bodily movements (here I refer to the limitations of patriarchal language, as we discussed earlier), reflection through meditation and music has the power to locate the individual in a different time and space. This is a movement outside the realms of control and discipline where women can focus on the creation of healing and connected life-affirming energies. Ritual within a Goddess feminist context addresses the emotional and spiritual needs of women in a non-masculine context. If patriarchal religions are understood as damaging for female embodiment and more generally dis-spiriting to the whole web-of-life, then Goddess feminism, within the context we have employed throughout this book, can be conceptualized as a soothing and healing discourse. As Raphael writes 'to be healed is to be made whole/holy, and therefore (re)charged with a spiritual and physical power'.[148] Ritual, as understood within a political framework, allows me to explore its employment as a psychological mechanism for dismantling the patriarchal power presiding over the construction of the feminine within contemporary society. Relating to the ritualization of food as a direct consequence of patriarchal values (control and discipline over the body), a method of dismantlement may result as a consequence of ritual development where the individual woman is engaging and reflecting upon the assumptions underpinning her utilization of the anorexic expression. Here she could reflect on the task she has taken on by defining her embodiment through anorexia, namely to deny her needs and escalating struggle in the pursuit of the creation of a new person and a search for self-esteem[149] as she seeks to meet society's demanding idealizations surrounding the female form. In Goddess feminist ritual creation she can address this denial head-on, identifying the daily and hourly obligations she has instigated. Here she can address the central questions surrounding how it started. Why are the rules and regulations in place? Why are they increasing? And, what would be the real consequence of stopping their enactment? Preoccupation with the performance of these rules and regulations through compulsive enactment distracts her from engaging with these issues. Goddess feminist ritual must allow the time and space for women struggling with anorexia to face these issues, to question and probe. Here all forms of healing (private, collective, environmental trauma etc.) contribute – through the regeneration of women's energies – to political and personal change. This is the case for Starhawk (an active member of the American anti-war movement) who draws upon a Goddess feminist framework to inform her rituals on reversing the desecration of sites due to patriarchal destruction. She writes:

> If magic is "the art of causing change in accordance with will", then political acts, acts of protest and resistance, acts that speak truth to power, that push for change, are acts of magic. . . . I once defined a spell as "a symbolic act done in a deepened state of consciousness". When political actions move into the realm of symbols, it becomes magical. If we apply the principles of magic to politics, we can understand political actions better and make them more effective.[150]

Within this context, Starhawk suggests that the healing energies created through group activities, 'their chanting, web-weaving and other non-violent direct actions magically name and will an Other, non-patriarchal, reality and infuse the profaned site with purifying, biophilic, sacred female energy'.[151] It is clear from the work of Starhawk that she understands ritual as intrinsically linked to human divine nature and her emphasis on interconnection and interdependence. In participating in these rituals, the individual does not just connect with divinity but with all her living creatures and the four elements. However, for many Goddess feminists, Starhawk included, ritual practices alone are not enough. These practitioners advocate the strength of ritual integrated with social action. For example, Riane Eisler writes that isolated rituals would amount to little more than 'dancing in the woods. Goddess rituals do change our consciousness and help us to bond, but if we stop there, it is like fireworks, which quickly dissipate'.[152] Mary Grey in *Introducing Feminist Images of God* writes about the "excesses" of Goddess practice as 'self-indulgent rituals affirming female sexuality'.[153] She argues that contemporary Goddess religion will ultimately fail because there is no 'adequate role for men'[154] and criticizes what she perceives, on the whole, as an inactive attitude towards addressing the need for 'structural justice'.[155] Criticisms such as these are not uncommon.[156] Addressing the charge that rituals affirming female sexuality are indulgent and the criticism that contemporary Goddess religion takes an inactive attitude towards the global need for structural justice, we need look no further than the work of Christ to see that thealogical academic consideration is given to these issues. In her book, *Rebirth of the Goddess*, Christ discusses the structural nature on injustice in offering Nine Touchstones of Goddess ethics. She writes:

> Nurture life. Walk in love and beauty. Trust the knowledge that comes through the body. Speak the truth about conflict, pain, and suffering. Take only what you need. Think about the consequences of your actions

> for seven generations. Approach the taking of life with great restraint. Practice great generosity. Repair the web.[157]

Furthermore, as mentioned earlier in this chapter, there are Goddess feminists and members of various Goddess movements who utilize the energy and awareness raised in ritual for direct action. For example, the work of Starhawk and her protests against the nuclear industry and globalization[158] and Charlene Spretnak's involvement with the Green Party in California.[159] Of course, not all who are interested in the Goddess are social activists but the same can be said of any religious denomination. However, because of the core principles inherent to Goddess feminism, it might be the case that there is more awareness of issues of social and structural justice than within other religious traditions.

Goddess-focused ritual is a tool that can be used for any number of psychological maladies, but my focus here is on the deconstructive possibilities for addressing the anorexic expression. Central elements of the ritual- creating process include grounding and connecting the circle to the earth, symbolically and physically cleansing the body, and the creation of energy for the purpose of relieving pain and tensions through meditation and reflection, body movement and music with the purpose of addressing elements of the anorexic expression directly. Reflecting on the compulsive ritualization of food consumption and preparation as exampled within the account of Rossi, the creation of a safe space for reflection, engaging the mind and body creatively, whilst consciously connecting to her surrounding environments, all of which informed by a positive female symbolic (within this work, located within Goddess mythology), for me, demonstrate the opportunities for challenging the disembodied anorexic rhetoric. Ritual creation and enactment requires the whole of the mind and body in an act of unification as both are creatively engaged in healing.

Pulling the work of Goldenberg on the creation of individually meaningful myth, the commonalities between Goddess feminism and psychoanalysis in the form of object relations theory together, I focus on active engagement through ritual,[160] namely, the underpinning of everyday rituals by a developing Goddess feminist consciousness as informed by the three steps I touched upon earlier in this chapter of active reflection on embodiment, a questioning of the patriarchal discourses that underpin the construction of anorexia and an engagement in the creation of ritual and individually meaningful myth to inspire healing and liberation. As we explored throughout this work, the anorexic expression develops as an unconscious protest towards displacing female stereotypes and idealizations which comes to represent her dissatisfaction with the limitations of the female role. It is within this understanding that treatment and the possibility of healing can take place. The anorexic woman needs a safe space to reconnect and rediscover her own feminine core and this can take place within ritual as a safe space that takes its form outside of patriarchal power relations as women engage in reflections (psychological and physical), challenging disembodied rhetoric and the contemplation of symbolic structures located in the context of their lives. A reconnection takes place here within the context of Goddess mythology in its contextualizing and informing of female embodiment for women's lives today. Subversion of the anorexic expression and the slender performance takes its form when women collectively incorporate a female divine construct into their daily lives and daily rituals. Over time, this repetition of female-empowering psychologies can change the way women experience their embodiment. Ritual and ceremony create a sacred space for women to embody aspects of the feminine in new performances and it is through this repetition that we can slowly disable the disembodiment at the heart of this expression. These ritual performances lie in everyday practices that can be understood to hold symbolic meaning. As we discussed in Chapter 3, these rituals are not limited to religious practice. The path to physical and psychological integration comes from a willingness to value and interact with memory as those that repress it are doomed to repeat it over and over again. Ultimately, the ritual is to re-balance patriarchy with a matriarchal lineage where female principles are given space and freedom to develop and it is within these ritual performances that transformation occurs. For some, this ritual can take place within a guided religious setting or through daily acts, as simply reflecting on everyday activities which, once bestowed with additional meaning, can allow for the development of new creative possibilities. These acts have the power to destabilize the anorexic expression and the slender performance. As Woodman writes: '[e]ach new situation is filled with new energies, new demands . . . and that . . . goes with us into the daisies we are arranging, the omelette we are cooking, the new prospectus we are preparing'.[161] The female body as thealogically mediated is actively engaged in challenging the gender status quo whilst creatively working with the core principles of Goddess feminism with a view towards broadening female embodiment and empowerment within society today.

As we have already explored, I draw upon ritual as a means of subverting and displacing society's female beauty and slender idealizations that I have argued lead to the development of eating disorders such as anorexia. Ritual here is located within a political framework through which we can start to weave an alternative model for embodiment within society today. If we understand anorexia as an attempt to protest against and at the same time escape from the continued subordination of women represented by way of the powerfully promoted slender ideal, we can see how the reimagining of female identify and embodiment can provide an attractive forum for women. Within thealogy and Goddess feminism we find not only a rich heritage of female empowerment and embodiment, but we find flexible and translatable creative energies that can be taken into many walks of life.

Notes

1 Reid-Bowen, P. (2007) *Goddess as Nature: Towards a Philosophical Thealogy*. Hampshire: Ashgate, 6.

2 Raphael, M. (1999) *Introducing Thealogy: Discourse on the Goddess*. Sheffield: Sheffield Academic Press, 13.

3 Slee, N. (2002) The Holy Spirit and Spirituality. In: Parsons, S. F. (ed.) *The Cambridge Companion to Feminist Theology*. Cambridge: Cambridge University Press, 171–190 (178).

4 Here I refer to the stories of women throughout this chapter whose experience of the Goddess or of a female divine construct has positively and powerfully affected reflections on their embodiment.

5 Raphael (1999: 28).

6 Raphael, M. (1996) *Thealogy and Embodiment: The Post-Patriarchal Reconstruction of Female Sacrality*. Sheffield: Sheffield Academic Press, 42.

7 Raphael (1999: 22).

8 Raphael (1999: 22).

9 Raphael (1999: 22).

10 Raphael (1996: 22).

11 For example, Raphael writes about women who incorporate Goddess rituals, symbols and language into their existing religious traditions such as Judaism and Christianity. For more information, see Raphael (1996).

12 Raphael (1996: 13).

13 Raphael (1999: 18).

14 Criticisms we will explore later in this chapter and the conclusion.

15 That is not to say that Goddess feminism cannot be pursued on a more formal basis. The Women's Thealogical Institute offers formal training for those who are interested in ordination and receiving ministerial credentials through offering a number of categories of study: the Cella Program, the Crone Program and the Guardian Program that enable women to celebrate the Goddess in distinct and diverse ways, although it is not clear from the institute website how academically credible this is. For more information, see Women's Thealogical Institute (2009–2015) *WTI Study*. Available at: www.rcgi.org/study [02/07/2016].

16 Goldenberg, N. (2004) Witches and Words. In: *Feminist Theology* 12, no. 2.

17 Starhawk. (1989) *The Spiral Dance: A Rebirth of the Ancient Religion of the Great Goddess*. New York: HarperCollins Publishers, 10–11.

18 Androcentric perspectives have affected the language and images we use to name and understand the sacred and our underlying conceptualizations of God. Not only do we reflect upon God and divinity as male, but we conceptualize Him as separate and distinct from life on earth. He is transcendent and more perfect than humanity and nature. As humanity was created in the image of God, it is assumed that humans are more "godlier" than the rest of nature. This is the mind-set that helped to establish the divine hierarchy that permeates society today. God's transcendence is expressed mythically through heaven symbolism in which his ruling on earth is understood in terms of a King ruling his people, He created the heavens and earth from nothing, He is jury, judge and destroyer. Philosophically, His transcendence paints Him as a spirit, unencumbered and uncorrupted by a physical body. The body of a man – as the most in control and powerful – is the masculine symbol ascribed to Him when deemed necessary essential for Christian moral teachings. In contrast to the masculine transcendent divine 'woman is often viewed as the source of sin who through her sexuality leads man away from God, binding him to his animal passions'. We see this when reflecting on the Hebrew narratives such as the story of Adam and Eve. Women have been associated with the body in ways that men have

not, which serves to reinforce their distance from male divinity. Transcendence here means "beyond", "supreme" and "surpassing" as opposed to immanence meaning, "existing within". Quotation from: Christ, C. P., Plaskow, J. (1989b) Naming the Sacred. In: Plaskow, J., Christ, C. P. (eds.) *Weaving the Visions: New Patterns in Feminist Spirituality*. London: Harper & Row, 95.

19 Robinson, J. (1998) *The Inner Goddess: Feminist Theology in the Light of Catholic Teaching*. Herefordshire: Fowler Wright Books, 157.

20 Starhawk (1982a) *Dreaming the Dark: Magic, Sex & Politics*. Boston: Beacon Press, 55.

21 Raphael (1996: 25).

22 Christ, C. P. (1995) *Diving Deep and Surfacing: Women Writers on Spiritual Quest*. Boston: Beacon Press, xiv.

23 Christ, C. (1997) *Rebirth of the Goddess: Finding Meaning in Feminist Spirituality*. Reading: Addison-Wesley, 103.

24 Christ (1997: 103).

25 Morton, N. (1989) The Goddess as Metaphoric Image. In: Christ, C. P., Plaskow, J. (eds.) *Weaving the Visions: New Patterns in Feminist Spirituality*. London: Harper & Row, 111–119 (111).

26 Morton (1989: 116).

27 Morton (1989: 115).

28 Morton (1989: 115).

29 Starhawk (1989: 10).

30 Griffin, S. (1989) This Earth Is My Sister. In: Plaskow, J., Christ, C. P. (eds.) *Weaving the Visions: New Patterns in Feminist Spirituality*. London: Harper & Row, 105–110 (105).

31 Walker, A. (1989) God Is Inside You and Everybody Else. In: Plaskow, J., Christ, C. P. (eds.) *Weaving the Visions: New Patterns in Feminist Spirituality*. London: Harper & Row, 101–104 (103).

32 Christ, C. P. (1982) Why Women Need the Goddess. In: Spretnak, C. (ed.) *The Politics of Women's Spirituality*. New York: Anchor, 71–86 (76).

33 Christ 1997: xiii.

34 Christ, C. P. (2012) Why Women, Men and Other Living Things Still Need the Goddess: Remembering and Reflecting 35 Years Later. In: *Feminist Theology* 20, no. 3: 247.

35 Christ (2012: 248).

36 Christ, C. P. (1979) Why Women Need the Goddess: Phenomenological, Psychological, and Political Reflections. In: Christ, C. P., Plaskow, J. (eds.) *Womanspirit Rising: A Feminist Reader in Religion*. London: Harper & Row, 273–286 (278).

37 This symbolism of the Goddess stands in sharp contrast to the female figures offered by our patriarchal heritage – Lilith, Eve and Pandora – women who have traditionally symbolized the dangerous and unrestrained female power that unleashes sin, pain and destruction on the world.

38 In her book *Thealogy and Embodiment* Melissa Raphael writes extensively on the de-sacralization of the female body by patriarchal structures. One of her central focuses is on the profane/sacred distinction between patriarchy and Goddess feminism in respect of menstruation and postpartum bleeding. She writes that Goddess feminism understands the female body as being particularly close to the source of life. Thus, it seeks to reverse patriarchal denigration and subjugation of female power. For example, where patriarchy might refer to menstrual or postpartum bleeding as unclean, dirty and sometimes even dangerous, Goddess feminists refer to these bodily processes as sacred. She writes that: 'most cultures have regarded menstrual blood as profane and have accordingly subjected women to varying degrees of segregation from the sacred. But

religious feminists (both Jewish and neo-pagan) now choose to experience their menstruation as a time to recharge themselves through the beneficent power of their blood'. For more information, see Raphael (1996).

39 Christ (2012: 248).

40 Goldenberg, N. (1979) *Changing of the Gods: Feminism and the End of Traditional Religions*. Boston: Beacon Press, 89.

41 Goldenberg (1979: 89).

42 As explored in Chapter 3.

43 Eller, C. (1993, 1995) *Living in the Lap of the Goddess: The Feminist Spirituality Movement in America*. Boston: Beacon Press, 74.

44 These traditions are usually encountered in the context of their presence within the emergent religious traditions in the West and occasionally through individual pilgrimage. Eastern religions with their emphasis on meditation and chanting rituals (Hinduism and Buddhism for example), alternative forms of healing (acupuncture) and movement traditions such as Hatha Yoga, Taiji, Sufi dancing and traditional Indian dance provide, for some women, a refreshing and embodied alternative to Western religions.

45 Eller (1995: 68).

46 Christ, C. (1987) *Laughter of Aphrodite: Reflections on a Journey to the Goddess*. New York: Harper & Row, 154.

47 Christ reminds us that many symbols of the Goddess have come from patriarchal cultures. It is important for women undertaking research in these areas to assess these Goddess constructions utilizing a feminist hermeneutic and identify the elements that legitimize the power of men. Not all goddesses serve female empowerment; we need look no further than India and the goddesses of Hinduism to see that. For more information on the tensions surrounding appropriation within the work of Christ, see Christ (1987: 154).

48 Sjoo, M., Mor, B. (1991) *The Great Cosmic Mother: Rediscovering the Religion of the Earth*. New York: HarperCollins Publishers, 221.

49 Such a case is exampled within the work of Christine Downing who was led to the Goddess through a dream. Within this dream she drove alone into the desert, driven by a desire to search for something not yet named. Her car developed a puncture, so she began to walk until she found herself at the entrance of a small cave. She enters the cave and prepares herself for sleep 'as though to fall asleep were part of my way to Her'. For Downing the Goddess became her anchor, leading her through dreams with a view towards aiding in reflections on her life. For more information, see Downing, C. (1981) *The Goddess: Mythological Images of the Feminine*. New York: Crossroad, 3.

50 This is the case for London-based Jungian analyst Ann Shearer who draws upon Athena's female, gynocentric traits, understanding her as the archetypal image of ancient female power, rather than an instrument of Zeus or patriarchy. For more information, see Shearer, A. (1998) *Athene: Image and Energy*. London: Penguin Books. Christine Downing also draws upon a "relationship" with Athena to inform reflections on her life and career. Her evolving understanding of the Goddess helped her to deal with the tensions of working within a male-dominated world. For more information, see Downing (1981).

51 Gross, R. (2009) *A Garland of Feminist Reflections: Forty Years of Religious Exploration*. London: University of California Press, 196.

52 Gross (2009: 196).

53 Gross (2009: 196).

54 Austen, H. I. (1990) *The Heart of the Goddess: Art, Myth, and Meditations of the World's Sacred Feminine*. Berkeley: Wingbow Press, xxiii.

55 Eller (1995: 78).

56 Budapest, Z. (1997) *Holy Book of Women's Mysteries*. Essex: New Leaf Distribution Company, 239.

57 There are many mythologies that can attest to the patriarchal denigration of female creativity and life-giving forces and one such account can be found within the Babylonian creation myth *Enuma Elish* (668–626 BCE) which was later recognized as being related to the early creation narratives in Genesis. As Christ writes, the creators of patriarchal mythologies aimed to 'dethrone the Goddess and to legitimate the new culture of the patriarchal warriors'. In the Babylonian creation myth Tiamat, the Goddess of the Salty Sea, is slain by the God Marduk. The Goddess murder is justified by vilifying Her. As Reid-Bowen writes: 'the myth provides the first textually accessible account of how universal order is established by the conquest/murder of a primordial Mother Goddess'. Anne Baring and Jules Cashford write '[t]he *Enuma Elish* is the first story of the replacing of a mother goddess who generates creation as part of herself by a god who "makes" creation as something separate from himself'. In order of quotation, see Christ (1997: 62); Reid-Bowen (2007: 86); and Baring, A., Cashford, J. (1991) *The Myth of the Goddess: Evolution of an Image*. London: Viking Arkana, 273.

58 Goldenberg, N. (1995) The Return of the Goddess: Psychoanalytic Reflections on the Shift From Theology to Thealogy. In: King, U. (ed.) *Religion and Gender*. Cambridge: Blackwell, 145–165 (150).

59 Stephen Benko in *The Virgin Goddess, Studies in the Pagan and Christian Roots of Mariology* argues that devotion to Mary stems from, and is the result of, pagan Goddess worship. He writes that 'veneration of the motherhood of Mary, is much more indebted to pagan belief and practice than many scholars are willing to admit . . . the conclusion seems inevitable that Mary eventually fulfilled the same role and filled the same need in Christian theology and piety'. Baring and Cashford write that 'Mary is the unrecognised Mother Goddess of the Christian tradition' as they demonstrate all the traditional roles she has assumed over time. These include the Great Mother Goddess, the Goddess of the Heavens, the Nature Goddess, to name a few. In order of quotation, see Benko, S. (2003) *The Virgin Goddess, Studies in the Pagan and Christian Roots of Mariology*. Danvers: Brill, 81; and Baring, Cashford (1991: 548).

60 Goldenberg (1995: 150).

61 Whilst it is not central to this work, as I operate from a non-realist position, due to the contentious nature of discussions surrounding a matriarchal prehistory, a short synopsis may be helpful at this juncture. One of the most well-known proponents of the past existence of a matrifocal society was Marija Gimbutas whose work catalogues the evidence (radiocarbon dating and spiritual feminist archaeological data) for believing that society would have been made up of small theocratic kingdoms presided over by a queen-priestess and a male family member to oversee agriculture and trade movements, arguing that there is absolutely no indication that society at that time was patrilinear or patriarchal. In her work, she argues that these cultures were peaceful, egalitarian, agrarian, art-loving and primarily worshipped lunar, earth and sea deities until Indo-European horsemen and warrior tribes began their 2,000-year onslaught (from approximately 2,000 BCE) of the matrifocal civilizations of Europe and India. Her research (taken from figurines, temples, artefacts and shrines for example) showed that grave goods were equally distributed between the sexes and that the number of objects/wealth accompanying the bodies was synonymous with age rather than sex, that children's lineage was traced through the mother and that ownership and inheritance of property was equal to both genders (to name three examples). For her, the evidence showed that females occupied pivotal roles such as carrying out ritual preparation alongside the supervision

and leading of ritual proceedings and that the male god was an adjunct of the female Goddess embodying the role of Her consort or son. Gimbutas identified two primary representations of the Goddess: 1) "she who is the giver of all" as the provider of life, water, food and happiness alongside the image of the Goddess as the "taker of all" representing death and thus representing the cyclical nature of existence; and, 2) representations of the Goddess as linked with the periodic awakening of nature; 'she is springtime, the new moon, rebirth, regeneration, and metamorphosis'. For more information, see Gimbutas, M. (1982) Women and Culture in Goddess-Oriented Old Europe. In: Spretnak, C. (ed.) *The Politics of Women's Spirituality: Essays by Founding Mothers of the Movement*. New York: Anchor Books, 22–32. Quotation from page 28. This hypothesis is also written about extensively by Merlin Stone. For more information, see Stone, M. (1976) *When God Was a Woman: The Landmark Exploration of the Ancient Worship of the Great Goddess and the Eventual Suppression of Women's Rites*. London: Harcourt Inc.

62 Raphael (1999: 78).

63 Stone (1976: xii).

64 Stone (1976: xiii).

65 Cynthia Eller argues that evidence for this prehistory is slim and should therefore not provide the inspirational basis for personal and social change based on studying of female figures and forms depicted in ancient artefacts and architecture. For more information, see Eller, C. (2001) *The Myth of Matriarchal Prehistory: Why an Invented Past Won't Give Women and Future*. Boston: Beacon Press. For a well-conceived rebuttal of Eller's argument, see Goldenberg (2004: 207–208).

66 Goldenberg (1995: 150–155).

67 Starhawk (1982b) Ethics and Justice in Goddess Religion. In: Spretnak, C. (ed.) *The Politics of Women's Spirituality: Essays by Founding Mothers of the Movement*. New York: Anchor Books, 415–422 (415–416).

68 Addressing the contentious nature of a matriarchal prehistory, Goldenberg advises feminist matriarchalists to 'portray themselves more explicitly as poets and visionaries and less as empiricists' arguing that '[a]ll religions interpret history to serve their aspirations. Feminist theology could demonstrate a high level of honesty and sophistication by freely admitting the speculative nature and inspirational objectives of its historical reconstructions'. For more information, see Goldenberg (2004: 208).

69 This draws upon the work of Chapter 3 and the idea that the most important feature of religion is its myth and that power and understanding comes from creating your own symbolic structures in the context of your life.

70 For more information on feminist writers engaged in critically analyzing the patriarchal nature of language, see Mills, S., Mullany, L. (2011) *Language, Gender and Feminism: Theory, Methodology and Practice*. Oxon: Routledge.

71 Salvaggio, R. (1999) *The Sounds of Feminist Theory*. New York: State University of New York Press, 45.

72 Cameron, D. (1998) *The Feminist Critique of Language: A Reader*. London: Routledge, 2.

73 Daly, M. (1991) *Gyn/Ecology: The Metaethics of Radical Feminism*. London: The Women's Press Ltd, 188.

74 Daly (1991: xxiv).

75 Daly (1991: xlvii).

76 Daly (1991: 3).

77 Daly, M. (1993) *Outercourse: The Be-Dazzling Voyage*. London: The Women's Press Ltd, 221.

78 Daly (1991: 47).

79 Daly (1991: 319).
80 Daly (1991: 315).
81 Daly (1991: 315).
82 Daly (1991: li).
83 This is more clearly seen in her co-created book *Websters' first new intergalactic wickedary of the English language* which highlighted the playful and empowering potential of non-sexist language. For more information, see Daly, M., Caputi, J. (1994) *Websters' First New Intergalactic Wickedary of the English Language*. New York: HarperSanFrancisco.
84 Goldenberg (2004: 205).
85 Goldenberg (2004: 210).
86 Goldenberg (2004: 210).
87 Christ (2012: 242).
88 Plaskow, J. (1983) The Right Question Is Theological. In: Heschel, S. (ed.) *On Being a Jewish Feminist*. New York: Schocken Books, 230.
89 Christ (1995: xiii–xiv).
90 Mantin, R. (2007) 'Dealing With a Jealous God': Letting Go of Monotheism and 'Doing' Sacrality. In: Isherwood, L. (ed.) *Patriarchs, Prophets and Other Villains*. London: Equinox Publishing, 37–49 (41).
91 Morton, N. (1985) *The Journey Is Home*. Boston: Beacon Press, 170.
92 Morton (1985: 143).
93 Morton (1985: 166).
94 Woodman, M. (1980) *The Owl Was a Baker's Daughter: Obesity, Anorexia Nervosa and the Repressed Feminine*. Toronto, Canada: Inner City Books, 112–113.
95 Woodman (1980: 113).
96 Morton (1985: 173).
97 Sands, K. (1994) *Escape From Paradise: Evil and Tragedy in Feminist Theology*. Minneapolis: Fortress Press, 115.
98 Reid-Bowen 2007: 63.
99 Reid-Bowen (2007: 64).
100 Starhawk writes that the Goddess has no genitalia and that Goddess as Mother is intended to refer to the creative and empowering possibilities of female-hood as opposed to biological realities or the decision to procreate and may also be used to refer to the fact that all humans had/have a mother. For more information, see Starhawk (1989: 244).
101 Discussed in detail in Chapter 3.
102 Goldenberg (1979).
103 Raphael (1999: 16).
104 Spirituality within this work can be broadly defined as a search for a greater meaning within which we can locate our individual experiences. This sparks a connection to a divinity that draws us into the totality of existence, symbolizing interdependence and interconnection as we are bound to a broader network of life. I employ feminist spirituality as 'an expression of the creative transformations envisioned by feminist approaches to the study and practice of religion' (Carrette, King 2005: 1).
105 Despite my employment of the term spirituality, I am wary of its disembodied heritage and the implication that some things are profane and some things sacred, that we are still employing judgemental hierarchical notions of which experiences are worth having and which are not. Goldenberg writes that feminist thought about religion often goes further and deeper than the concept of spirituality allows and so the term spirituality might limit our conceptions of what we are doing through the mystification of the direction of theories on embodiment and female power. Despite these reservations, I continue to work

with the term spirituality as a model within which to explore healing strategies for addressing female maladies, such as anorexia, today.

106 Goldenberg (1993: 1).

107 Goldenberg (1993: 1).

108 Goldenberg writes that object relations theory stresses the interconnectedness of people. Within this framework, we are always seeking relationships with "objects" (in this case people) and defining ourselves, our identities, against these relationships. Everyone is conceptualized as being part of a larger whole. What affects me, affects you, and so on. One of the central concepts of object relations theory is the idea that our earliest experiences have a significant impact on our development of character and behaviour in later years. Thus, object relations theorists stress the developmental significance of infancy and the early years of childhood and therapy focuses on reaching back to childhood in order to understand how the here and now came to be. Here we see many commonalities between the therapeutic approach of object relations theory and the drive of Goddess feminism in identifying a strong connection to the past in order to benefit the present and foster individual growth for the future. For more information on Goldenberg's work with object relations theory, see Goldenberg (1993: 190–210).

109 Goldenberg (1993: 193).

110 Goldenberg (1993: 194).

111 Goldenberg (1993: 194).

112 Goldenberg (1993: 193).

113 As we have already addressed, drawing upon the association of women with symbolism of the mother is not without its complications.

114 Goldenberg (1993: 202).

115 For example, Melanie Klein, a female theorist in the area of psychoanalysis, writes that the male fear of castration is actually derived from earlier anxieties about feeding and the disappearance of the mother's breast. Klein suggests that the child perceives the breast as part of their body, a part that sometimes disappears creating anxiety and discomfort. For more information, see Klein, M. (1975) *Envy and Gratitude and Other Works, 1946–1963*. New York: Delacorte Press; and Klein, M. (1975) *Love, Guilt, and Reparation and Other Works, 1921–1945*. New York: Delacorte Press. Taking this further, Luce Irigaray theorizes that this castration fear backdates to the severing of the umbilical cord and the lost physical connection with the mother. For more information, see Irigaray, L. (1985) *The Sex Which Is Not One*. Ithaca: Cornell University Press.

116 Goldenberg (2004: 205).

117 Christ (2012: 242).

118 Goldenberg (2004: 207).

119 Goldenberg (2004: 207).

120 Goldenberg (1993: 197).

121 Riviere, J. (1955) The Unconscious Phantasy of an Inner World Reflected in Examples From Literature. In: Klein, M. (ed.) *New Directions in Psychoanalysis*. New York: Basic Books, 358–359. Quoted in Goldenberg 1993: 200.

122 Goldenberg 91993: 195).

123 Goldenberg (1993: 203).

124 Goldenberg (1993: 203).

125 Goldenberg (1993: 204).

126 Goldenberg (1993: 204).

127 For more information on the ritual dimensions of anorexia, see Garrett, C. (1998) *Beyond Anorexia: Narrative, Spirituality and Recovery*. Cambridge: Cambridge University Press, 103–105; and Orbach, S. (1993) *Hunger Strike: The Anorectic's Struggle as a Metaphor for Our Age*. London: Penguin Books, 82.

128 Starhawk (1982a) *Dreaming in the Dark: Magic, Sex & Politics*. Boston: Beacon Press, 155.
129 Starhawk (1982a: 155).
130 Starhawk writes that Covens (her own Coven is based on the Faery Tradition) create their own rituals drawing influences from many traditions as they collaboratively create ways to worship the various manifestations of the Goddess. She writes that 'some covens follow practices that have been handed down in an unbroken line since before the Burning Times. Others derive their rituals from leaders of modern revivals of the Craft . . . feminist covens are probably the fastest growing arm of the craft'. For more information, see Starhawk (1982c) Witchcraft as Goddess Religion. In: Spretnak, C. (ed.) *The Politics of Women's Spirituality: Essays by Founding Mothers of the Movement*. London: Anchor Books, 49–57 (53).
131 This was expanded upon in Chapter 3 within discussions surrounding displacing the slender performance.
132 Goldenberg (1995: 148).
133 Mystical aspects of the Goddess are accessed especially when engaging with the Goddess's outer manifestations in the natural world, through annual community Sabbats or rituals. Eight Sabbats occur annually based on the lunar calendar. As groups of people engage in group ritual practices in which the self becomes connected to the earth and the Goddess in all her manifestations, the seasonal, creative, communal, celestial and the personal meet in communal ceremony. Ritual might be carried out for a number of purposes, for meditation, healing, trance or prayer but each of these relies heavily on an overriding divine dependency that is often understood as the true path towards creativity, freedom and embodied confidence. This may create an environment of belonging whilst providing a forum for engaging with the past for life in the present. It reinforces the cyclical nature of existence and locates the individual in a community of transformations. Ritual practices may find their focus in overcoming obstacles and promoting the flow of relational energy that fosters human and planetary health. Group rituals bond women together as sisters. Some rituals invoke assistance from the Goddess and others do not.
134 Barrett, R. R. (2013) The Power of Ritual. In: Griffin, W. (ed.) *Daughters of the Goddess: Studies of Healing, Identity, and Empowerment*. Walnut Creek: AltaMira Press, 185–201 (191).
135 Raphael (1999: 121).
136 Barrett (2013: 191).
137 Barrett (2013: 196).
138 Berry, J. (2009) *Ritual Making Women: Shaping Rites for Changing Lives*. New York: Routledge, 1–2.
139 Berry (2009: 2).
140 Berry (2009: 2).
141 de Rossi, P. (2010) *Unbearable Lightness: A Story of Loss and Gain*. New York: Atria Books, 5. It is worth noting that de Rossi is a Hollywood actress and therefore under increased body and aesthetic scrutiny. Being on "display" in such a visual way contributed to her disordered eating behaviour.
142 Rossi (2010: 6).
143 Rossi (2010: 6).
144 Rossi (2010: 6, author's emphasis).
145 Rossi (2010: 7).
146 Woodman, M. (1985) *The Pregnant Virgin: A Process of Psychological Transformation*. Toronto, Canada: Inner City Books.
147 Roth, G. (2010) *Women, Food and God: An Unexpected Path to Almost Everything*. London: Simon and Schuster UK LTD.

148 Raphael (1999: 121).

149 Within the anorexic expression it is through the creation of rules and regulations in relation to food, exercise, habits of work and study that she creates for herself a self-image to counteract her feelings of worthlessness and meaningless she feels herself to be. This provides her with a false and fleeting sense of comfort and security. For more information, see Orbach (1993) and Bordo, S. (2003) *Unbearable Weight: Feminism, Western Culture, and the Body*. London: University of California Press.

150 Starhawk (1982a: 169).

151 Raphael (1999: 121–122).

152 Eisler, R. (1995) Envisioning a Partnership Future. In: *Woman of Power* 24: 20–27.

153 Grey, M. (2001) *Introducing Feminist Images of God*. Sheffield: Sheffield Academic Press, 32.

154 Grey (2001: 33).

155 Grey (2001: 33).

156 Rosemary Radford Ruether is well known for her criticisms of Goddess religions. In *Gaia and God* she writes that religions need both God and Gaia. Religions without Gaia 'run the risk of sacrificing the world to the (alleged) judgement of God, while religions of Gaia alone lack the principle of prophetic judgement which [Ruether believes] is the ground of ethics'. Responding to these criticisms Christ argues that participants of contemporary Goddess religion have strong ethical concerns rooted in 'reverence and love for life and the web of life' as opposed to rooting it in 'a transcendent or prophetic principle of judgement' (Christ quoting and subsequently responding to Ruether's critique). Extrapolating, she writes that '[r]ecognising that ethics do not have to be rooted in a transcendent principle of justice uncovers the fallacy (or phallacy?) of theories that assume that earth-based, Goddess, or 'Gaian' religions are unethical'. For more information, see Ruether, R. R. (1992) *Gaia and God: An Ecofeminist Theology of Earth Healing*. San Francisco: HarperSanFrancisco, 24; and Christ, C. P. (2005) Musings on the Goddess and Her Cultural Despisers, Provoked by Naomi Goldenberg. In: *Feminist Theology* 13, no. 2: 143–149 (145–146).

157 Christ (1997: 167).

158 Christ asks if it is still 'self-indulgent narcissistic navel-gazing when Starhawk and members of Reclaiming [an activist branch of modern Pagan religion] are arrested in the direct action movement against globalization in the name of the Goddess'. See Christ (2005: 147). For more information on Starhawk, see Starhawk (1982a; 1982b; 1982c) and Starhawk (1982d) Consciousness, Politics and Magic. In: Spretnak, C. (ed.) *The Politics of Women's Spirituality: Essays by Founding Mothers of the Movement*. London: Anchor Books, 172–184; and Starhawk (2002) *Webs of Power: Notes From the Global Uprising*. Gabriola Island, British Columbia, Canada: New York Society Publishers. For more information on Reclaiming, see Anon. (2015) *Reclaiming*. Available at: www.reclaiming.org/ [22/08/2016]; and Starhawk (2016) *Regenerative Culture, Earth-Based Spirituality, and Permaculture*. Available at: http://starhawk.org/ [22/08/2016].

159 For more information on the work of Spretnak with the Green Party, see Spretnak, C. (1982) The Politics of Women's Spirituality. In: Spretnak, C. (ed.) *The Politics of Women's Spirituality: Essays by Founding Mothers of the Movement*. London: Anchor Books, 393–399; and Capra, F., Spretnak, C. (1984) *Green Politics*. New York: Dutton.

160 My work on the commonalities between psychoanalysis and discourses on the Goddess provided an overview of object relations theory as identified by

Goldenberg but is far from a comprehensive study of the use of object relations theory. In the context of my work this demonstrates the positive potential of Goddess feminism within therapeutic settings for addressing the anorexic expression.

161 Woodman, M. (1982) *Addicted to Perfection: The Still Unravished Bride*. Toronto, Canada: Inner City Books, 189–190.

Conclusion

The spirituality of anorexia

The Spirituality of Anorexia marks a pursuit towards female-embodied consciousness that utilizes some of the core features of Goddess feminism within a political framework. As mentioned at the inception of this work, this book marks the start of a broader research project concerned with developing alternative therapeutic responses to anorexia within thealogical frameworks with an aim towards providing women with access to empowering and embodied symbols of the feminine.

At the centre of this book is the argument that anorexia within Western society results as a direct consequence of our environments which have been significantly influenced by the patriarchy at the heart of the Judeo-Christian tradition. In framing religion as fictitious, drawing upon the work on myth and reality within the work of Goldenberg,[1] we have the power to create new fictions, new realities and new embodied opportunities for women. Direct application to the anorexic expression provides us with a mechanism for displacing the disembodied rhetoric. Thus, the aim of this study was to explore the aspects of thealogical discourse which can be employed to (co) construct an alternative reality for girls and women utilizing the anorexic expression within society today.

My argument is that some of the central tenets of Goddess feminism directly address the female experience of anorexia and lend themselves to a reconnection of feminine nature in our culture. For directly addressing the anorexic expression in this study, I identified several key features. First, in and of itself, Goddess feminism provides us with the resources for subverting the damaging patriarchal agenda that has presided over the lives of women. In its focus on female experiences, the immanency of the Goddess and the female body as divine alongside the political dimensions which focus on challenging androcentrism and male supremacy, we have a strong tool for addressing the disembodied rhetoric which underpins the anorexic expression. Second, if we agree that the creation of individually meaningful myths are central to healing psychological development, the experiential nature of Goddess feminism (and the culture of shared experiences it has fostered) is endowed with additional meaning as women come together to give serious consideration to their own mythic development as they actively engage in work towards displacing the damaging discourses at play in their lives. Third, I draw upon a broadly defined, but Goddess-located, ritual practice to somatically address this mythic development and developing consciousness in daily life and as a safe space for reflections and creative engagement in this process of healing. Through the use of ritual within a Goddess framework, communication can take place outside of the limitations of patriarchal language as women employ the use of movement, meditation and music to engage with their bodies. A physical interaction between the mind and body is played out here. Within this framework, daily rituals, when underpinned by a Goddess feminist philosophy, take on new levels of meaning as embodied consciousness starts to permeate all aspects of life. Here, we have the power to challenge and subvert the anorexic expression – and by extension, the slender performance – through the individual creation of myth and healing stories as women address the various strands of their own disembodiment.

My aim in drawing upon the commonalities between Goddess feminism and object relations theory was to demonstrate the potential for Goddess feminism within a therapeutic setting through drawing on certain key features such as the past as an important source of meaning, deconstructing images of patriarchal authority, the individual as interconnected in the web-of-life and the potential of fantasy and myth creation as both a deconstructive and healing tool. Unpacking these elements, we know that un-relatedness feeds the anorexic expression and so importance lies in the universal inclusion of conceptualizations of interdependence and interconnection into healing frameworks. Here a developing understanding of the connectedness of the web-of-life nourishes the individual's perspective and reflections on their existence. Additionally, reflections on the myth of matriarchal prehistory provide us with a rich heritage to contextualize female consciousness in contemporary society which, when informed by a wish within fantasy, can tease out opportunities for positive reflections on change and growth. Here we are drawing on the belief in Goddess feminism of fantasy as valuable in its ability to focus the mind and mobilize willpower as we work towards positive and creative change. Alongside what we know about the anorexic expression and the negativity that permeates thoughts on life, through an engagement in positive and life-affirming thinking whilst engaging in the isolation of anorexia through displacing the patriarchy at its heart, we can address the specific strands of the anorexic identity.

My use of ritual to dismantle the rigidity, strictness and the compulsive nature of the anorexic expression (and the slender performance) was discussed in Chapters 3 and 5. Here we understood ritual as a transformative practice, locating our everyday rituals within a larger framework where the individual is engaged in a conscious development from one level of awareness to another. This process was later underpinned by a developing Goddess feminist consciousness as ritual, which was employed to identify empowering associations from disempowering rhetoric through taking a closer look at how we might disable the anorexic expression and the slender performance. Discussions here surrounded reconnection to a female-empowering embodied construct as a vehicle towards addressing the disembodiment at the heart of this expression. Understanding the strands of their own disembodiment is central to the process of healing. Picking up on themes of reconnection and female embodiment, we explored the work of Goldenberg on myth creation. Her purpose was to reconnect women with their bodies, to work towards female embodiment and she saw this happening as a movement away from traditional patriarchal religions and towards female-empowering psychological frameworks located within the process of myth development. For her it is the process of discovering myth that is most important for the individual. For Goldenberg, the value of psychoanalysis (within this framework) lay in the importance it placed on the necessity of myth in providing meaning and divine connection for people. This significantly influenced her argument for the creation of individually meaningful myths. This work on the development of myth was directly related to discourses on the Goddess as "living" and dynamic movements which encourage people to look inwards to understand the forces at work in their lives. Locating this alongside the anorexic expression, the process of myth development becomes a resource for the process of co-creating healing models of embodiment as women address the mythic structures that inform the story of their lives and explore avenues for creating alternative narratives. Picking up on these themes, in Chapter 5 we explored the psychological benefit of matriarchal prehistory as myth. Here the idea of a matriarchal past can inform reflections on embodiment today as we call upon conceptualizations of the past to improve our situation in the present. Utilizing a matriarchal prehistory in the form of an ancient myth of the superiority of the Goddess provides women with a higher place within social and religious structures of power. This provides new avenues for strengthening women's conceptualizations of self today. Goddess feminism here is understood as providing women with reconnection to a repressed femininity within a "living" religion whereby the individual has access to, and a growing appreciation of, the psychological and healing benefit of locating their existence within a broader network of connections. The anorexic woman needs a safe space to reconnect and rediscover her own feminine core and this can take place within ritual as a safe environment that takes its form outside of patriarchal power relations as women engage in reflections (psychological and physical), challenging disembodied rhetoric and the contemplation of symbolic structures located in the context of their lives. A reconnection takes place within the context of Goddess mythology in its contextualizing and informing of female embodiment for women's lives today. In this context ritual can be utilized as the safe space that allows the anorexic individual to explore her embodiment outside of patriarchal discourse. Here we have a framework for dismantling the fragmented anorexic identity and the ritualistic and regulated compulsion that underpins the anorexic women's disembodiment. Drawing on this work, there are three features central to this framework and these are as follows: active reflection on embodiment, a questioning of the patriarchal discourses that underpin the construction of anorexia, and an engagement in the creation of ritual and individually meaningful myth to inspire healing and liberation.

Extending beyond this, I argue that thealogy has the potential to positively affect the lives of many women within society, the women tightrope walking from one diet to another, the women who spend hundreds and thousands of pounds and time on narrowing the boundaries of their bodies not for the purpose of health but for social acceptance and legitimacy. There are several central features to this process as women utilizing the anorexic expression must play an active role in healing their inner wounds, in addressing the underlying features which became manifest in this somatic expression. As the roots are manifold, constructing a standardized theory on the form the Spirituality of Anorexia would take is a problematic task. There is a need for bespoke therapeutic approaches to address the myriad underlying features that develop as a consequence of the individual's experiences. As discussed, Goddess feminism will need to be employed to inform the use of existing therapeutic approaches, such as narrative therapy, as the individual and therapist engage in the underlying features. The individual will be called to creatively address contributing factors such as family, peer, fashion and media influences, the sexism that underpins her experience of contemporary life, obsessions surrounding personal fitness and the compulsion to exercise and issues surrounding nutrition and perceived beauty pressures to name a number of contributing factors. Women utilizing the anorexic expression will also need to address underlying assumptions about happiness, love, acceptance and legitimacy as they redefine what these concepts really mean to them. In turn this will lead to the dismantling of unconsciously absorbed patriarchal rhetoric that underpins reflections on their disembodiment.

My conceptualization of the Spirituality of Anorexia as a pursuit towards female-embodied consciousness will be unable to reflect the infinite diversity of female experience but should provide a malleable framework for women to work towards empowered change. The symbols, motifs, stories and myths will change as we develop, as our perspectives shift and our embodied living evolves. Any therapeutic response needs to take this fluidity into consideration and is an additional strength of working with Goddess feminism given its flexible and adaptive nature. This is a living process located within a living and body/experience loving spiritual framework. There is no universal spiritual quest for all women; rather there is meaning in the unique experiences of women. The women utilizing the anorexic expression need to seek new stories outside the boundaries of patriarchal discourse. This is the calling of the Spirituality of Anorexia: the individual must create new female-empowering stories and myths that hold meaning for their lives. As Goldenberg writes: 'witches know that their physical lives are changed by their images of the Goddess. A woman's feeling's about her body undergo joyous transformation if she imagines herself to be in some sense divine'.[2] Even though I have shied away from the radicalness of the witchcraft movement, there are elements which, when diluted, are helpful for my reflections here. For example, Goldenberg writes that

> [t]hose who cast spells and work hexes know that thought has effects on the world – that thought *certainly* influences the one who casts the spells and works the hexes and that thought *seems* to operate on other things as well.[3]

Thoughts, feelings and words have embodied consequences. We must realize this power in all forms of life and incorporate this knowledge into working therapies if we are to truly transform the landscape of embodiment.

An example of one way this is played out can be found within the work of Goldenberg and her use of dreams to inform her spiritual development. In a dream about travelling to a new and previously untravelled destination, she finds herself overwhelmed with anxiety, nervousness and excitement. This anxiety is compounded by the restriction of having to stay in a certain area for a specified period of time. On her journey to buy provisions for this period she sees a 'far-off figure'[4] walking about a mile away from the car. This person, a man, came to the foreground in subsequent dream analysis whilst participating in group work. Becoming this figure and absorbing the feelings she had projected onto him, she felt a 'wonderful sensation of peace . . . he was a brave, clear-sighted person who was pioneering alone in Australia'.[5] She felt the strength and independence of his character and her fear and anxiety slipped away, she felt calm and at peace with her environment. Taking this into her conscious living, Goldenberg writes: '[t]he Australian Pioneer is a psychic figure to whom I have access whenever I feel fearful of the directions that my research, my writing or any other part of my life are taking'.[6] Becoming this pioneer, she sees with clarity and experiences her environment as being charged with mystical significance. Subsequent work encouraged her to transform this male pioneer into a woman, inspiring her to undertake her own pioneering work. She uses this example to reinforce the message that people do not need an enforced standardized set of religious images to feel a sense of community, that instead 'a common ground may be developed around the activity of image-making itself . . . [where] the psychic creativity of individuals can be encouraged within the company of a supportive social group'.[7] This is also exampled in her story of the wise woman and the purple ellipse as we discussed in Chapter 3 where she argued that power is lost when people collectively create mythic systems based on the life of others. Power comes from the creation of your own symbolic structures for your own life, and this is of central importance when focusing on creative avenues of healing for anorexia as healing must address the features that culminated in its manifestation. Drawing upon the spiritual development of Goldenberg through utilizing dream analysis in a group setting, we could reflect upon the work of Woodman in Chapter 3 and her reflection on the dreams of anorexic women often focusing on feelings of entrapment, enclosure, pain and death. Here we may be able to develop creative avenues through subsequent reflection by drawing on elements outside the immediate environment of the dream which, when endowed with additional meaning, can be transformed into embodied reflection on the nature of empowerment and embodiment in present life circumstances.

For example, recalling the work of Woodman as discussed earlier in this book and her dream analysis work which led to her assertion that the dreams of anorexic patients are often filled with themes of being trapped, caged, hurt or dying, there may be opportunities through analysis to focus on alternative features. Maybe, whilst reflecting on the cage that traps her, she can examine her surroundings and discover elements that when focused upon, provide opportunities for Goddess feminist reflection. I do not want to labour the importance of dreams here, but I do want to highlight the myriad opportunities for challenging the underlying features of the anorexic expression and exploring alternative avenues for reflection. Employing the use of fantasy and wishful thinking, if a woman experiences herself as trapped and hurt in a nightmare, maybe there are opportunities, on reflection, to build in new elements to open up creative possibilities for healing. In this dream there could be a small window beyond which an owl sits. The owl here could symbolize the Goddess as the window is representative of a disconnection from nature. Healing may involve earth- and nature-focused ritual as the woman learns to reconnect with nature and her surrounding environment. This could take place as a broader group ritual with other women or just walking outside in nature, barefoot in the grass whilst reflecting on the reasons for this perceived isolation. Placing herself within the owl, there may be creative avenues for experiencing the immanentism of the Goddess and in flight the owl may provide an opportunity for the anorexic women to address feelings surrounding her embodiment. This is just an example of how we might creatively address anorexic symptoms whilst drawing on some of the central features of Goddess feminism. Whilst professional guidance will be undoubtedly necessary for women who have become absorbed by the anorexic expression, this spiritual development should not be limited to therapy. This is a project to take place outside of these spaces and into the individual's daily life to challenge and reform daily reflections with friends and family; the Spirituality of Anorexia must be a fully transferable and approachable mechanism for change.

Throughout this book I have argued that the aetiology of anorexia can be found within reflections on society, the politics of the female body and understanding the body as a historically mediated form. The purpose of all this is twofold, first and foremost this work has been concerned with displacing the damaging rhetoric which underpins the development of anorexia within contemporary society, but I have also explored the broader slender ideal and the pressure on women to reduce their boundaries to meet increasingly oppressive body standards. For me the Goddess is a symbol of hope, love, compassion and acceptance and a strongly immanent divinity participating in and through our bodies and our lives. She embodies a breaking down of the dualisms that would see us destroy our bodies and our environments through self-hate, hierarchy etc. As Morton and Christ reinforce, she is not "out there" or "back there" but "in here" – the Goddess 'has taken root in our bodies and become part of the fabric of our lives'.[8] Thus, we focus on an immanent divinity as we construct a challenge and alternative spiritual framework for those individuals for whom a male divinity and patriarchal agenda does not satisfy. Thealogy in the context of this work is a political framework towards reclaiming the female body and identifying with our own immanent and powerfully embodied divinity in all her manifestations. It is not just about a Goddess or goddesses but it is more broadly concerned with 'imagining the divine with qualities traditionally or biologically associated with being female'.[9] In terms of how this affects the embodiment of women in contemporary society, Goldenberg writes that the Goddess, when understood as a psychological tool to build individual strengths, helps women to learn to 'visualize and bring [themselves] to birth in the world'.[10] Here, each part of the life cycle is respected as a valued aspect of the individual's existence. These models provide powerful positive images that may psychologically help the individual grow and develop throughout life as opposed to desperately clinging onto a particular stage in one's development (i.e. fighting to retain a youthful aesthetic in a society that celebrates one ideal regardless of age, experience or profession). For Goldenberg the Goddess is central to this process of development as a 'concept to give women positive self-images in all stages of life'.[11] These are life-affirming and powerful models for many women within the Goddess movement as female divinity is valued throughout life; it is not a member's only club for a select few who most successfully meet the prerequisites (here I refer to the increasing propensity within society to worship beauty as divine). It is not just the idea of a female divinity and the celebration of life in all its stages that draws a lot of women (and men) towards the various Goddess movements but the emphasis on experience. The experiential nature of thealogy and Goddess feminism is one of its fundamental strengths. It is through listening to the voices and stories of women, accounts that have traditionally been omitted from Judeo-Christian religious discourse, that we start to conceive of an alternative model of embodiment and broaden the parameters (if not disable them completely) of normative notions of being. Beverley Clack writes that academic study requires us to

> detach the individual and their academic concerns the one from the other, creating the idea of "the intellectual" as something like a brain on a stick whose situation, interests and experiences are irrelevant to the kind of arguments they forge.[12]

In using experience as a starting point for academic analysis 'women have been able to challenge the dominant discourse developed by patriarchy over a millennium and perhaps it is only by maintaining the importance of the personal that we will be able to affect the political'.[13]

For me personally, having always struggled with body acceptance and a compulsion to narrow my boundaries, research into the Goddess has been transforming. The features that most resonate with me are the political elements of Goddess feminism in its challenging of patriarchal power, the calling for women to actively engage in the creation of their own embodied stories, alongside the appreciation of our interdependence and the Goddess as immanent in ourselves and the world that surrounds us. Feeling this connection to our environments helps to develop new ways of reflecting on embodiment as we open ourselves up to understanding that our health, physical and mental, is contingent on the health and well-being of the world that surrounds us and equally, the health of the environment is contingent on our actions and thoughts. To send love, living energy and creative vitality out into the world, to work for change in whatever way we can. To expand knowledge, both in ourselves and for others who would like to grow and develop within this spiritual framework and to work, not for financial gain or personal profit, but for the health and well-being of all. In this respect, the natural development of this project would be to see this approach embedded into therapy work. Here Goddess feminism would find its location in society as we incorporate the Goddess into creative healing strategies. Transformation happens when we broaden our conceptualizations on embodiment, when we see through Her eyes, developing new models for embodied praxis and new avenues for empowered living. Thus, over time, we become more and more distanced from the patriarchal power dynamics endemic to contemporary living. The change does not take place overnight. This process of dismantling the elements of life that constrain and limit our development takes time and dedication. The women with anorexia engaging with these themes and motifs will be starting a life-long journey.

As I draw this thealogical examination towards its end, having discussed at length the female body in contemporary society, the political dimensions of such extreme self-starvation behaviours, the patriarchal rhetoric underpinning these expressions and finally, discourses on the Goddess as a forum for displacing patriarchal female constructions, I reflect upon what this Spirituality of Anorexia may feel like for the individuals engaged in this activity. The goal I had imagined for myself at the inception of this book had been to unpack the destructive rhetoric at the heart of the anorexic expression and to work within a thealogical framework, utilizing the symbolism of the Goddess, to explore methods of deconstruction and embodied re-creations with a contribution towards disrupting the gender status quo and challenging slender and reductionist rhetoric that so many women are caged by. As I demonstrated whilst reflecting on the work of Goldenberg and her application of myth and fantasy, reflecting on thealogy as a framework within which women can participate in the co-creation of healing psychologies, which reflect upon the Goddess, we have a potential avenue for eradicating the foundational principles of the anorexic expression. I have demonstrated how reflections on the Goddess, as conceptualized as a powerful female construct, can provide an empowering and liberating symbolic for women, particularly for women utilizing the anorexic expression, but also for all those women and girls chasing the slender ideal. Beyond this application, I suggested that the mass adoption of this framework by society would provide fertile ground for the development of gender equality as our patriarchal society is rebalanced with an equally powerful female principle. However, there are Goddess constructs that I argued are in need of deconstruction (such as the conceptualization of the Goddess as maiden-mother-crone). Here we have the potential to understand each new situation as filled with new energies, new demands. Positive and creative energy is interacting with healing energy and transformation happens because we recognize each other and in that recognition is the love that encourages the full humanity of all. We see with new eyes. This transformation permeates life as healing love and vitality flows into our daily activities. It becomes part of our response to the whole world. In living through this embodiment, through embodied praxis, we disrupt the power this reductionist and sexist rhetoric has on us as we consciously acknowledge our connection with life-affirming and meaningfully lived realities. This is a pursuit towards female consciousness which embodies an awakening from the patriarchal discourses that would otherwise see many young women fade away. In this we have *The Spirituality of Anorexia*.

Notes

1 Here I am picking up on the influence work of Chapter 3 on myth creation, and Chapter 5 on the psychological benefit of new realities, have on healing this disembodied reflection on embodiment.
2 Goldenberg, N. (1979) *Changing of the Gods: Feminism and the End of Traditional Religions*. Boston, MA: Beacon Press, 126.
3 Goldenberg (1979: 126, author's emphasis).
4 Goldenberg (1979: 139).
5 Goldenberg (1979: 139).
6 Goldenberg (1979: 140).
7 Goldenberg (1979: 127).
8 Christ, C. P. (2012) Why Women, Men and Other Living Things Still Need the Goddess: Remembering and Reflecting 35 Years Later. In: *Feminist Theology* 20, no. 3: 253.
9 Raphael, M. (1996) *Thealogy and Embodiment: The Post-Patriarchal Reconstruction of Female Sacrality*. Sheffield: Sheffield Academic Press, 15.
10 Goldenberg (1979: 97).
11 Goldenberg (1979: 97).
12 Clack, B. (2012) The Future Is Female: Revisioning Feminism For/With the Next Generation. In: *Feminist Theology* 20, no. 3: 256–261 (256).
13 Clack (2012: 256).

Bibliography

Anam, T. (2013) Things Your Mother Never Told You (For Fear You Would Demand a Sex Change). In: Appignanesi, L., Holmes, R., Orbach, S. (eds.) *Fifty Shades of Feminism*. London: Hachette Digital, 17–23.

Anon. (2011) *Airbrushed Make-Up Ads Banned for 'Misleading'*. Available at: www.bbc.co.uk/news/uk-14304802 [24/11/2014].

Anon. (2014) *The Dove Campaign for Real Beauty*. Available at: www.dove.us/Social-Mission/campaign-for-real-beauty.aspx [19/11/2014].

Anon. (2014) *Eating Disorders Not Exclusive to those Who Are Underweight*. Available at: www.mcri.edu.au/news/2014/august/eating-disorders/ [31/01/2015].

Anon. (2015) *General Information*. Available at: www.anad.org/get-information/about-eating-disorders/general-information/ [03/01/2015].

Anon. (2015) *Reclaiming*. Available at: www.reclaiming.org/ [22/08/2016].

Anon. (2016) *Men Get Eating Disorders Too*. Available at: http://mengetedstoo.co.uk/ [15/01/2017].

Anon. (2017) *Anne Hathaway Has Psychic Connection to Giant Monster in Colossal Trailer*. Available at: www.theguardian.com/film/2017/jan/19/anne-hathaway-colossal-trailer [23/01/2017].

Anon. (2017) *Eating Disorders Can Strike in Mid-Life*. Available at: www.bbc.co.uk/news/health-38635082 [24/01/2017].

Anon. (2017) *Global Protests on Donald Trump Inauguration Day*. Available at: www.bbc.co.uk/news/world-us-canada-38699844 [24/01/2017].

Arnold, C. (2013) *Decoding Anorexia: How Breakthroughs in Science Offer Hope for Eating Disorders*. East Sussex: Routledge.

Asgari, S., Dasgupta, N., Stout, J. G. (2012) When Do Counterstereotypic Ingroup Members Inspire Versus Deflate? The Effect of Successful Professional Women on Young Women's Leadership Self-Concept. In: *Personality and Social Psychology Bulletin* 38: 370–383.

Austen, H. I. (1990) *The Heart of the Goddess: Art, Myth, and Meditations of the World's Sacred Feminine*. Berkeley: Wingbow Press.

Banyard, K. (2010) *The Equality Illusion: The Truth About Women and Men Today*. London: Faber and Faber.

Baring, A., Cashford, J. (1991) *The Myth of the Goddess: Evolution of an Image*. London: Viking Arkana.

Barker, P. J. (2004) *Assessment in Psychiatric and Mental Health Nursing: In Search of the Whole Person*. Cheltenham: Nelson Thornes Ltd.

Baron-Cohen, S. (2003) *The Essential Difference*. London: Penguin Books.

Barrett, R. R. (2013) The Power of Ritual. In: Griffin, W. (ed.) *Daughters of the Goddess: Studies of Healing, Identity, and Empowerment*. Walnut Creek: AltaMira Press, 185–201.

Bartky, S. L. (1988) Foucault, Femininity and the Modernization of Patriarchal Power. In: Diamond, I., Quinby, L. (eds.) *Feminism and Foucault: Reflections on Resistance*. Boston: Northeasten University Press.

Bartky, S. L. (2003) Foucault, Femininity, and the Modernization of Patriarchal Power. In: Weitz, R. (ed.) *The Politics of Women's Bodies: Sexuality, Appearance, and Behavior*. Oxford: Oxford University Press, 25–45.

Bates, L. (2017) *The Pocket Money Gap- and 10 Other Ways Girls Are Taught They're Worth Less*. Available at: www.theguardian.com/commentisfree/2017/jan/24/gender-pay-gap-boys-girls-pocket-money?CMP=fb_gu [25/01/2017].

Baxter, E. (2000) Cutting Edge: Witnessing Rites of Passage in a Therapeutic Community. In: Isherwood, L., Althaus-Reid, M. (eds.) *Controversies in Body Theology*. London: SCM Press, 48–70.

B-eat. (2016) *Eating Disorder Statistics*. Available at: www.b-eat.co.uk/about-beat/media-centre/information-and-statistics-about-eating-disorders?gclid=CMSWhIKync4CFUJmGwod17kFMQ [03/08/2016].

B-eat. (2016) *New Report Gives Insight Into Body Image Issues Among Boys*. Available at: www.b-eat.co.uk/latest/5397-new-report-gives-insight-into-body-image-issues-among-boys [15/01/2017].

Beauvoir, S. D. (1997) *The Second Sex*. London: Vintage Classics.

Becker, A. E., Keel, P. K., Anderson-Fye, E. P., Thomas, J. J. (2004) Genes (and/or) Jeans?: Genetic and Socio-Cultural Contributions to Risk for Eating Disorders. In: *Journal of Addictive Diseases* 23: 81–103.

Behar, R. (2007) Gender-Related Aspects of Eating Disorders: A Psychosocial View. In: Rubin, J. S. (ed.) *Eating Disorders and Weight Loss Research*. New York: Nova Science Publishers, 39–65.

Bell, R. M. (1987) *Holy Anorexia*. London: The University of Chicago Press.

Benhabib, S. (1995) Feminism and Post Modernism. In: Benhabib, S., Butler, J., Cornell, D., Fraser, N. (eds.) *Feminist Contentions: A Philosophical Exchange*. London: Routledge, 17–35.

Benko, S. (2003) *The Virgin Goddess, Studies in the Pagan and Christian Roots of Mariology*. Danvers: Brill.

Berry, J. (2009) *Ritual Making Women: Shaping Rites for Changing Lives*. New York: Routledge.

Bidisha. (2013) The Red Room. In: Appignanesi, L., Holmes, R., Orbach, S. (eds.) *Fifty Shades of Feminism*. London: Hachette Digital, 38–44.

Bird, P. (1974) Images of Women in the Old Testament. In: Ruether, R. R. (ed.) *Religion and Sexism: Images of Woman in the Jewish and Christian Traditions*. New York: Simon and Schuster, 41–88.

Bly, R., Woodman, M. (1998) *The Maiden King: The Reunion of Masculine and Feminine*. New York: Henry Holt and Company Inc.

Bordo, S. (1999) *Twilight Zones*. Berkeley: University of California Press.

Bordo, S. (2003) *Unbearable Weight: Feminism, Western Culture, and the Body*. London: University of California Press.

Bruch, H. (1973) *Eating Disorders*. New York: Basic Books.

Bruch, H. (2001) *The Golden Cage: The Enigma of Anorexia Nervosa*. London: Harvard University Press.

Brumberg, J. (2000) *Fasting Girls: A History of Anorexia Nervosa*. New York: Vintage Books.
Budapest, Z. (1997) *Holy Book of Women's Mysteries*. Essex: New Leaf Distribution Company.
Butler, J. (1985) *Embodied Identity in De Beauvoir's the Second Sex*. Paper presented at the American Philosophical Association, Pacific Division, March 22, 1985.
Butler, J. (1990) Performative Acts and Gender Constitution: An Essay in Phenomenology and Feminist Theory. In: Case, S. E. (ed.) *Performing Feminisms: Feminist Critical Theory and Theatre*. Baltimore: The Johns Hopkins University Press, 270–83.
Butler, J. (1990, 2007) *Gender Troubles*. London: Routledge.
Butler, J. (1993, 2011) *Bodies That Matter: On the Discursive Limits of "Sex"*. New York: Routledge.
Bynum, C. W. (1987) *Holy Feast and Holy Fast: The Religious Significance of Food to Medieval Women*. London, England/Berkeley and Los Angeles, California: University of California Press.
Cameron, D. (1998) *The Feminist Critique of Language: A Reader*. London: Routledge.
Campos, P. (2004) *The Obesity Myth: Why America's Obsession With Weight Is Hazardous to your Health*. London: Penguin Books.
Capra, F., Spretnak, C. (1984) *Green Politics*. New York: Dutton.
Carrette, J., King, R. (2005) *Selling Spirituality: The Silent Takeover of Religion*. London: Routledge.
Chappell, K. (2008) Celeb Workout Secrets: You Can Have a Body Like The Stars. In: *Ebony* 164–168. Available at: http://books.google.co.uk/books?id=l9MDAAAAMBAJ&pg=PA166&dq=beyonce's+exercise&hl=en&sa=X&ei=tylqVLOuBYHeaMH4gJgJ&ved=0CCAQ6AEwAA#v=onepage&q=beyonce's%20exercise&f=false [16/11/2014].
Chernin, K. (1985) *The Hungry Self: Women, Eating and Identity*. New York: HarperCollins Publishers.
Chernin, K. (1987) *Reinventing Eve: Modern Woman in Search of Herself*. New York: HarperCollins Publishers, Inc.
Chernin, K. (1994) *The Obsession: Reflections on the Tyranny of Slenderness*. New York: HarperPerennial.
Christ, C. P. (1979) Why Women Need the Goddess: Phenomenological, Psychological, and Political Reflections. In: Christ, C. P., Plaskow, J. (eds.) *Womanspirit Rising: A Feminist Reader in Religion*. London: Harper & Row, 273–286.
Christ, C. P. (1982) Why Women Need the Goddess. In: Spretnak, C. (ed.) *The Politics of Women's Spirituality*. New York: Anchor, 71–86.
Christ, C. P. (1987) *Laughter of Aphrodite: Reflections on a Journey to the Goddess*. New York: Harper & Row.
Christ, C. P. (1995) *Diving Deep and Surfacing: Women Writers on Spiritual Quest*. Boston: Beacon Press.
Christ, C. P. (1997) *Rebirth of the Goddess: Finding Meaning in Feminist Spirituality*. Reading: Addison-Wesley.
Christ, C. P. (2005) Musings on the Goddess and Her Cultural Despisers, Provoked by Naomi Goldenberg. In: *Feminist Theology* 13, no. 2: 143–149.
Christ, C. P. (2012) Why Women, Men and Other Living Things Still Need the Goddess: Remembering and Reflecting 35 Years Later. In: *Feminist Theology* 20, no. 3: 242–255.

Christ, C. P., Plaskow, J. (1989a) *Weaving the Visions: New Patterns in Feminist Spirituality*. London: Harper & Row.

Christ, C. P., Plaskow, J. (1989b) Naming the Sacred. In: Plaskow, J., Christ, C. P. (eds.) *Weaving the Visions: New Patterns in Feminist Spirituality*. London: Harper & Row.

Clack, B. (2012) The Future Is Female: Revisioning Feminism For/With the Next Generation. In: *Feminist Theology* 20, no. 3: 256–261.

Clifford, A. M. (2002) *Introducing Feminist Theology*. Maryknoll: Orbis Books.

Cloe, A. (2014) *Average American Women's Weight and Height*. Available at: www.livestrong.com/article/357769-weight-height-for-the-average-american-woman/ [16/11/2014].

Coleman, K. (2010) *Re-riting Woman: Dianic Wicca and the Feminine Divine*. New York: AltaMira Press.

Condren, M. (2002) *The Serpent and the Goddess: Women, Religion and Power in Celtic Ireland*. Dublin: New Island Books.

Craft-Fairchild, C. (1993) *Masquerade and Gender: Disguise and Female Identity in Eighteenth- Century Fictions by Women*. University Park: Pennsylvania State University Press.

Crilly, L. (2012) *Hope With Eating Disorders*. London: Hay House Insights.

The Critical Religion Association. (2016) *Critical Approaches to the Study of Religion*. Available at: www.criticalreligion.org/ [09/08/2016].

Critser, G. (2003) *Fat Land: How Americans Became the Fattest People in the World*. New York: Houghton Mifflin Company.

Daly, M. (1991) *Gyn/Ecology: The Metaethics of Radical Feminism*. London: The Women's Press Ltd.

Daly, M. (1992) *Beyond God the Father: Towards a Philosophy of Women's Liberation*. Boston: Beacon Press.

Daly, M. (1993) *Outercourse: The Be-Dazzling Voyage*. London: The Women's Press Ltd.

Daly, M., Caputi, J. (1994) *Websters' First New Intergalactic Wickedary of the English Language*. New York: HarperSanFrancisco.

Davis, D. (1996) Logocentrism. In: Enos, T. (ed.) *Encyclopedia of Rhetoric and Composition: Communication from Ancient Times to the Information Age*. London: Routledge.

Dignon, A. (2007) *All of Me: A Fuller Picture of Anorexia*. Oxford: Peter Lang.

Disney. (2017) *Bibbidi Bobbidi Boutique-Disney Springs*. Available at: https://disneyworld.disney.go.com/shops/disney-springs/bibbidi-bobbidi-boutique-marketplace/ [25/01/2017].

Douglas, M. (2002) *Purity and Danger: An Analysis of Concept and Taboo*. London: Routledge.

Downing, C. (1981) *The Goddess: Mythological Images of the Feminine*. New York: Crossroad.

Dwyer, J. (1985) Nutritional Aspects of Anorexia Nervosa and Bulimia. In: Emmett, S. W. (ed.) *Theory and Treatment of Anorexia Nervosa and Bulimia: Biomedical Sociocultural, and Psychological Perspectives*. New York: Brunner/Mazel Inc, 20–51.

Eisler, R. (1995) Envisioning a Partnership Future. In: *Woman of Power* 24: 20–27.

Eller, C. (1993, 1995) *Living in the Lap of the Goddess: The Feminist Spirituality Movement in America*. Boston: Beacon Press.

Eller, C. (2001) *The Myth of Matriarchal Prehistory: Why an Invented Past Won't Give Women and Future*. Boston: Beacon Press.
Ezzell, M. B. (2008) Pornography, Lad Mags, Video Games, and Boys: Reviving the Canary in the Cultural Coal Mine. In: Olfman, S. (ed.) *The Sexualization of Childhood*. Westport: Praeger Publishers Inc., 7–32.
Fallon, P., Wooley, S. C., Katzman, M. A. (1994) *Feminist Perspectives on Eating Disorders*. New York: The Guilford Press.
Faludi, S. (1993) *Backlash: The Undeclared War Against Women*. London: Vintage.
Favaro, A., Ferrara, S., Santonastaso, P. (2004) Impulsive and Compulsive Self-Injurious Behaviour and Eating Disorders: An Epidemiological Study. In: Levitt, J. L., Sansone, R. A., Cohn, L. (eds.) *Self-Harm Behaviour and Eating Disorders: Dynamics, Assessment, and Treatment*. New York: Brunner-Routledge, 31–45.
Featherstone, M. (1996) *The Body: Social Process and Cultural Theory*. London: Sage Publications.
Featherstone, M. (2001) The Body in Consumer Society. In: Banks, D., Purdy, M. (eds.) *The Sociology and Politics of Health: A Reader*. London: Routledge, 228–237.
Fedele, A. (2013) *Looking For Mary Magdalene: Alternative Pilgrimage and Ritual Creativity at Catholic Shrines in France*. Oxford: Oxford University Press.
Fine, C. (2010) *Delusions of Gender: The Real Science Behind Sex Differences*. London: Icon Books.
Flax, J. (1990) *Thinking Fragments: Psychoanalysis, Feminism and Postmodernism in the Contemporary West*. Oxford: University of California Press Ltd.
Foucault, M. (1991) *Discipline and Punish: The Birth of the Prison*. London: Penguin Books.
Fox, M. (2009) *The Hidden Spirituality of Men: The Metaphors to Awaken the Sacred Masculine*. Novato: New World Library.
Garrett, C. (1998) *Beyond Anorexia: Narrative, Spirituality and Recovery*. Cambridge: Cambridge University Press.
Gentles-Peart, K. (2016) *Romance with Voluptuousness: Caribbean Women and Thick Bodies in the United States*. Lincoln: University of Nebraska Press.
Gilman, S. L. (1980) *Diets and Dieting: A Cultural Encyclopaedia*. New York: Routledge.
Gimbutas, M. (1982) Women and Culture in Goddess-Oriented Old Europe. In: Spretnak, C. (ed.) *The Politics of Women's Spirituality: Essays by Founding Mothers of the Movement*. New York: Anchor Books.
Glucklich, A. (2001) *Sacred Pain: Hurting the Body for the Sake of the Soul*. New York: Oxford University Press.
Goldenberg, N. (1992) *Changing of the Gods*. Boston: Beacon Press.
Goldenberg, N. (1993) *Resurrecting the Body: Feminism, Religion, and Psychoanalysis*. New York: Crossroads.
Goldenberg, N. (1995) The Return of the Goddess: Psychoanalytic Reflections on the Shift from Theology to Thealogy. In: King, U. (ed.) *Religion and Gender*. Cambridge: Blackwell, 145–165.
Goldenberg, N. (2004) Witches and Words. In: *Feminist Theology* 12, no. 2: 203–211.
Goldhill, O. (2014) *A Nation of Weight Watchers: Is Our Obsession With Thin Making Us Fat?* Available at: www.telegraph.co.uk/women/womens-health/11003614/A-nation-of-weight-watchers-Is-our-obsession-with-thin-making-us-fat.html [15/10/2016].

Goldstein, L., Rissman, J. (2008) Anorexia. In: Gilman, S. L. (ed.) *Diets and Dieting: A Cultural Encyclopaedia*. New York: Routledge, 7–11.

Gordon, R. (2000) *Eating Disorders: Anatomy of a Social Epidemic*. Oxford: Blackwell Publishers Ltd.

Greer, G. (2006) *The Female Eunuch*. London: Harper Perennial.

Gremillion, H. (2003) *Feeding Anorexia: Gender and Power at a Treatment Centre*. London: Duke University Press, 193.

Grey, M. (2001) *Introducing Feminist Images of God*. Sheffield: Sheffield Academic Press.

Griffin, R. M. (2004) *Born Again Bodies: Flesh and Spirit in American Christianity*. London: University of California Press.

Griffin, S. (1989) This Earth Is My Sister. In: Plaskow, J., Christ, C. P. (eds.) *Weaving the Visions: New Patterns in Feminist Spirituality*. London: Harper & Row, 105–110.

Groesz, L. M., Levine, M. P., Murnen, S. K. (2002) The Effects of Experimental Presentation on Thin Media Images on Body Satisfaction: A Meta-Analytic Review. In: *International Journal of Eating Disorders* 31: 1–16.

Gross, R. (2009) *A Garland of Feminist Reflections: Forty Years of Religious Exploration*. London: University of California Press.

Grosz, E. (1995) *Space, Time and Perversion: Essays on the Politics of Bodies*. London: Routledge.

Hamermesh, D. S. (2011) *Beauty Pays: Why Attractive People Are More Successful*. Oxford: Princeton University Press.

Henley, N. (1977) *Body Politics: Power, Sex, and Non-Verbal Communication*. Englewood Cliffs: Prentice Hall.

Heywood, L. (1996) *Dedication to Hunger: The Anorexia Aesthetic in Modern Culture*. Berkeley: University of California Press.

Hill, R., Haslett, C., Kumar, S. (2001) Anorexia Nervosa in an Elderly Woman. In: *Australian and New Zealand Journal of Psychiatry* 35: 246–248.

Hochschild, A. R. (2012) *The Managed Heart*. Berkeley: University of California Press.

Hogan, M. (2014) *Horizon: Is Your Brain Male or Female?, BBC Two, Review: 'Thought-Provoking'*. Available at: www.telegraph.co.uk/culture/tvandradio/tv-and-radio-reviews/11129004/Horizon-Is-Your-Brain-Male-or-Female-BBC-Two-review-thought-provoking.html [09/12/2014].

Holmes, A. (2007) *Memo To Women's Magazine Editors: White Women Hate Themselves After Reading Your Magazines*. Available at: http://jezebal.com/248484/memo-to-womens-magazine-editors-white-women-hate-themselves-after-raeding-your-magazines [22/11/2014].

Howard-Taylor, L. (2008) *Biting Anorexia*. Sydney: Finch Publishing.

Irigaray, L. (1985) *The Sex Which Is Not One*. Ithaca: Cornell University Press.

Isherwood, L. (2000) Sex and Body Politics: Issues for Feminist Theology. In: Isherwood, L. (ed.) *The Good News of the Body: Sexual Theology and Feminism*. Sheffield: Sheffield Academic Press, 20–35.

Isherwood, L. (2007a) *The Fat Jesus: Feminist Explorations in Boundaries and Transgressions*. London: Darton, Longman and Todd Ltd.

Isherwood, L. (2007b) *Patriarchs, Prophets and Other Villains*. London: Equinox Publishing.

Isherwood, L. (2007c) 'Eat, Friends, Drink. Be Drunk With Love' [Song of Songs 5:2] – A Reflection. In: Isherwood, L. (ed.) *Patriarchs, Prophets and Other Villains*. London: Equinox Publishing, 149–157.

Isherwood, L. (2008) Will You Slim for Him or Bake Cakes for the Queen of Heaven. In: Althaus-Reid, A., Isherwood, L. (eds.) *Controversies in Body Theology*. London: SCM Press, 174–207.

Isherwood, L., McEwan, D. (2001) *Introducing Feminist Theology*. Sheffield: Sheffield Academic Press.

Isherwood, L., Stuart, E. (1998) *Introducing Body Theology*. Sheffield: Continuum International Publishing Group.

Jaafar, N. R. N., Daud, T. I. M., Rahman, F. N. A., Baharudin, A. (2007) Mirtazapine for anorexia nervosa and depression. In: *Australian and New Zealand Journal of Psychiatry* 41: 768–769.

Jasper, A. (2015) Womanspirit Still Rising? Some Feminist Reflections on 'Religious Education' in the UK. In: *Feminist Theology* 23, no. 3: 240–253.

Jefferys, S. (2005, 2015) *Women and Misogyny: Harmful Cultural Practices in the West*. London: Routledge.

Jones, E. (1956) *Sigmund Freud: Life and Work*. London: Hogarth Press.

Keel, P. K. (2005) *Eating Disorders*. Upper Saddle River: Pearson Prentice-Hall.

Keel, P. K., McCormick, L. (2010) Diagnosis, Assessment, and Treatment Planning for Anorexia Nervosa. In: Grilo, C. M., Mitchell, J. E. (eds.) *The Treatment of Eating Disorders: A Clinical Handbook*. London: The Guildford Press, 3–28.

Kindersley, T., Vine, S. (2009) *Backwards in High Heels: The impossible Art of Being Female*. London: Fourth Estate.

Klein, M. (1975) *Envy and Gratitude and Other Works, 1946–1963*. New York: Delacorte Press.

Klein, M. (1975) *Love, Guilt, and Reparation and Other Works, 1921–1945*. New York: Delacorte Press.

Klein, R. (2001) Fat Beauty. In: Braziel, J. E., LeBesco, K. (eds.) *Bodies Out of Bounds: Fatness and Transgression*. London: University of California Press, 19–37.

Kotz, L. (1992) The Body You Want: Liz Kotz Interviews Judith Butler. In: *Artforum* 31, no. 3: 82–89. Available at: www.mariabuszek.com/kcai/PoMoSeminar/Readings/KotzButler.pdf [05/06/2014].

Lamb, S. (2003) *The Secret Lives of Girls: What Good Girls Really Do – Sex Play, Aggression, and their Guilt*. London: Simon and Schuster.

Langley, J. (2006) *Boys Get Anorexia Too: Coping With Male Eating Disorders in the Family*. London: Sage Publications.

Lawrence, L. (1995) *The Anorexic Experience*. London: The Women's Press Ltd.

Lawrence, M. (2008) *The Anorexic Mind*. London: Karnac Books.

Lelwica, M. M. (1999) *Starving for Salvation: The Spiritual Dimensions of Eating Problems among American Girls and Women*. New York: Oxford University Press.

Lipsedge, M., Littlewood, R. (1997) *Aliens and Alienists: Ethnic Minorities and Psychiatry*. London: Routledge.

Lloyd, M. (2007) *Judith Butler*. Cambridge: Polity Press.

Long, A. P. (1992) *In a Chariot Drawn By Lions: The Search for the Female in Deity*. London: The Women's Press Ltd.

Lunn, P. (1993) Do Women Need the GODDESS? Some Phenomenological and Social Reflections. In: *Feminist Theology* 4: 17–38.

Lynn, C. (2012) *Hope With Eating Disorders*. London: Hay House UK LTD.

Maine, M. (2000) *Body Wars: Making Peace with Women's Bodies*. Carlsbad: Gurze Books.

Malson, H. (1998) *The Thin Woman: Feminism, Poststructualism and the Social Psychology of Anorexia Nervosa*. East Sussex: Routledge.

Mantin, R. (2001) Carol Christ: Feminist Spirituality and Narrative Thealogy. In: Erricker, C., Erriker, J. (eds.) *Contemporary Spiritualities: Social and Religious Contexts*. London: Continuum, 93–113.

Mantin, R. (2007) 'Dealing With a Jealous God': Letting go of Monotheism and 'Doing' Sacrality. In: Isherwood, L. (ed.) *Patriarchs, Prophets and Other Villains*. London: Equinox Publishing, 37–49.

Martin, C. E. (2007) *Perfect Girls, Starving Daughters: The Frightening New Normalcy of Hating Your Body*. London: Piatkus Books Ltd.

Martin, F. (2011) *The Feminist Question: Feminist Theology in Light of Christian Tradition*. Eugene: Wipf & Stock Publishers.

McCormick, L. M., Keel, P. K., Brumm, M. C., Bowers, W., Swayze, V., Anderson, A. (2008) Implications of starvation-induced change in right dorsal anterior cingulate volume in anorexia nervosa. In: *International Journal of Eating Disorders* 41: 602–610.

McKim, D. K. (2014) *The Westminster Dictionary of Theological Terms*. Louisville: Westminster John Know Press.

Metcalfe, K. (2006) *Anorexia: A Stranger in the Family*. Mid-Glamorgan: Accent Press Ltd.

Mills, S. (2003) *Michael Foucault*. London: Routledge.

Mills, S., Mullany, L. (2011) *Language, Gender and Feminism: Theory, Methodology and Practice*. Oxon: Routledge.

Moorey, J. (1991) *Living With Anorexia and Bulimia*. Manchester: Bell and Bain Ltd.

Morton, N. (1985) *The Journey Is Home*. Boston: Beacon Press.

Morton, N. (1989) The Goddess as Metaphoric Image. In: Christ, C. P., Plaskow, J. (eds.) *Weaving the Visions: New Patterns in Feminist Spirituality*. London: Harper & Row, 111–119.

Mosley, M. (2014) *Is Your Brain Male or Female?* Available at: www.bbc.co.uk/news/science-environment-29405467 [13/12/2014].

Nelson, J. (2012) *Airbrushed Nation: The Lure and Loathing of Women's Magazines*. Berkeley: Perseus Books Group.

NHS. (2016) *Anorexia Nervosa – Treatment*. Available at: www.nhs.uk/Conditions/Anorexia-nervosa/Pages/Treatment.aspx [15/10/2016].

Oakley, A. (2015) *Sex, Gender and Society*. New York: Routledge.

O'Connor, M. (2014) *Eating Disorders Awareness Week Shows that Student Hunger for Greater University Support Still Exists*. Available at: www.independent.co.uk/student/student-life/eating-disorders-awareness-week-shows-that-student-hunger-for-greater-university-support-still-9160524.html [22/10/2016].

Olfman, S. (2008) *The Sexualisation of Childhood*. Westport: Praeger Publishers Inc.

Orbach, S. (1993) *Hunger Strike: The Anorectic's Struggle as a Metaphor for Our Age*. London: Penguin Books.

Orbach, S. (1998) *Fat Is a Feminist Issue*. London: Arrow Books.

Orbach, S. (2009) *Bodies*. London: Profile Books Ltd.

Peacore, L. D. (2008) Feminist Theologies. In: Dyrness, W. A., Karkkainen, V.-M. (eds.) *Global Dictionary of Theology: A Resource for the Worldwide Church*. Nottingham: Inter-Varsity Press, 317–322.

Phillips, K. A. (2005) *The Broken Mirror: Understanding and Treating Body Dysmorphic Disorder*. Oxford: Oxford University Press.

Pjetri, E., Schmidt, U., Kas, M. J., Campbell, I. C. (2012) *Epigenetics and Eating Disorders*. Available at: www.researchgate.net/profile/Martien_Kas/publication/225056288_Epigenetics_and_eating_disorders/links/0deec51a335cb9dce2000000.pdf [15/08/2015].

Plaskow, J. (1983) The Right Question Is Theological. In: Heschel, S. (ed.) *On Being a Jewish Feminist*. New York: Schocken Books, 223–233.

Potts, A. (2005) Phallocentrism. In: Harrington, A., Marshall, B. L., Muller, H. P. (eds.) *Encyclopedia of Social Theory*. Oxon: Routledge.

Rachelle, L., Lilenfeld, R. (2016) Suicidal Behavior in Eating Disorders. In: Latzer, Y., Stein, D. (eds.) *Bio-Psycho-Social Contributions to Understanding Eating Disorders*. New York: Springer International Publishing, 65–77.

Raphael, M. (1996) *Thealogy and Embodiment: The Post-Patriarchal Reconstruction of Female Sacrality*. Sheffield: Sheffield Academic Press.

Raphael, M. (1999) *Introducing Thealogy: Discourses on the Goddess*. Sheffield: Continuum Publishing Group.

Reel, J. J. (2013) *Eating Disorders: An Encyclopedia of Causes, Treatment, and Prevention*. Santa Barbara: Greenwood Press.

Reid-Bowen, P. (2007) *Goddess as Nature: Towards a Philosophical Thealogy*. Hampshire: Ashgate.

Reid-Bowen, P. (2008) Why Women Need to be Ripped, Shredded and Sliced. In: Isherwood, L., Althaus-Reid, M. (eds.) *Controversies in Body Theology*. London: SCM Press, 207–227.

Rhode, D. (2011) *The Beauty Bias: The Injustice of Appearance in Life and Law*. Oxford: Oxford University Press.

Riviere, J. (1955) The Unconscious Phantasy of an Inner World Reflected in Examples from Literature. In: Klein, M. (ed.) *New Directions in Psychoanalysis*. New York: Basic Books, 358–359.

Riviere, J. (1986) Womanliness as a Masquerade. In: Burgin, V., Donald, J., Kaplan, C. (eds.) *Formations of Fantasy*. London: Methuen.

Robinson, J. (1998) *The Inner Goddess: Feminist Theology in the Light of Catholic Teaching*. Herefordshire: Fowler Wright Books.

Rossi, P. de. (2010) *Unbearable Lightness: A Story of Loss and Gain*. New York: Atria Books.

Roth, G. (2010) *Women, Food and God: An Unexpected Path to Almost Everything*. London: Simon & Schuster UK Ltd.

Rothblum, E. D. (1994) "I'll Die for the Revolution But Don't Ask Me Not to Diet": Feminism and the Continuing Stigmatization of Obesity. In: Fallon, P., Katzman, M. A., Wooley, S. C. (eds.) *Feminist Perspectives on Eating Disorders*. New York: The Guildford Press, 53–77.

Ruether, R. R. (1974) *Religion and Sexism*. New York: Simon and Schuster.

Ruether, R. R. (1992) *Gaia and God: An Ecofeminist Theology of Earth Healing*. San Francisco: HarperSanFrancisco.

Russell, G. R. M. (1997) The History of Bulimia Nervosa. In: Garner, D. M., Garfinkel, P. E. (eds.) *Handbook of Treatment for Eating Disorders*. New York: The Guilford Press, 11–25.

Salih, S. (2007) On Judith Butler and Performativity. In: Lovaas, K. E., Jenkins, M. M. (eds.) *Sexualities and Communication in Everyday Life*. Thousand Oaks: Sage Publications, 55–68.

Salomonsen, J. (2002) *Enchanted Feminism: The Reclaiming Witches of San Francisco*. London: Routledge.

Salvaggio, R. (1999) *The Sounds of Feminist Theory*. New York: State University of New York Press.

Samelson, D. A. (2009) *Feeding the Starving Mind: A Personalised, Comprehensive Approach to Overcoming Anorexia and Other Starvation Eating Disorders*. Oakland: New Harbinger Publications.

Sands, K. (1994) *Escape from Paradise: Evil and Tragedy in Feminist Theology*. Minneapolis: Fortress Press.

Sarup, M. (1992) *Jacques Lacan*. London: Harvester Wheatsheaf.

Saukko, P. (2008) *The Anorexic Self: A Personnel, Political Analysis of Diagnostic Discourse*. New York: State of New York Press.

Sax, L. (2007) *Why Gender Matters: What Parents and Teachers Need to Know About the Emerging Science of Sex Differences*. New York: Crown Publishing Group.

Sceats, S. (2005) *Food, Consumption and the Body in Contemporary Women's Fiction*. Cambridge: Cambridge University Press.

Selby, J. (2014) *Emma Watson: Noah and Harry Potter Actress 'Excited About the Aging Process.' She's Only 23*. Available at: www.independent.co.uk/news/people/emma-watson-is-excited-about-the-aging-process-aged-23-9225728.html [23/11/2014].

Shearer, A. (1998) *Athene: Image and Energy*. London: Penguin Books.

Silverman, J. A. (1997) Anorexia Nervosa: Historical Perspectives on Treatment. In: Garner, D. M., Garfinkel, P. E. (eds.) *Handbook of Treatment for Eating Disorders*. New York: Guilford Press.

Sjoo, M., Mor, B. (1991) *The Great Cosmic Mother: Rediscovering the Religion of the Earth*. New York: HarperCollins Publishers.

Slater, L. (1997) *Welcome to My Country*. London: Penguin Books.

Slee, N. (2002) The Holy Spirit and Spirituality. In: Parsons, S. F. (ed.) *The Cambridge Companion to Feminist Theology*. Cambridge: Cambridge University Press, 171–190.

Spretnak, C. (1982) The Politics of Women's Spirituality. In: Spretnak, C. (ed.) *The Politics of Women's Spirituality: Essays by Founding Mothers of the Movement*. London: Anchor Books, 393–399.

Starhawk. (1982a) *Dreaming the Dark: Magic, Sex & Politics*. Boston: Beacon Press.

Starhawk. (1982b) *Ethics and Justice in Goddess Religion*. In: Spretnak, C. (ed.) *The Politics of Women's Spirituality: Essays by Founding Mothers of the Movement*. New York: Anchor Books, 415–422.

Starhawk. (1982c) Witchcraft as Goddess Religion. In: Spretnak, C. (ed.) *The Politics of Women's Spirituality: Essays by Founding Mothers of the Movement*. London: Anchor Books, 49–57.

Starhawk. (1982d) Consciousness, Politics and Magic. In: Spretnak, C. (ed.) *The Politics of Women's Spirituality: Essays by Founding Mothers of the Movement*. London: Anchor Books, 172–184.

Starhawk. (1989) *The Spiral Dance: A Rebirth of the Ancient Religion of the Great Goddess*. New York: HarperCollins Publishers.

Starhawk. (2002) *Webs of Power: Notes From the Global Uprising*. Gabriola Island, British Columbia, Canada: New York Society Publishers.

Starhawk. (2016) *Regenerative Culture, Earth-Based Spirituality, and Permaculture.* Available at: http://starhawk.org/ [22/08/2016].

Steiner-Adair, C. (1990) New Maps of Development, New Models of Therapy: The Psychology of Women and the Treatment of Eating Disorders. In: Johnson, C. (ed.) *Psychodynamic Treatment of Anorexic Nervosa and Bulimia.* New York: Gilford Press, 225–245.

Stone, M. (1976) *When God Was a Woman: The Landmark Exploration of the Ancient Worship of the Great Goddess and the Eventual Suppression of Women's Rites.* London: Harcourt Inc.

Tanner, R. S. (2007) *The Female Trickster: The Mask That Reveals, Post-Jungian and Postmodern Psychological Perspectives on Women in Contemporary Culture.* London: Routledge.

Treadgold, R., Treadgold, A., Treadgold, D. (2009) Rediscovering a Daughter. In: Malson, H., Burns, M. (eds.) *Critical Feminist Approaches to Eating Disorders.* London: Routledge, 233–245.

Treasure, J., Alexander, J. (2013) *Anorexia Nervosa: A Recovery Guide for Sufferers, Families and Friends.* London: Routledge.

Turner, V. (2008) *The Ritual Process: Structure and Anti-Structure.* Piscataway: Aldine Transaction.

Vandereycken, W. (1994) *From Fasting Saints to Anorexic Girls: The History of Self-Starvation.* New York: New York University Press.

Vernon, J. (2007) *Hunger: A Modern History.* London: The Belknap Press of Harvard University Press.

Walker, A. (1989) God Is Inside You and Everybody Else. In: Plaskow, J., Christ, C. P. (eds.) *Weaving the Visions: New Patterns in Feminist Spirituality.* London: Harper & Row, 101–104.

Wallace, A. (2002) *Jamie Lee Curtis: True Thighs.* Available at: www.more.com/news/womens-issues/jamie-lee-curtis-true-thighs [23/11/2014].

Walter, N. (2010) *Living Dolls: The Return of Sexism.* London: Virago.

Warner, M. (1985) *Monuments and Maidens: The Allegory of the Female Form.* London: Weidenfeld & Nicolson.

Weiss, S. I. (2002) *Coping With the Beauty Myth: A Guide for Real Girls.* New York: Rosen Publishing Group.

Weitz, R. (2003) *The Politics of Women's Bodies: Sexuality, Appearance, and Behavior.* Oxford: Oxford University Press.

Wex, M. (1984) *Let's Take Back Our Space: "Female" and "Male" Body Language as a Result of Patriarchal Structures.* Munich, Germany: Frauenliteratur Verlag.

Wilson, L. (2015) Starvation and Self-Mutilation in Religious Traditions. In: Juergensmeyer, M., Kitts, M., Jerryson, M. (eds.) *The Oxford Handbook of Religion and Violence.* Oxford: Oxford University Press, 242–250.

Wolf, N. (1990) *The Beauty Myth: How Images of Beauty Are Used Against Women.* London: Vintage Books.

Wolf, N. (1994) Hunger. In: Fallon, P., Katzman, M. A., Wooley, S. C. (eds.) *Feminist Perspectives on Eating Disorders.* New York: The Guildford Press, 94–115.

Women's Thealogical Institute. (2009–2015) *WTI Study.* Available at: www.rcgi.org/study [02/07/2016].

Woodman, M. (1980) *The Owl Was a Baker's Daughter: Obesity, Anorexia Nervosa and the Repressed Feminine.* Toronto, Canada: Inner City Books.

Woodman, M. (1982) *Addicted to Perfection: The Still Unravished Bride*. Toronto, Canada: Inner City Books.

Woodman, M. (1985) *The Pregnant Virgin: A Process of Psychological Transformation*. Toronto, Canada: Inner City Books.

Woodman, M. (1987) From Concrete to Consciousness: The Emergence of the Feminine. In: Mahdi, L. C., Foster, S., Little, M. (eds.) *Betwixt and Between: Patterns of Masculine and Feminine Initiation*. Chicago: Open Court Publishing Company, 201–223.

World Health Organisation. (2012) Anorexia Nervosa. In: World Health Organisation (eds.) *International Statistical Classification of Diseases and Related Health Problems*. Geneva: WHO.

Wykes, M., Gunter, B. (2004) *The Media and Body Image: If Looks Could Kill*. London: Sage Publications.

Young-Eisendrath, P. (2001) *Women and Desire: Beyond Wanting to Be Wanted*. London: Judy Piatkus Ltd.

Index

For Product Safety Concerns and Information please contact our EU representative GPSR@taylorandfrancis.com
Taylor & Francis Verlag GmbH, Kaufingerstraße 24, 80331 München, Germany

www.ingramcontent.com/pod-product-compliance
Ingram Content Group UK Ltd.
Pitfield, Milton Keynes, MK11 3LW, UK
UKHW011015180926
475701UK00004B/764
* 9 7 8 0 3 6 7 5 8 9 5 7 8 *